BOSTON UNIVERSITY
African Research Studies
Number Three

SOCIAL CONTROL IN AN AFRICAN SOCIETY

A Study of the Arusha:
Agricultural Masai
of Northern Tanganyika

by
P. H. GULLIVER

African Studies Program
Boston University

BOSTON UNIVERSITY PRESS
1963

CONTENTS

v

Contents

PART THREE: ROLES AND PROCESSES RESULTING
FROM ORGANISED GOVERNMENT

PART FOUR: PROCESSES OF DISPUTE SETTLEMENT

FIGURES

PLATES

(between pages 146 and 147)

1. The Mountain (Mt. Meru, 14,979 ft.) viewed from the lower slopes
   (*courtesy of the Director, Information Services, Government of Tanganyika*)
2. (a) A homestead on the mountain slopes
   (b) Homesteads in the open country of the peripheral region
3. Girls and women on a ceremonial occasion
4. A young wife (*courtesy of the Director, Information Services, Government of Tanganyika*)
5. A notable of a senior elder age-group (*courtesy of the Director, Information Services, Government of Tanganyika*)
6. (a) Junior murran spokesmen leading their age-mates and girl-friends in singing and dancing
   (b) The senior elder notables of a parish in ceremonial procession
7. A parish assembly in progress in the peripheral region
8. Waiting for beer to be served after the successful settlement of a dispute

PREFACE

IN 1956, as research sociologist for the Government of Tanganyika, I was requested to make an investigation into the economic, social and administrative problems which had arisen in the country of the Arusha people, as the result of an increasingly acute shortage of agricultural land and the comparative slowness of economic development. These matters had come to be a matter of serious concern to the Government because of its general responsibility and the threatening unrest among the people. The Arusha had been protesting to the Government about the great severity of the land shortage, and unverified claims were being made that hundreds of families were without land in this entirely rural society. Not only did the Arusha consider it the duty of the Government to help them in their modern and novel plight; but many of them believed that this duty was imperative because it was the policies of the Government in the past which had prevented their natural expansion of agricultural settlement into the adjacent lands. Those lands were now either controlled forest, or farms occupied by foreigners. It was my task to discover the nature and extent of the land problem, to report on the attitudes and ideas of the Arusha, to relate all this to their social life and traditions, and to suggest steps which would alleviate the situation.

Field-work began in August 1956, and continued with minor breaks until May 1958. The first part of this period was devoted primarily to land and economic matters, including demography, land tenure, agriculture and the recent history of settlement. Necessarily this involved some concern with virtually every aspect of Arusha social life, and therefore a general ethnographic survey was made; but it was possible in the later part of the field-work period to concentrate on certain features of the social system of the Arusha which seemed to be of particular importance and interest, and going beyond purely economic considerations. My account of contemporary conditions in the area, together with some recommendations for future policy, were presented in my *Report on Land and Population in the Arusha Chiefdom* (1957), and in a number of other official memoranda. The present volume contains some of the results which came from the continuation and specialisation of research in the latter part of my period in the field.

During my enquiries into land tenure and the fairly recent expansion of the Arusha into unoccupied bushlands, I quickly became aware of the large number of disputes occurring over land matters—such as the ownership of farms and fields, the alignment of boundaries, the rights of tenants, the validity of inheritance settlements or of sales of land. One obvious way to investigate both the norms and practices of land tenure, and to distinguish the particular kind of issues arousing conflict, was to record and analyse as many of these disputes as possible—both those which came before the local courts, and those more numerous which did not. My enquiries were later widened to take in other kinds of disputes but gradually my interests were drawn beyond the details of the disputes themselves, to the processes involved in achieving and enforcing settlements. Thus I was led to a renewed study of the social contexts in which these disputes and processes occurred, and the nature of the systems of social relationships in which the disputants were involved: i.e. the age-group system and the patrilineal descent system. This patterning of my field research fitted well with another principal interest:—the inter-relations between these two major and markedly contrasting types of social systems, based on age and unilineal descent respectively. In addition, because of the Government's request for information, during the course of the reorganisation of the local administration, it was possible to make an examination of the work of the local courts and the influence of the chief, headmen and magistrates.

I have chosen to describe firstly, and in relative isolation, each of these three sub-systems of the total society. This, it must be conceded, raises some difficulties, chief of which is that my description and analysis of each sub-system is necessarily concentrated and rather abstract. At the risk of confusing the reader, I have followed this plan in order that I may attempt the essential synthesis, in Part 4 of the book, focusing on the processes of dispute settlement and social control. Especially I am conscious that my account of Arusha patrilineages is inadequate. That is, it does not provide the wealth of data nor the depth of analysis which, in this aspect of social anthropology, have been a distinctive contribution of British scholars working in Africa. It has not been my specific intention to add to that here; rather, I wish to give only an account sufficient to allow me to address the problem of social control in Arusha society.

Because of my official association with the Government—an alien, imposed government as Arusha saw it—and the suspicion with which the people regarded much of the Government's activity, I began my research at a disadvantage which was never altogether overcome. Acutely aware of their severe and novel shortage of land, and with marked feelings of insecurity under the pressure of modern conditions (of which land shortage was a part), many Arusha feared that my enquiries might bring danger of some kind—even the loss of some of the land they already had. My first attempt to establish a small field-camp was hindered for fear that I might seize the land on which my tent was pitched; and even many months later, similar apprehensions in other areas interfered with my relations with my temporary neighbours and potential informants. People thought I might be surveying the land against their real interests; others suspected that I might be preparing the way for the diversion of mountain water-supplies to the town or to alien farms, or investigating tax defaulters (of whom there were many at that time). My campaign to learn and use their language, and other anthropological techniques, together with my growing and obvious sympathy over their economic difficulties and respect for their opinions and ideas, gradually lessened mistrust. The knowledge that, in my 1957 *Report*, I had strongly recommended that further arable land be made available to them, was also in my favour. Nevertheless a completely independent anthropologist might have fared better, and at least would have become generally accepted more easily and quickly.

Fortunately, almost never was there unwillingness for me to attend meetings at which discussion and negotiation occurred in the attempt to settle particular disputes. Many of these are public affairs, but I was usually admitted to the semi-private conclaves also. Often spokesmen or counsellors took pains, and pride, in explaining events to me and discussing their significance. This was, in fact, a further reason for concentrating on these matters in the field. On the other hand, I frequently was not able to overhear or obtain adequate accounts of the vital gossip and informal discussion and conversations which are an essential part of the processes by which Arusha settle their disputes. The work of Colson (1953)a, Frankenberg (1957) and others has shown the sociological significance of those kinds of informal interaction, and I must acknowledge that failure in this aspect of field-work has produced an unavoidable defect in my account of social control.

Eventually I had a number of friends who were not only good informants, but who were prepared to stand surety for me with less trusting neighbours. Among these, special mention must be made of Ndikala Koinase and Mevukie Mengadieki for whose friendship and assistance I am deeply grateful. Many others gave me their toleration, hospitality and help; without their generosity and kindness my work would have been impossible. It has been my endeavour not to betray any personal confidences; and in deference to the requests of many informants, as well as to avoid offending individual susceptibilities, all names of persons mentioned in this book are fictitious. Minor details of a number of case-histories have been changed where otherwise particular people might be readily identified.

One could not hope for a more permissive yet more helpful organisation under whose aegis to conduct both applied anthropology and basic research than that provided by the then Government of Tanganyika. A general debt of gratitude must go to the many officials who provided help and information, and who gave me the benefit of their experience from time to time, without intruding at all into my field operations. It is impossible to mention all their names here; but in particular, Mr. H. L. Snaith, then District Officer responsible for the Arusha Chiefdom, and Mr. J. Lewton Brain, Social Development Officer, gave me considerable assistance beyond their official requirements. The present Government of independent Tanganyika is, of course, in no way responsible for, nor is it necessarily in agreement with, any expression of opinion in this book. By the courtesy of the Director of Information Services of that Government, I am able to reproduce some official photographs here, as noted in the list of plates.

Preface

By coincidence and great good fortune, Alan Jacobs arrived in Tanganyika to begin anthropological field-work among the pastoral Masai a few months after I had begun work among the Arusha. Although the nature of our field-work differed tremendously, much of the material we obtained was, of course, fairly closely related. We discussed our data at intervals and gained insight and stimulus from the similarities and differences which became evident. This was particularly advantageous for me because the Arusha have always been strongly aware of and influenced by their pastoral neighbours, but published information on the Masai, though seemingly plentiful, is generally inadequate and sometimes grossly so. Mr. Jacobs was often able to give me information on Masai affairs which would otherwise have remained obscure to hamper my full understanding of Arusha. Thus I was the more easily able to obtain a balanced view of Arusha cultural affinities and history, as well as an improved sociological appreciation of the Masai-speaking peoples.

A draft of this book was read by a number of colleagues, whose comments have been most valuable in making the final version more satisfactory: Professor Elizabeth Colson of Brandeis and Boston Universities, Professor I. Schapera and Dr. A. Allott of London University, Dr. Robert Gray of Tulane University, and Mr. Axel Somerfelt of the University College of Rhodesia and Nyasaland. In addition, I must acknowledge the personal stimulus which I gained in the field from re-reading Dr. Colson's paper on social control among the Plateau Tonga of Northern Rhodesia (1953)b: it suggested to me new ways of thinking about conflict resolution in a society without courts, even though Tonga and Arusha societies are by no means similar.

Finally I wish to express my gratitude to Professor William O. Brown, Director of the African Studies Program at Boston University, on whose staff I was given both the time and the freedom to write this book. He was a sure source of encouragement and confidence and I can scarcely thank him sufficiently. He made all the facilities of the Program available to me and eased many of the tiresome chores of turning a draft into a completed manuscript. Under his direction the final typescript was prepared at the Program by Dr. Elaine Hagopian. It is for me the happiest culmination that this book should appear in the United States under the auspices of

Preface

the African Studies Program, and with the imprint of the Boston
University Press.

P. H. GULLIVER

Boston, U.S.A., 1959
London, England, 1962

Orthography: the Arusha speak a dialect of the Masai language. All
Arusha words are therefore written in the orthography suggested
for Masai in the grammar by Tucker and Mpaayei (1955), but without
the use of the velar n.

CHAPTER ONE

INTRODUCTION

I

STATED initially, and therefore over-simply, I seek to show in this book how, in cases of a more or less serious breach of the norms of social behaviour, the people involved attempt to reach a settlement of the subsequent dispute. In any society there must, by definition, exist regularised procedures which can be used to deal with alleged breaches of norms and the injuries they cause: there must be ways by which it can be established whether in fact a breach has occurred, and what is the extent of the injuries; and there must be means of determining and enforcing decisions which provide a settlement of the dispute, and perhaps also means which tend to prevent recurrence of the matter. In some societies, of course, the principal means to these ends are contained in the complex of political authorities, police, courts, judges, lawyers and codes of law—in other words, the judicial component of organised government. In indigenous Arusha society there was no such government, and hence no established and specialised judicial system. Arusha dispute processes, as part of the wider political system, are to be discovered only by an examination of more general social roles, relationships and group activities. When one person is alleged to have committed an injury against another—when, therefore, the two persons come into dispute—the significant jural factors are not only the kind of injury involved, but the social relationship between the two persons and the position of each in the structure of his society. By position here, I mean primarily the social status of each person, and the various groups to which he belongs. Especially are the groups important, because it is very largely through them that an Arusha has access to the ability and power to take jural action, there being no traditional institutionalised authority existing over and above these groups to exercise regulatory coercion and judicial competence.

An offender may, of course, readily submit to the consequences of his deed and accede to the demands of the injured person. There is then no real dispute, as the matter remains on a purely inter-personal basis—as it well may in the case of civil (as opposed to criminal) injuries committed in a society with organised government. Where there is no immediate submission, the injured party must look to his potential supporters with whose assistance only can he attempt to tackle the matter. The kind and number of supporters among the Arusha depends partly on the nature of the matter in dispute, but more importantly it depends on his relationship to the offender. In brief, other men should support that disputant to whom they are more nearly related within the smallest sector of society which includes both disputants. Those people who, in respect of the particular dispute, do not belong to that minimal sector are neutral; they are not directly involved, although they may be of some general importance in the expression of public opinion.

The expectation of support presupposes the fact that men may also bring pressure to bear on the person to whom they are responsible. That is, pressure in a general way to encourage conformity to norms and to deter him from breach of them; and pressure to accept such consequences of his actions which, after consultation with the other disputant and his supporters, are seen to be unavoidable. A man, of course, claims support from his associates in return for support which he has given them in the past, or promises to give in the future—there is a considerable degree of reciprocity here. Nevertheless, by being dependent on his associates, he is necessarily subject to their opinion and action—i.e. their constraint.

The dispute procedures of Arusha in their simplest form operate in meetings of the two conflicting parties—each a disputant and his supporters—at which discussion, advocacy and negotiation occur, and in which various pressures of both a moral and a practical kind are brought to bear by each against the other. Ideally, by Arusha standards, the ultimate settlement is one to which both parties agree, and in which, because they *do* agree, the question of enforcement does not arise. Needless to say, this is not always realised in actual life—though something like it often is—but the ideal provides a guiding principle for the people. It should be added, even at this introductory stage, that a party's agreement to a settlement does not at all imply that the party likes it in any absolute way, but rather that it is accepted as the most advantageous one which can be obtained in the total circumstances.

In order to understand the indigenous judicial procedures of the Arusha, it is necessary, first, to understand the more general structure and processes which comprise their society. For this reason, the first two parts of the monograph are concerned with a description and analysis of the two principal sub-systems of the society:—the age organisation in its territorial setting, and the patrilineal descent system respectively. The social role and the social relationships of a person in these sub-systems are never static, but always tending to change as people mature and age, as a new generation emerges and an old one retires and dies away, and as shifts of population occur. Therefore it is necessary to look beyond the formal structure to the dynamics of roles and relationships, and of the changing composition of the groups through time. It is impossible to have a genuine understanding of either the age-group system or the lineage system of the Arusha unless each is considered as a totality of continuous processes, rather than as a single, static structure. Both age-groups and shallow lineages are markedly affected by the physiological and social ageing of their members. Their developmental processes are most important, for the same reason that they are among the family or domestic group.[1] Developmental processes through time are far less easily seen in the larger-scale system of Arusha clanship, and I must admit that the limited period of field-work, unassisted by adequate records of earlier decades, has prevented me from a proper consideration of this aspect. On the other hand, whilst giving a structural account of clanship, I have attempted to show the empirical activities and their significances which clothe the analytic structural model. The nature of the various groups—age-groups and combinations of them, lineages, and clanship groupings—are described in the early part of this monograph, therefore, in order that their significance, their potential strength and weaknesses, the nature of their integrity and of their corporate action, may be appreciated in the particular context of dispute settlement. To comprehend why on one occasion the operative group is a lineage of a certain kind, and on another an age-group, and on another a clan or sub-clan, it is necessary to know not only what these social units

---

[1] In an earlier work I have examined the development processes of the family and other small-scale groups in two other African societies; Cf. *The Family Herds*, 1955.

3

are, but how they operate in general and non-judicial ways. Although analytically we may wish, for the moment, only to comprehend their operation in dispute contexts, such contexts are not really separated from other social situations, interests and processes by the people themselves, and we must follow them in that.

Secondly, each of these sub-systems produces a number of specific roles of influence and leadership—but not of authority—which Arusha describe by the generic term *olaigwenani*, directly translatable as 'spokesman'. Men occupying these roles, in an age-group or a maximal lineage, are chosen by their fellow-members because of their assessed abilities for leadership, counsel, advocacy and negotiation. They are never judges; they do not have authority, except insofar as they directly represent the agreed and expressed will of their groups. Their influence, however, is marked, especially as they are generally some of the most able members of the society; and they are the prime movers, in conjunction with particular disputants, of Arusha dispute procedures. An account of the basis and nature of their roles in those sub-systems is, therefore, a required preliminary before their parts in dispute procedures can be described.

Thirdly, each of these sub-systems provides regularised means for dealing with disputes between its members. There is the possibility of an assembly in which disputes are argued and settlements negotiated in public, and by rather formal rules of procedure. Additionally or alternatively there can be a conclave, comprising each disputant and his closest associates, in which discussion and negotiation are informal and intimate. Both assembly and conclave are defined in terms of the structure of the sub-system which is operative in respect of the relationship between two disputants, the kind of dispute, and certain other considerations. Here again, although it might be possible merely to assert the existence of such institutionalised gatherings, their full import can only be realised in the light of their wider structural and processual context.

The Arusha have for sixty years been subject to the general authority of an organised government established by colonial power. One of the results of this has been the establishment of a local government under an appointed chief, and with regular courts headed by salaried magistrates. A new kind of judicial procedure was thus introduced, involving new powers of coercion and the

concept of neutral arbitration and judgment. Although the Arusha were compelled to accede to the new power, and although after several decades they have come in part to accept it, most of their
: courts. The indigenous procedures
ts are used, the authority of both
knowledged; the courts have become,
nethod of dispute settlement. Princi-
of seeking a settlement where indi-
umbersome or inefficient. At the time
reciable period previously, the local
ef with his subordinate officials were
ge of juridical opportunities available
have to some extent influenced per-
both by their existence as a practical
r methods followed in them. It is not
herefore in Part 3 of this monograph
ocal government is given, so that this
nination of the total system of social

of the processes of dispute settlement,
r Parts are brought together to focus
here I am chiefly concerned with the
he choice of the social locus where a
nd the chain of successive procedures
which is followed in the attempt to obtain a settlement; and secondly, the nature of the process in seeking and establishing a conclusion of a dispute.

ERRATUM

Page 5, paragraph under II, line 3:
for 41,979 read 14,979.

II

The Arusha live on the lower, south-western slopes of Mt. Meru and the immediately peripheral area. Meru is an extinct volcano, 41,979 feet in altitude, and about fifty miles west-south-west of Kilimanjaro in northern Tanganyika. In contrast with the surrounding arid steppe, the mountain slopes are well watered, cool and, because of volcanic soils, notably fertile. The people are principally agricultural: their traditional economy was based on a number of staples—bananas, maize, beans and (for beer) finger millet—with lesser cultivation of tobacco, gourds and squashes, and honey-

FIGURE 1.

The location of Arusha and Masailand in East Africa

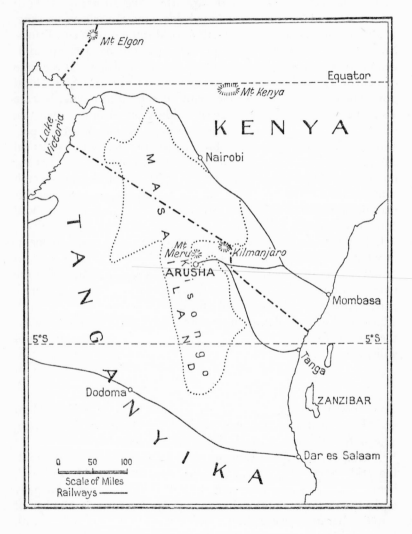

gathering in the forest. Only in the last few years has deliberate cash-crop cultivation begun—mainly coffee and onions, but also beans and seed-beans, peas and some wheat and pyrethrum.

A panoramic view of the mountain slopes shows a patchwork quilt of small arable fields and grassy paddocks, bounded by hedges of mauritius thorn, with banana groves among them, and everywhere scattered trees—remnants of the old forest cover, or newly planted for timber, firewood and shade. Many homesteads are hidden in the banana groves, but some are visible by their palisade fences, black-thatched houses, and open spaces. Each married woman has her own semi-spherical house, up to ten or twelve yards in diameter, and thatched down to the ground with dried fibre of banana trunks. Some homesteads are now enclosed by a hedge rather than a fence, and on one or more sides many of them give off directly into the banana grove. Paths wind between the fields, often sunken between the hedges by long usage and by the flow of rain water over the years. Scarcely a patch of ground is not in use, other than the precipitous banks of some streams and the areas around the springs. Fields are usually small—an acre or so, often less; only in the highest areas, the last to be pioneered some forty years ago, does the arable land sometimes remain unenclosed.

In the peripheral region, pioneered between about 1930 and 1955, the land is mainly without trees or bush. Many homesteads remain as unenclosed clusters of houses, for timber for fencing is scarce and hedges will not grow. Because of the much lower density of population, the homesteads are scattered much more widely apart. The fields are all open, bounded only by paths, dry water-courses or roughly hoed ridges. Cattle pastures are merely the uncultivated areas. Most men attempt to plant a few trees at their homesteads, to serve as windbreaks and shade, and for their timber; but often these are stunted by the long-hot dry season and the harsh winds of those times.

The lush verdancy of the mountain slopes,[1] even in the dry season, is striking and provides an environment of great contrast from the dry Masai steppe which surrounds Arusha country. Even in the open peripheral region the stamp of agriculture is marked, but this is especially the case in the traditional mountain lands. When the Germans arrived at the end of last century, Arusha settlement was

[1]The average annual rainfall ranges between 45 and 70 inches, according to altitude.

FIGURE 2.

The Arusha Chiefdom, 1957

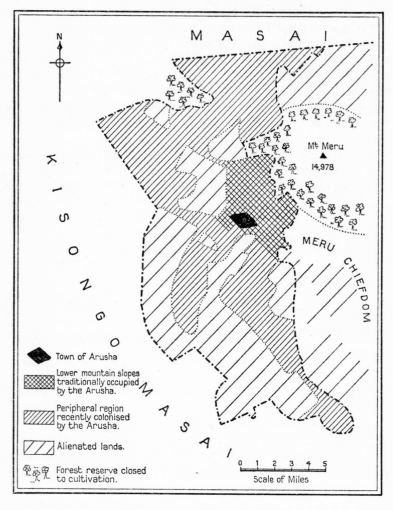

Town of Arusha

Lower mountain slopes traditionally occupied by the Arusha.

Peripheral region recently colonised by the Arusha.

Alienated lands.

Forest reserve closed to cultivation.

confined to the south-western slopes between the altitudes of roughly 4,400 and 5,300 feet. The peripheral region, lately vacated by the Masai, was used as occasional pastures only, for the Arusha had no wish to live there whilst forest land was available. A Government forest reserve was established beyond the upper limit of settlement; but this was overrun during the interregnum of World War I, and the lower forest boundary was later re-established at about 5,700 feet.

Arusha upward expansion was thus halted by about 1920; but population increase continued so that by about 1930 the Arusha began to be forced to settle in the less favourable peripheral region. It is a dry region with low and uncertain rainfall (25-30 inches annually on the average) and poor soils. There is little water for human and stock consumption, and none for irrigation. The staple banana will not grow there, but only maize and beans. The cultivation cycle is quite different from the established one of the mountain. Nevertheless, increasing numbers of younger men had no choice but to pioneer there, and by 1957 a third of the total population lived in that region.

In 1957 the total population was 62,900. Since the previous census in 1948 the population of the Arusha country had increased at an average annual rate of 2·6%. On the mountain slopes the people live at a density of about 1,000 persons per square mile, and in the poorer peripheral lands the density ranges between 100 and 200 persons per square mile. Despite the fact that about one-fifth of the mountain population in 1948 had migrated to the periphery by 1957, the density of population on the mountain scarcely fell—and in some areas it actually increased during that period. The outer limits of agricultural settlement were reached by the middle of the nineteen-fifties, but population growth continued. In their favourable mountain environment, the Arusha are as densely concentrated as any African people; but even the lighter densities in the periphery are rather higher than for most comparable environments in tropical Africa.[1]

Gradually confronted with the scarcity of land, which was the agricultural concomitant of these conditions, the Arusha have been compelled to make major adaptations in their economy and in their social life generally. It became no longer possible to persist with

[1] See my 'The population of the Arusha chiefdom, a high density area of East Africa', *Rhodes-Livingstone Journal*, 1960.

the established subsistence agriculture because increasing numbers of men had not land enough to produce sufficient food. Since the late nineteen-forties and beginning in the east, where population density is greatest, the production of crops for the market has slowly begun to spread as a means of livelihood. With the acceptance of the introduction of a cash economy has come the initial desire to earn more money and to raise living standards, and this seems to have triggered off other changes.[1]

These changes were only just starting in the nineteen-fifties and their significance was then indeterminate, though promising to be considerable. At the time of fieldwork it was impossible to make an assessment. Fundamentally the older social norms and relations, and the values and attitudes involved in them, seemed scarcely to have begun to change. The local communities, the age-group system, the lineage and clanship system, all appeared still to be only slightly affected. But in any case this present study deals primarily with the period of the nineteen-fifties and no special significance is attached to the degree of change which may have occurred in the society.

III

The Arusha have often been referred to as 'agricultural Masai'.[2] In many ways it is a reasonable description of them for it emphasises the two main bases of their lives. In their history and culture the Arusha have a dominant connection with the Masai, and they speak a dialect of the Masai language. But they have always been primarily cultivators with a sedentary life: this bias orginated in and has been fostered by factors which are not Masai inspired, for those latter people are mobile pastoralists who despise agriculture.

As a settled and established tribe the Arusha date from about 1830, at which time a few small groups of Masai-speaking peoples came to settle near the upper Burka river, at the south-western edge of the rain forest of Mt. Meru. Although the approximate date of first-settlement is reasonably well affirmed by reference to age-set chron-

---

[1] Cf. my 'The evolution of Arusha trade', in Bohannan, P. (ed): *Markets in Africa*, 1962.

[2] Early travellers called them *Kwavi*, a word of possibly Bantu origin, which in one of its meanings has the same connotation.

ology and Masai history,[1] it is still uncertain who precisely these first-settlers were. Briefly, present-day Arusha agree that almost all these settlers came from the upper Ruvu valley to the south of Kilimanjaro. Some are said to have been *Ilogolala*—a Masai-speaking, 'Kwavi'-like people who probably had earlier been driven out of the Kenya Rift region and scattered by the Masai-proper. Other first-settlers are referred to as residents of *Kikoin*, nowadays called Arusha Chini (Lower Arusha), who may have been both Kwavi and Bantu-speakers. One or two modern lineages claim a separate but still Masai-like origin, and a slightly earlier arrival on Mt. Meru. Despite the uncertainties, some important points are clear: all the first-settlers came at roughly the same time, they were predominantly Masai-speaking and Masai-like in their culture, and they immediately began cultivation and had very few or no livestock.

At the time of settlement the people made contact with the Masai tribe (the Kisongo) surrounding Mt. Meru; principally with the tribal ritual expert (*olaiboni*), Subet. The Masai must have tacitly approved the settlement for they controlled the area, and the Arusha were in an exposed position on the open, lower edge of the mountain forest. In the event the Kisongo Masai profited by the Arusha settlement: in trade, obtaining gourds, tobacco, honey and beer;[2] from the new water supplies off the mountain along Arusha-made channels; and in the herding labour of Arusha youths. The Kisongo remained confidently superior to their agricultural associates, but tolerated them far more than their Bantu-speaking, agriculturalist neighbours. For their part the Arusha accepted their ascribed inferiority. They took the Masai as their preceptors and endeavoured in all ways, short of renouncing agriculture, to maintain and consolidate their Masai orientation and association.

In their virtually virgin forest-land, with fertile volcanic soils, good rainfall and plentiful springs and streams, the Arusha quickly prospered as farmers. They began to push up the mountain slopes, clearing the forest as they went. Apart from a natural increase, they soon began to be augmented by refugees from internecine warfare among the Chagga, and from frequent raiding among the

[1] See Fosbrooke, H. A., 1956. Fosbrooke's estimates are probably as good as we may expect to make, though perhaps some of his assumptions are open to question.

[2] See my 'The evolution of Arusha trade', in Bohannan, P.: *Markets in Africa*, 1962.

Meru.[1] After the first generation, the Meru were subjugated by the Arusha, and many of them forcibly taken to live in the Arusha country. Population grew rapidly because of this, and continued to do so for the same reason until the end of the century and the advent of German rule. The non-Arusha element in the total population began to predominate numerically,[2] but the immigrants were all absorbed as Arusha and adopted the premises of Arusha-Masai culture. It is impossible to assess properly the effect of this large influx of Bantu-speaking agriculturalists. It is likely that persistent adherence to a dominantly agricultural and sedentary life—as against the typical Masai mobile and pastoral life—was much encouraged, despite continued or intensified admiration for the Masai. Arusha society is in some ways markedly different from that of the Kisongo Masai: not only in its agricultural basis, but also particularly in the lineage system and ancestor worship, and in political leadership, both of which may have been derived in part from the Chagga-Meru.

On the other hand, the structure and internal processes of the Arusha age-set system are, with few modifications, typically Masai, although the significance of the system has a peculiarly Arusha cast by virtue of their sedentary life. Arusha have consistently acknowledged the authority of the Kisongo ritual expert (*olaiboni*) as they have continued to participate in the two major *rites de passage* of the Kisongo age-set cycle which recur roughly every twelve to fifteen years. Thus the whole developmental process of Arusha age-sets is geared to that of the Kisongo. In addition the structure of the

[1] The Meru, or Rwo, were earlier settlers on Mt. Meru, occupying the south-eastern slopes. They are closely related to the western (Machame) Chagga of Kilimanjaro.

[2] Surveys among adult males in a number of mountain areas by my field assistants in 1957 produced the following results of patrilineal origins:—

Area	True-Arusha	Meru	Chagga	Masai	Dorobo	Iraqw	Total
Kidinga	201	88	84	12	12	—	397
Kimunyak	41	187	11	—	—	—	239
Siwandet	—	85	66	—	—	—	151
Sambasha	33	52	33	—	2	—	120
Kirevi (west)	38	30	21	—	—	6	95
Kioga (south)	29	32	19	5	—	—	85
Totals	342	474	234	17	14	6	1087
%	31	44	22	3			100

Arusha clanship system is essentially Masai, although (insofar as Masai data are available) there again seems to be a distinctive Arusha mode of operation of the system in working human relations.

This is not the place to attempt a full discussion of Arusha-Masai history, nor an explanation of the marked persistence of Masai values and attitudes (including opposition to western-type innovations) among the Arusha today.[1] The point may perhaps be most vividly and briefly made in a sketch of the dress and general appearance of Arusha in the nineteen-fifties, in which respect they are not easily distinguished from the Masai.

A young Arusha man (*olmurrani*) plaits and ochres his hair, wears a length of cloth over his shoulders and bead and wire decorations on his body—all in the true Masai fashion. Girls and women wear skirts and cloaks of dressed skin (preferably calf or goat) on which are sewn beaded patterns; they apply red ochre and animal fat liberally, and on the neck, arms and legs they wear beads and metal wire decoration. Like the Masai, most Arusha have their ears pierced, and the lobes stretched into large hanging loops from which are suspended decorations. Because both of the cooler and wetter climate, and the beginnings of the introduction of money, Arusha men (but seldom women) wear more of the western-style clothing than Masai—shirts and trousers under their cotton-cloth cloaks, raincoats and great coats and blanket-cloaks are common in the wet and cool seasons (March to August). Caps and hats early became popular to protect carefully ochred hairstyles against the rain. Nevertheless it remains difficult for the outsider to distinguish Arusha from Masai. Doubtless many of the casual accounts of Masai in Northern Tanganyika really refer to Arusha, who are readily encountered by visitors and residents in the township and its environs. I found that the Arusha themselves were not always able to determine whether a stranger in a crowd was a Masai or not—especially if the stranger is a man. Female fashions tend to differ between the two peoples, and deportment and dialect differ for both sexes and all ages; but the differences are subtle and in total far smaller than the general similarities.

Arusha are not unwilling to be referred to as Masai, as they often

[1] A preliminary field report was made in my paper, 'A history of relations between the Arusha and the Masai', read before the midyear conference of the East African Institute of Social Research, 1957, and circulated in cyclostyled form.

are both by other Africans and by non-Africans. Among themselves, however, they use that name only for the Masai proper, the pastoralists. Themselves they designate *Ilarusa*, s. *Olarusai*. For all their conscious admiration for the Masai, they are well aware of certain distinctions in their own culture—above all, in the agricultural basis of their lives. They keep cattle but, despite recent increases in numbers, still relatively few—rather less than one head per human being, compared with perhaps ten to fifteen per human among the Kisongo. There is no indication that the Arusha have attempted to renounce or even to diminish their cultivation; and, unlike the Masai, its practice carries no stigma at all, but only commendation.

PART ONE

ROLES AND PROCESSES RESULTING

FROM RESIDENCE AND AGE

CHAPTER TWO

THE PARISH

THE settled and cultivated part of the Arusha country is divided into a number of named areas with fixed boundaries, the residents of which comprise corporate local groups. Such an area and the group of residents are called *embalbal*, pl. *imbalbali*; or sometimes *eserit*, a vaguer word with the general meaning of 'group'. In this account these local groups are referred to as 'parishes'. The use of this word in the Arusha context refers to the smallness of size and to the autonomy of these local groups, and is not intended to imply any particular religious connotations. Nowhere do the Arusha live in compact residential clusters of the village type. A parish is a socially and geographically defined collection of scattered homesteads, each of which is built on the separate land-holding worked by the family which occupies it.

At the time of the German invasion at the end of the nineteenth century, there were fifteen parishes covering the then settled area, wholly on the mountain slopes, but not the region of common pasturelands on the lower borders. Since that time, as settlement continued to expand, new parishes have been established both on the mountain slopes and in the peripheral region of former pasturelands and what had formerly been Masai territory. Since 1948 there have been twenty-eight parishes.

On the mountain slopes, although parish boundaries do not precisely follow natural, geographical features, yet in general these have been significant guides in the identification of each parish as a single entity as the process of pioneering new farm land and new settlement developed. On the whole the mountain slopes are fairly regular in their gentle declination, but they are divided by the numerous streams flowing down from mountain springs. Between these streams are low, usually broad ridges. Pioneer settlement tended to be on the upper or flat parts of the ridges, with cultivated fields extending across and down to the streams in fairly narrow strips. This provided drier sites for homesteads and paths in the wet season, and also allowed irrigation channels to keep to the higher ground with subsidiary channels running down through the fields to the streams. Arusha say that narrower fields are easier to work and to irrigate, and that the lengthy perimeter boundaries with neighbours' fields make for greater and easier mutual cooperation and protection at the time of pioneering. The evolution of a parish occurred as the pioneering group worked its way up a broad ridge, or sometimes as it followed a stream upwards creating new farms on either flank. Some parish boundaries therefore embrace one or more ridges, or they follow the adjacent ridges with a stream in between. Usually there is some mixture of both patterns according to the historical nature of pioneering. In each mountain parish there is a well-authenticated tradition of a known group of first pioneers who established the general outlines of the local group. Final boundaries often wind erratically down the slopes as a result of the particular points at which pioneers from adjacent sides met on the ridge.

In the peripheral region pioneering was less clearly patterned and parish formation was more artificial, coming from superimposed administrative convenience, rather than from the territorial and social growth of a local community. It is a flatter, more featureless country. Continuity of expansion was broken: partly because of blocks of intervening alienated land, and partly because new pioneering was stimulated by provision of artificial water points, and by new roads and tracks, which gave rise to something like a ribbon development. Parish boundaries here have little or no natural basis but are largely arbitrary. Peripheral parishes are all much larger than those in the mountains, and in the nineteen-fifties they still had less active unity. It is possible that, without administrative interference, they would have been smaller in conformity with the organisational norms of the people. On the other hand, and administrative convenience apart, the environment is markedly different from the traditional mountain slopes, and the population is necessarily much more thinly distributed; so that the social as well as the territorial forms of the peripheral parishes are bound to be somewhat different.

On the mountain slopes the parishes are all small, both in area and population. The average size is about two square miles, though some are rather less. In 1957 they ranged between 1,200 and 3,000 people with an average of about 2,000 people. It is likely that mountain parishes were about this same size in the early part of this century; for the later, new parishes have accommodated the increase in population (more than double) since that time. With the large-scale expansion into the periphery since 1945, some mountain parishes had decreased slightly by 1957, but it is highly probable that the persisting population growth had erased these decreases by 1960. Some mountain parishes, whose members were unable to obtain access to the peripheral region, have increased rapidly in population size. With an average density of population of rather more than 1,000 people per square mile, the mountain parishes are congested, so that neighbours are close together, and day-to-day contacts are frequent.

In the peripheral region, parishes range between twenty and forty square miles in extent; and they contained from 3,000 to 5,000 people in 1957. Their populations have roughly doubled in the first decade of their formal existence. Population density is relatively low—between 100 and 200 people per square mile—and thus neighbours are farther apart, and day-to-day contacts less. Members of such a parish may live several miles apart and have little contact with one another.[1]

A parish is readily defined territorially. Traditionally almost no one owned and cultivated fields outside the parish boundaries. Even with an increase in pledges and sales of land, and the novel possibility of pioneering and using land in the peripheral region whilst retaining residence in a mountain parish, still no more than one man in ten cultivates outside his parish.[2] Nevertheless, a parish is in no way a land-owning or land-controlling group. Land is held and worked by autonomous family heads; and the public limitations on individual control are exercised through patrilineal groups, and not the parish. Membership of a parish has no basis in kinship: Arusha lineages and clanship groups are all widely dispersed territorially. Fundamentally, a parish is a local community: especially on the mountain slopes, it comprises neighbours (*elatia*) and near-neighbours who in everyday life engage in more or less regular face-to-face contact; and who, out of a historical evolution geographically based, find it mutually convenient and advantageous to

[1] On demography and historical development, see my, 'The population of the Arusha Chiefdom: a high density area in East Africa'; *Rhodes-Livingstone Journal*, 1960.
[2] *Loc. cit.*, Table 3.

AS3

recognise, and promote, a degree of cooperation and unity. A parish is, however, an organised community. It is politically autonomous; containing its own institutional machinery for determining its affairs, settling internal disputes, and dealing corporately with adjacent parishes in amity, or animosity. Each parish contains its own autonomous age-group system, from which is derived the means to self-organisation and social control which, in the context of neighbourhood-community, creates and preserves group identity and cohesion. The age-group system as described later, provides a comprehensive status system, a set of interlocking, corporate groups embracing all adult males, and a number of leadership roles which operate principally within the parish. The nature and operation of this system is described in the following chapter.

Membership of a parish is acquired and maintained by continuous residence, and cultivation within its boundaries. Because of the central importance of the age-group system, Arusha sometimes say that membership is only acquired, by a male, at his initiation into an age-group of the parish, along with his coevals. In so far as a youth, after initiation and in joining an age-group, takes the first step towards adult maturity and towards playing a responsible part in his parish, this assertion is correct. It also occurs, that a man is strongly inclined to retain interests in, and ties with, the parish where he was initiated—i.e. normally where his father lived—even if he later goes to live elsewhere. Nevertheless, a man can effectively change his parish by going to live permanently in another, by accepting and cooperating with his new neighbours, by joining (automatically) the age-group in his new parish, equivalent to that in which he was initiated, and by accepting the leadership of parish notables. The act of residence and cultivation in a parish produces unavoidable obligations, and particular status in the age-group system; and it provides complementary privileges and protection. Nowadays each parish has an official headman and parish membership tends to be endorsed by a man's inclusion on the headman's tax-roll. Children and wives participate in parish affairs through their father's or husband's membership.

Each parish maintains its own ritual grove, a sacred place dedicated to Engai, the high-god of the Arusha. The grove consists of a small patch of uncleared forest or bush, centered on a huge *oreteti* tree (probably a giant fig tree). Here occasionally—at intervals of a year or two nowadays—rituals are performed to Engai, seeking fertility for the women of the parish, and the general welfare of all. The ceremony is attended by all elders, senior murran and married women of the parish. Each newly formed parish in modern times has established its own ritual grove for this purpose.[1] It is said that special rituals are also performed by each parish at its ritual grove to combat particular major crises such as epidemics affecting humans (e.g. smallpox, influenza) or livestock, or prolonged failure of rain; but this seems not to have occurred recently. On any of these occasions, the rituals are administered by the diviner (*olaiboni*), among those resident in the parish, who is considered to be senior-most. This is partly an hereditary role, since the acknowledged diviner should be a member of the maximal lineage of that diviner who first established the grove, when the parish emerged as an autonomous unit. The grove itself is used only for these infrequent rituals involving the whole parish. It is not a site of rituals of particular parish members or sub-groups (e.g. age-groups) nor is it used for mundane assemblies.

The unity of a parish is expressed and renewed in a number of other ritual manifestations. Every stage in the age-group cycle is marked by ritual performance of some or all parish members, and is consciously described by Arusha as being in the general interests of the parish, even when primarily devoted to a particular age-segment. Parish members are free to attend one another's major ceremonies (e.g. birth, initiation, pre-marital feasts, ancestor worship, etc.) and often special portions of beer or meat are allocated to them. Anti-witchcraft drives are arranged, and carried out within the confines of a parish by the women every two or three years, as seems to them necessary by the rate of occurrence of witchcraft allegations and fears. On such an occasion, every separate homestead in the parish is visited by all the women together, and a dancing and singing ritual is performed which is believed to kill any witches who live there and to prevent new witchcraft occurring. It is mandatory on all women to participate, for those who do not are declared to be witches attempting to avoid the ritual cleansing.

The parish has acquired new corporate qualities under modern

---

[1] An *oreteti* tree is reported to be used by women of the Masai Matapatu tribe in fertility rituals to Engai—Dallas, 1931, pp. 30-41. In the Arusha country there are many *oreteti* trees, but only one in each parish is sacred to Engai.

local government, as it has become the smallest administrative unit under its appointed headman. The traditionally irregular parish assemblies have been given semi-official recognition as pseudo-judicial and consultative bodies, and regular meetings are encouraged by the chief and the government so that administrative information can be disseminated, or opinion collected through the headman. Each parish is compelled to accept responsibility for the maintainance of motor tracks and main paths which run through its area. Younger men, supervised by the headman and by the elders in general, give two or three days of free labour after the wet season. Additionally, some parishes have by corporate effort cleared new motor tracks, in efforts to make transport available to all farmers wishing to take produce to market.

Each of the parishes of the mountain slopes, both the old and the newer ones, contains two geographically discrete parts the name for which, *engashata*, is here translated as 'parish-division'. In every parish where inquiries were made—about half of the total—it was found that the two divisions arose at the development of early pioneering. One division, the geographically lower of the two, was cleared, cultivated and settled first, and the other, higher up the slopes, was pioneered later by the sons and younger brothers of the first settlers and by immigrants from other established parishes lower down. The two principal waves of settlement came roughly to distinguish two areas. Later as settlement became consolidated, the two parts came to represent areas of relatively greater neighbourhood contact and cooperation than exist throughout the parish as a whole. The divisions have, however, more significance than this, in that they are the basis of the dichotomous sub-division of each age-group and age-group leadership as described later (see p. 48). The sections are named, and because of this age-group significance their boundaries must be well defined.

The larger peripheral parishes, which are all of quite recent origins, have not developed fixed internal divisions. In these parishes a fully autonomous age-group system is not yet established, for the older men were initiated elsewhere in a number of different mountain parishes. For some time, youths returned to their fathers' natal parishes to be initiated; and in at least two peripheral parishes, autonomously controlled initiation began only with the age-group which commenced recruitment in 1955. Age-group leadership in

FIGURE 3.

The Boru sub-tribe

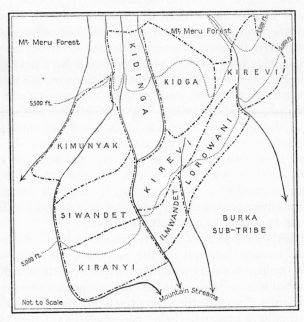

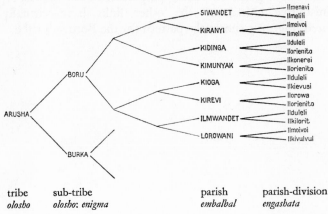

tribe	sub-tribe	parish	parish-division
olosho	*olosho: enigma*	*embalbal*	*engashata*

these parishes has tended to be erratic and disorganised, and there has been no demand for the traditional dichotomous divisions. They may emerge in due course if the age-group system persists in the future. These parishes are too extensive geographically, however, for only two parish-divisions to emerge as areas of more concentrated neighbourly cooperation and interaction; nor was pioneering so simple as in the mountain region. Instead, in each of the peripheral parishes, a number of local neighbourhoods have developed, each based on local geographical features which encourage their growth —common wet season water supply, a common cattle track or major path, a shallow valley. These neighbourhoods are not well defined, though many of them are named, and they correspond only approximately to the more precise parish-divisions of the mountain slopes. They have not yet become connected with the age-group system of their parishes. Nevertheless they provide a form of smaller community within the artificially imposed, unconsolidated and extensive parishes of the peripheral region: and for that reason they are important in everyday social life.

Formerly fixed pairs of adjacent parishes were linked together in friendly cooperation, and for the purpose of creating war-parties of the smallest scale. For military purposes, each pair of parishes was linked to an adjacent pair, and the two groups of pairs made up the sub-tribe. Two sub-tribes comprise the whole tribe. Although the sub-tribes have persisted—being perpetuated until 1948 as separate administrative chiefdoms—the other links have virtually disappeared. Figure 3 shows the pattern for the Boru sub-tribe.

CHAPTER THREE

THE AGE ORGANISATION

WITH only a few qualifications, the formal structure of the Arusha age-set system and that of the Kisongo Masai seem to be the same. And although there are important differences in the operation and significances of the two systems, the general principles of the social processes are clearly similar. Almost certainly the Arusha first-settlers brought their system with them as a result of their Masai-like origins; but their general dependence on and admiration for the Kisongo, and their acceptance of Kisongo leadership in the major rituals, must have been responsible for the close conformity between the two systems during the last few generations.[1] That structural similarity should be accompanied by functional differences is not unexpected, for the wider social contexts within which the systems operate are so strikingly dissimilar: the Arusha—a primarily sedentary, agricultural people, living at a very high density in a small country; the Kisongo—a mobile, pastoral people, living thinly dispersed over an extensive territory. Despite a number of accounts of the Masai system, none are sociologically satisfactory and therefore I do not rely on any of them directly.[2]

The Formal Structure

First I wish to distinguish clearly between what I identify as the 'age-group' and the 'age-set'. An *age-group* comprises the men of about the same age in a single parish who were initiated during a single period of four to six consecutive years. It is a corporate entity the members of which are not only conscious of their unity and of their distinctiveness from both older and younger groups in the parish, but they often act as a single body; they recognise common rights and obligations and acknowledge their own, selected leaders.

---

[1] The Kwavi (Baraguyu) of east-central Tanganyika also have a Masai-like age-set system, but in its timing, naming and rituals there is no direct conformity with the Kisongo, on whose south-eastern borders they live. Cf. Beidelman 1960.

[2] The most useful are Fosbrooke 1948 (directly on the Kisongo) and Bernardi 1955.

It is the age-group which a young man joins as a consequence of his completed initiation.

The Arusha word for this group, *olporror*, is extended to age-groups of all parishes the members of which were initiated during the same single period. An *age-set* is this set of concurrent age-groups: it bears a common name and all its members pass through the institutionalised series of promotions and transfers at the same time. The age-set has only a loose unity; only infrequently does it act as a single entity, and then principally in relation to the internal development processes of the system rather than in relation to more general social activities and processes. A wider extension of the same word, *olporror*, includes both Kisongo Masai and Meru men who were initiated in the same period as members of an Arusha age-set.

Thus an Arusha man belongs to both an age-group and an age-set; but it is the age-group which is primarily important in social life, and it is the organisation of the total chronological range of such groups within a parish which is emphasised in this present account.

Each age-group is a face-to-face unit and is operationally autonomous of other groups in the same age-set. As described later, age-group leaders have influence largely within their own parish. Institutionalised relations between older and younger groups are chiefly confined to the parish so that the total range of groups in that community comprises a self-sufficient system. The synchronisation of certain activities during the maturation of an age-set is periodically required but not continuously, and for those purposes *ad hoc* assemblies are convened as required.

As in Masailand, there are a number of institutionalised *age-grades* each comprising a formal status and a cluster of norms of behaviour, obligations and privileges. These grades or normative roles must be clearly distinguished from the corporate age-groups. Verbally the Arusha recognise two principal grades—*olmurrani*, 'murran', and *olwayian* (or *olmoruo*), 'elder'—with one pre-group grade of *olayioni*, 'youth'. In practice, however, the number of effective grades is six as a result of the differentiation of junior and senior murran and junior, senior and retired elders.

The Arusha word *olmurrani*, pl. *ilmurran*, is not translated here because in its social context there is no English synonym other than the inconvenient 'young man'. The term 'warrior', commonly used by writers on the Masai, is specifically rejected because it tends to give a distorting emphasis to a single aspect of both normative and actual social roles. It is true, of course, that for about two decades at the end of the nineteenth century raiding and offensive warfare were an important part of Arusha murran activities; but there were, even then, other equally significant features which after sixty years of enforced peace are of well-established primary importance. It is highly pertinent that, despite sixty years of peace, the age-group system has continued to flourish without appreciable lack of coherence and vitality as far as can be ascertained. To use the term 'warrior' of Arusha murran of the nineteen-fifties serves only to confuse the real significance of the role by giving it a romantic and out-dated gloss.[1]

FIGURE 4.
The Arusha Age-Set Cycle—the formal stages

(The numbers in brackets at each stage give approximately the number of years which have elapsed since the beginning of the cycle. These are indicators only, for in practice there is much variation.*)

1. *Edungore o lpiron*: closure of circumcision period of the immediately preceding age-set by the ceremonial-leader and patrons of the incipient set.
2. *Esoit narok*: the formal depositing of a ritual 'black stone' by the ceremonial-leader to enforce the prohibition of circumcision.
3. *Olamal* (5/6): deputation of representatives of each parish's potential initiates and their patrons to the Kisongo Masai ritual expert near Monduli, to obtain permission to recommence circumcision and to receive the name of the new set.
4. Deputation to the Arusha chief (6) similarly to obtain his permission.
5. Ritual treatment of the 'black stone' (6) to permit the resumption of circumcision, by ceremonial-leader together with parish representatives of patrons and wards.

[1] There is greater justification for the use of 'warrior' in reference to the Masai, for they were always a war-like people as far back as tradition goes; and they have managed to retain something of that character to the present day in their extensive and lightly administered territory. Mr. A. H. Jacobs, in a personal letter states that there were 'over a hundred cases of raiding in the first half of 1957 in Masailand.' This condition marks an important distinction from the Arusha who, with an administrative headquarters and police posts in their small country, have been unable to continue raiding. It is unlikely that the Arusha engaged in raiding before about 1880.

*For the purpose of simplified exposition it has been assumed, somewhat arbitrarily, that:—(a) 6 years elapses between the closure of one circumcision period and the beginning of the next; (b) a circumcision period lasts 6 years; (c) 2 years elapse between the closure of initiation into a set and its promotion to senior murranhood; (d) the transfer of a set to elderhood occurs one year before the promotion of the next succeeding set to senior murranhood. In practice, of course, these periods are not regular, and thus the total progression of age-sets and the chronological inter-relation of successive age-sets are not regular: cf. the actual dates given in Figure 5.

6. *Engipata* (6): proclamation of the resumption of circumcision, by ceremonial-leader at Eleree, the site of the original Arusha settlement in this country.

A. Formal period of junior murranhood (6-14)

7. Circumcision period (6-12): three main spells of activity separated by intervals of virtual inactivity.
8. *Edungore o lpiron* (12): closure of circumcision period by ceremonial-leader and patrons of the immediately succeeding set (as yet incipient only—cf. 1 above).
9. *Olamal* (14): deputation of representatives of each parish's age-group and its patrons to the Kisongo Masai ritual expert, to obtain permission to proceed to promotion.
10. *Eunoto* (14): promotion to senior murranhood at the Kisongo ceremonies at Mkulat. The set receives a new name from the ritual expert.

B. Formal period of senior murranhood (14-25)

11. *Olngesher* (25): transfer to elderhood at the Kisongo ceremonies at Oldonyo loo lmoruak. The set receives its final name from the ritual expert.
12. *Engirin aji* (25/26): ceremonial removal of all murran restrictions on meat-eating by each age-group independently in its own parish. CONCLUSION OF MATURATION CYCLE.

C. Formal period of junior elderhood (25-37)

13. Promotion to senior elderhood (37), marked only by the transfer to elderhood of the next succeeding age-set.

D. Formal period of senior elderhood (37-49)

14. Retirement (49): marked only by the transfer to elderhood of the wards' set, and the promotion to senior elderhood of the intercalary set.

E. Formal period of retired elderhood (49-)

Thereafter the age-set gradually becomes extinguished as its members die.
N.B. At stage 8, in about the twelfth year of the cycle of a set, the next succeeding set begins its cycle; and in about the twenty-fourth year of the cycle, the set of its wards begins its cycle.

As a first approximation, an age-group simultaneously with other groups of the same, named set follows a *maturation cycle*—a series of institutionalised stages—as it passes into and through the two murran grades and eventually achieves elderhood by a continuous process lasting some twenty-five years. The total *age-set cycle* involves additionally a subsequent but less well marked progress through elderhood, and ends with the extinction of a group in retired elderhood by the deaths of its members.

A concise table of the age-group cycle is given in Figure 4. It is geared to that of the adjacent Kisongo Masai by Arusha participation in the Kisongo-controlled ceremonies of promotion of junior murran to senior murran (*eunoto*), and transfer of senior murran to elderhood (*olngesher*)—stages 10 and 11 in the Figure. Other stages are not rigidly determined by Kisongo activities, not even the commencement and closure of the initiation period; and some are peculiar to the Arusha alone—i.e. stages 2, 4, 5 and parts of others. Nevertheless the Arusha are aware of comparable Kisongo progress at any time, and the two systems are subject to some similar sociological requirements.

Age-groups of the same set pass through these formal stages together by cooperative ceremonies at a tribal level, and these events are attended by deputations from each separate parish. Each stage is, however, subsequently marked ceremonially by each age-group in its own parish. The termination of the maturation cycle when the newly transferred elders publicly and ritually affirm their new status and their rejection of murran-like restrictions on meat-eating (stage 12) is entirely the affair of each separate age-group.

Recruitment to an age-group is by circumcision in the Masai fashion. One to three youths are circumcised together at the homestead of their father or their father's near agnate. Each age-group contains three 'circumcision-sections' (*emurrata*) which emerge successively as a result of the three spells of circumcision activity within the total initiation period. These spells are separated by virtual lulls which may last as long as eighteen months. The three sections thus produced are named invariably *Ilkikurukur*, *Ilkereyen* and *Ilkirimbot*. These three active spells derive from the semi-institutionalised groupings of youths before the initiation season, and are based on a narrower coevality than that which embraces the whole age-group.

The circumcision-sections are important during the period in which the new age-group occupies the grade of junior murran—that is, whilst it is not yet fully integrated and the young men are learning the mores of murranhood. The unity of the total group only gradually emerges as its members find unity in common conflict with the immediately preceding (i.e. older) group and in the effort to gain corporate promotion to senior murranhood. After this promotion the sections become much less important as sub-units, though they never disappear entirely.

Age-groups are related alternately in the total range in a parish, so that the group in the grade of junior murran is always linked with that in the grade of junior elders; and similarly the groups occupying the grades of senior murran and senior elders are linked. This relationship is vital to the processes of the maturation cycle of an age-group for each murran group is supported and guided in this by its linked elders' group; and opposition between adjacent groups in the grades of murran is controlled by similar opposition between their two linked groups, themselves adjacent in the elders' grades. The older of a pair of linked groups is described as *iloowawa* (literally 'the fathers') and will be referred to in this account as the 'patrons'; the younger group is described as *ilayiok* (literally 'the sons') and will be referred to as the 'wards'. Not all of a man's sons are recruited into the wards' age-group—and Arusha readily concede this—but at least his eldest son often is.[1] The kinship idiom is, however, consciously utilised as a means of emphasising the nature of relations between the pair of linked groups—the responsibility of the patrons to look to the best interests of their wards and to guide and assist the young men in the light of their own experience; but also the patrons' authority, for without their approval and participation the wards cannot undertake a further stage in their maturation process. The similar link between an age-group in the elders' grades and its patrons, now in the retired elders' grade, bears little practical significance for the patron-ward relationship directly concerns only the maturation cycle of an age-group.

Each age-group recognises a 'father of the wards' (*menye laiyiok*) who is selected just before the beginning of the initiation period. He is a member of the patrons' age-group, and he represents his agemates in their responsibilities to the wards. He of all the patrons is continuously active in advising and assisting the young men in all matters concerning their group and their maturation cycle. Invariably he is a member of the parish's delegation which attends interparish meetings to arrange cooperation throughout the whole age-set, and he accompanies a parish deputation to the Kisongo ritual expert (stages 3 and 9, Figure 4) and to the chief (stage 4).

This linkage of alternate groups is endlessly repeated as the flow of men and groups continues. It creates a dichotomous division of

---

[1] A man's sons are distributed amongst the wards' age-group and the next one or two successive groups, in accordance with their age and thus the time when they are ready for circumcision.

active, initiated men, and two 'streams'[1] of age-groups which are
continuous, such that one contains groups . . . 5, 7, 9 . . ., and the
other groups . . .6, 8, 10 . . . Men ascribe approved qualities to
members of their own stream and disapproved qualities to members
of the other stream, whether living members of those long dead;
and there is thought to be a continuity through time in this way. Any
important stage in the maturation cycle of a group can be referred
to as *olepole* of its patrons' group—e.g. beginning initiation, promotion to senior murranhood, etc. This arises from the recognition of
the responsibility and privilege of the patrons to assist their wards at
all times. Because there are always two age-groups in the murran or
proto-murran grades, now one and then the other is at some specific
stage: thus the stream to which *olepole* is attributed frequently
changes. Most years are associated with one stream or the other, and
past events are sometimes dated by this procedure. Men of either
stream claim that favourable seasons (good rain and crops, absence
of disease and misfortune) occur only, or almost only, when a year
is *olepole* of their own stream. Arusha are tenacious of these assertions,
despite their obvious illogicality and demonstrable falsity in fact,
for to them they are assertions of important human relationships of
identity and of opposition. This dichotomous segmentation in the
age-group system—the two streams comprising all men living and
dead, and the two active groups in each stream—conforms to a
general sociological principle of structural dichotomy in this
society.[2]

At certain stages of the maturation cycle, procedural and ritual
cooperation is required between the age-groups of the total age-set,
and between their patrons' age-groups, in order to maintain a common continuity through the whole tribe and a tribal concensus in

[1] These streams are, of course, moieties of the total of initiated men. The term 'moiety'
is however normally restricted in anthropology to groups recruited by descent and is
so used in this book; cf. p. 112. The Arusha have no word equivalent to 'stream' and
refer to it by the names of the constituent age-groups.

[2] The operational significance of this in the age-group system is discussed later in this
chapter; on the general principle, see Chapter 7. A dichotomous division of men is a
feature of many East African age systems, although the sociological significance of this
structural principle is variable. It occurs among all Masai-like peoples; but it is also
demonstrated, for example, in the Turkana 'alternation' (Gulliver 1958, p. 902), the
linked alternate 'generations' of the Jie (Gulliver 1953, p. 148ff.), the Kikuyu 'generation'
(Lambert 1956, p. 40ff.), the Meru 'division' (Lambert 1947, p. 4), the Pokomo
'company' (Prins 1952, p. 24ff.), and the Longarim 'moiety' (Kronenberg 1961, p. 263).
Cf. also, Ruel 1962, p. 18ff.

relation to the Kisongo Masai and their ritual expert. This is arranged through and focuses upon the 'ceremonial-leader' (*olaunoni*) of the murran set involved. He is a member of the patrons' set, and he acts in close consultation with leading members of that set. There are at any time two age-sets following their maturation cycles (though always at different stages from each other) and therefore there are two ceremonial-leaders, one for each set: that is, one for each stream. The role is hereditary and there is a known line of succession in each stream. These lines are not genealogically related to each other and the founding ancestor of each originated in different areas, according to lineage histories.[1] A leader's responsibilities end with the completion of his wards' transfer to elderhood, and his position is then taken over by a son—a member of his wards' set—who immediately assumes responsibility for the next set in the same stream which is just about to commence its maturation cycle. The successor, selected by his father, is the first youth to be initiated into his age-set, so that the choice is made twenty or more years before he takes over the role. He is not normally the eldest son, for he should be at or just before puberty when initiated, having had no carnal experience.

A ceremonial-leader is responsible only for the organising and ritual processing of one age-set in its maturation cycle—notably, but not only, stages 1, 2, 5, 6 and 8 in Figure 4. He does not become involved with the other currently active leader, nor with the tensions and conflict between his wards and the other murran set. Although he is the only person with a tribe-wide competence for a whole set, he does not acquire a political or ritual significance beyond his narrow specialist role. This was so for both of the leaders in the nineteen-fifties, and there is no tradition that any of their predecessors were any more important. Cooperative consultation and decision making with regard to the wards' set are monopolised by the more prominent spokesmen of the various age-groups of patrons, who are by that time highly experienced men in public affairs. The ceremonial-leader gives a focus to their dispersed and otherwise uncoordinated activities, without challenging their local strength

[1] One came from Masailand and the other from Kikoin (Arusha Chini). The role of *olaunoni* is quite different among the Kisongo Masai: cf. Fosbrooke 1948, pp. 39-40. The hereditary succession of the Arusha leader has affinities with that of the senior men in a Jie generation, though their respective roles are operationally different: cf. Gulliver 1953, p. 149.

FIGURE 5.

Arusha age-sets up to 1959.

Final name of age-set	Commencement of initiation	Promotion to senior murran	Transfer to elderhood	Patrons' age-set	Lines of succession of ceremonial leaders	
Diyoki						
Kisaruni						
Merishari	(c.1811)					
Kidotu	(c.1825)					
Dwati	(c.1839)			Merishari	gggf	gggf
Nyangusi	(c.1853)			Kidotu	ggf	ggf
Laimer	(c.1867)			Dwati	gf	gf
Dalala	c.1881	c.1887	c.1905	Nyangusi	f	f
Dwati	c.1896	c.1905	1917	Laimer		
Dareto	c.1911	c.1919	1929	Dalala		
Derito	1926	1931	1948	Dwati		
Nyangusi	1942	1949	1959	Dareto		
(Kiwoni)	1955			Derito	son	son
?				Nyangusi		
?				(Kiwoni)	son	son

Notes:—

1. Age-set names are given in their plural form without the gender prefix (*il-*). All names except the most recent one are those acquired on transfer to elderhood.

2. For earlier dating the suggestions of Fosbrooke (1956) are followed.

3. Genealogical relationships of earlier ceremonial leaders are given by reference to the incumbents of the role in 1959. (f—father, gf—grandfather, etc.).

4. The two lines of patrilineal succession to the role of ceremonial leader indicate also, of course, the two streams in which alternate age-sets are placed.

5. The original pioneers who settled as adult men on the lower south-western slopes of Mt. Meru were members of the Merishari and Kidotu sets. It is possible that sets had been formed before that time, but the evidence is not clear. There may have been *ex post facto* reconstruction based on the known Kisongo Masai sets, as there almost certainly was by the Meru and, according to Fosbrooke (*ibid*, p. 16), among the Taveta.

nor exercising what Arusha consider to be undesirable political power at a supra-parish level. He is the key to the successful synchronisation of the activities of all the age-groups of a single age-set throughout the tribe, without affecting the valued autonomy of each in its own parish.

The age-group system provides the organisational basis for the administration and integration of the parish. The authority of age-groups and the influence of age-group leaders are almost entirely confined to the individual parish. As noted above, the age-set only loosely coordinates the activities of its component groups, whilst relations between age-sets are in effect only the sum of relations between age-groups in their own parishes. A further source of unity in the parish comes from the fact that all men of the community belong to one or other of the current age-groups. Intra-group relations extend across the whole parish. Similarly a man can satisfactorily place every other man in his parish in a more or less senior or junior position with respect to himself. That is, a man is meaningfully linked to all other men; such linkage is given significance because of the nature of inter-group relations, and because at least the initial basis of attitudes and behaviour towards any other man is thus provided.

Particularly important to an individual are the institutionalised links with his coevals, his age-mates, with whom he can be on terms of equality, familiarity and ease, who join him in many leisure activities, and who give him sympathy and support. This kind of evaluation is perhaps strongest amongst murran, and weakest among senior and retired elders; yet even amongst the oldest men it by no means disappears, and this is often demonstrated in the convivial comradeship and co-identification of retired elders both at beer-drinks, feasts and other gatherings, and in their everyday visiting and association.

Age-mates may refer to each other as 'brothers' (*ilalashera*) in recognition of the kind of fraternal feeling between them. This feeling is particularly marked in two ways beyond its generalised expression. Firstly, a man may not have sexual relations with an age-mate's daughter, for such a girl is 'like your own daughter'. This analogy is not extended to the members of the alternately-linked group, 'the fathers' (cf. page 38). A man can marry the daughter of one of these 'fathers' with no idea of incest with a classificatory sister.

The emphasis, that is, is placed on the fraternal relations between age-mates. Secondly, a man has the privilege of sexual access to an age-mate's wife. Occasional sexual intercourse with an age-mate's wife is not regarded as wrong unless the woman is suckling a child, or unless it occurs frequently enough to interfere with the husband's conjugal rights so as to alienate the couple. There is an adultery fine of an ewe and beer payable to members of other age-groups, and this is increased by a heifer in the case of a member of the patrons' group. The fine to be claimed against an age-mate is likely to be no more than some beer, and it is notoriously difficult for a man to establish his case and obtain even this amount. Arusha say that an age-mate's wife is like one's own wife, though this is true only in a limited sense as everyone is aware. This conception is emphasised when a girl undergoes clitoridectomy at her initiation. The man to whom she is betrothed, together with his age-mates, not only assemble to witness the operation, but they aggressively prevent other men from approaching near. At such a time the girl is referred to as the 'wife' of the age-group.

Leisure groups are commonly composed of age-mates. Murran, especially in the junior grade, spend a good deal of time roaming about in small bands—informal, local collections of age-mates—which coalesce to form the age-group proper at dances and singing displays. Elders attend beer-drinks and ceremonies in the company of their age-mates, and usually portions of food and drink are allocated to the members of each group for their own distribution and consumption. Men tend to find their closer friends within their own age-groups, and they are more likely to visit the homesteads of nearby age-mates than those of other neighbours; informal clusters of drinkers at beer clubs tend to comprise age-mates.

Finally, the death of a man is considered to be a loss to his age-group and he is publicly mourned by his age-mates. Fairly soon after his death they assemble at his homestead to slaughter and eat an animal taken from his herd. This occasion—*olkiteng le ngare*—is described as the last time his age-mates beg him for food and are fed by him. Although not confined only to members of the deceased's age-group, for neighbours and particularly affines also attend, the event is initiated by them. Some Arusha state that, until the feast has been held by the deceased's age-group, discussions on the inheritance of his estate cannot begin; but I failed to enquire if this is mandatory.

Roles and Processes

We are concerned with the age organisation as one of the sub-systems of Arusha society which is involved in dispute processes and social control. Its mode of operation in this connection can only be understood through an appreciation of the roles which individuals play as members of an age-group, and of the processes through which the age-groups of a parish develop and interact. This is the purpose of the present section.

As Arusha describe their age organisation, and as it may appear superficially to the outside observer, there is an ordered progression of chronologically successive, corporate groups through a regular series of defined age-grades. The progression is one of defined stages marked by the ceremonies already referred to (see Figure 4), and among which the more important are the 'proclamation' of the commencement of a new set, the 'promotion' of a set from junior to senior murranhood, and the 'transfer' of a set from senior murranhood to elderhood. The progression continues as a set passes through the elders' grades. Considerable emphasis is laid by the Arusha on the notion of the progression of men in groups rather than of individuals as such, so that men should conform to the standards of the grade in which their own age-set is currently located.

This conceptualisation of a most complicated set of social processes is adequate enough as a simplified and generalised picture. It is not true, as it stands, of concrete situations involving actual men. More than this—and it is probably true of all cases of significant divergence between the ideal and the actual—the generalised, ideal type version tends to conceal or distort the active principles of the system and its real operation. Nevertheless it is useful to begin with the simpler version, and therefore a brief summary is given first of the ideal roles appropriate to each grade. These roles can conveniently be subdivided:—the public aspect, concerning an individual in his parish, in political, jural and ritual affairs; and the private aspect, concerning him in his family and kinship setting, and in his particular inter-personal relations. The two aspects are, of course, complementary.

Youths: They have no part in public life. Their role is herding livestock and acting as servants to the older members of their families. Youths of about the same age who live in adjacent homesteads, or in adjacent cattle camps, tend to associate together in informal bands which have the nature of play groups (e.g. hunting birds, spear and stick throwing, imitating men's dancing, gossiping, hanging around the edge of an adult meeting or other event). They have nothing to do with unmarried girls. Theirs is a wholly pre-adult status.

Junior murran: The key feature is a general absence of responsibility in either public or private life. They do not participate in ritual affairs or in politico-jural discussion. They are used as servants in tasks requiring little judgment or skill (e.g. carrying unambiguous messages, fetching firewood at feasts, clearing an assembly place, etc.). Although initiated, they are not considered fully adult. They play little part in family affairs. They may supervise a cattle camp in the pasturelands but do not normally herd livestock; nor do they assist in agricultural work, although they share with senior murran heavy building labour and work on parish roads and paths. They spend a good deal of time in enthusiastically singing and dancing at the edge of any public event, and in general enjoying themselves easily. Their hair is fashioned into two or three mudded pigtails and they carry a plain-hafted spear. There are restrictions on meat and milk consumption and an absolution prohibition on drinking beer or honey wine. They may consort with girls and become betrothed, but they should not marry.

Senior murran: They assume a degree of responsibility and, formerly, were the experienced warriors. They are not mature enough to participate fully in ritual or politico-jural affairs nor knowledgeable enough to be of consequence in them. They may attend parish assemblies but even their spokesmen remain quiet unless specifically required to represent the interests of their age-group. They undertake 'police' duties and tasks requiring some discretion (e.g. carrying a diplomatic message, summoning a witness, seizing an animal as a fine or ritual reparation) on the orders of the elders. They are ineligible to be chosen as lineage counsellors. They are less hedonistic and they stay at home more, undertaking responsibilities to parents and younger siblings and assisting in agriculture. They are betrothed and marry, undertake affinal obligations and become involved in starting a household. Until land shortage prevailed, they pioneered new farms in the forest or bush and built new homesteads. They wear a single mudded pigtail and carry a black-hafted spear. Food restrictions are relaxed but not abolished.

Junior elders: They participate fully in all ritual and politico-jural affairs. Their spokesmen convene and administer parish assemblies and, in consultation with their age-mates, facilitate the approach to decisions on matters in discussion or dispute. Junior elders are fast learning Arusha custom, ritual procedures, ceremonial conventions, judicial techniques and the details of past precedents. They settle down as householders, heads of growing families, cultivators, and stock owners whose major concern is the development of homestead and farm. They no longer undertake the heavier labouring tasks. They no longer wear pigtails nor much other decoration, nor do they carry spears. They submit to no special food restrictions, and they drink beer freely—much of their leisure time away from home is spent at beer-drinks in the company of other elders.

Senior elders: Participation in public affairs is less than in junior elderhood; but they, and especially their spokesmen, become repositories of experience, knowledgeable of past affairs and specialists in the diplomacy essential to delicate matters and obdurate disputants. Ritually they are the acknowledged experts and most efficacious performers. In private life they are consolidating their families, farms and herds, and often they engage in a second pioneering enterprise. Their older sons are attaining adulthood, and their older daughters are marrying and new affinal ties are accumulating. Dispositions of land and livestock amongst their sons are begun. They tend to confine themselves more to their own homesteads and participate less in beer-drinks and feasts than junior elders.

Retired elders: They give up participation in public affairs unless personally involved; indeed they are specifically excluded and their experience ignored. They are rather pitied by younger men, and even despised as 'too old for anything'. Their families and homesteads shrink as children move out; and their influence, even authority, is usurped by adult sons (some of whom may be junior elders) impatient of old men's dilatoriness. There is a return almost to irresponsibility in both public and private life. They have no liabilities to a junior age-group in its maturation cycle; and although they retain ultimate control over both sons and property and ritual primacy in the ancestor cult, nevertheless day-to-day management is left to their sons. Thus a retired elder demands respect without responsibilities for supervision, and food and beer without the obligation to administer resources.

These summary descriptions are directly based on remarks and comments of Arusha in their everyday lives. It is noteworthy that they are stereotyped and vary little for different individuals whatever their own personal situation.

Although these ideal types are not incorrect in themselves as indigenous conceptualisations, nevertheless it is wrong to say that differences between successive types are clear-cut. More importantly, members of a single age-set do not necessarily all occupy a single age-grade, playing substantially the same role; nor are the *real* shifts from grade to grade made by whole sets at specific times through *rites de passage*. The Arusha, despite their simple idealisation of age-grades, recognise this and they give considerable cultural emphasis to the fact that men are individuals whose characters and particular personal maturation are not equal and orderly. They assume that men cannot, indeed should not, be closely regimented.

What occurs in reality is that there is a gradual, fairly continuous process of changing and becoming, and in this process there are a number of successive role-phases which tend to conform to the ideal age-grades, being influenced in this by cultural expectations. In their timing these phases are, however, correlated only to a limited extent with the ideal periods associated with the age-grades, as these are marked ceremonially and by their formal occupation by an age-set in its developmental cycle. Thus not only do members of an age-set not necessarily occupy the same actual grade—or role-phase—but many of them (even the majority sometimes) do not occupy it during the period when by ideal standards they should. As the system operates in actual practice the ceremonial events (the presumptive *rites de passage*) mainly give public recognition of an already established change for the majority of men in an age-set; they largely serve to bring formal categories into line with actual roles.[1]

In making this interpretative analysis I am strongly influenced

---

[1] A similar process occurs in the evolution of Kuria generation classes. Ruel states that each class ceremony 'commemorates the changing status of class members rather than actually effects it.' Ruel 1962, p. 22; cf. also pp. 26-7.

by conditions in the developmental cycles of the five existent age-sets during the period of field work, i.e. 1956-58.

During the period under review a new initiation period had begun (in 1955) and recruitment to a new set of age-groups was in progress. By 1957 (two years before formal, ritual transfer) the majority of the senior murran were already acting as if they were junior elders, for they had largely rejected the mores, attitudes, dress and status of murran. Few wore murran decorations, even at feasts and celebrations; few carried spears, flirted with girls or attended dances. They said that these things were for the junior murran. All without exception drank beer, and acknowledgement of this was made at beer-drinks where a portion was set aside for them just as for elders' groups. Surveys in three parishes revealed that over three-quarters of the senior murran were married, and one-fifth had more than one wife.[1] Virtually all the married men had their own homesteads and had been allocated the bulk of their farmland and livestock by their fathers. Many had in fact inherited as their fathers were already dead. The large majority of senior murran were preoccupied with consolidating their households, developing cultivation regimes and administering their herds. In public affairs they were attending parish assemblies and lineage moots as regularly as full elders and they were increasingly participating there in cross-questioning and the exchange of opinion; clearly they were consciously encouraged in this by the full elders. Although it was repeatedly asserted that only elders should be selected as lineage counsellors, yet in 1957 several counsellors were still formally senior murran, and a number of others were recognised by the people to be virtually counsellors in all but name. This adoption in practice by most senior murran of what was the role of junior elder went unchallenged by members of other age-sets and was, indeed, accepted by them as a normal development.

Concomitantly, the junior elders were beginning to give up their executive responsibilities, declaring that now there were sufficient members of the succeeding group (still formally in the senior murran grade) capable of taking over their duties. For example, a

[1] In a sample of 419 senior murran in 1957, 23% were unmarried. In the same sample survey nearly 7% of the junior elders were still unmarried, and it may be assumed that at least some of the senior murran would similarly remain permanently unmarried. Permanent bachelorhood is not impossible among the Arusha.

junior elder spokesman said in public in 1957: 'We are getting old now; we have no time for all this work and no energy for it. Let the (senior) murran do it! It is their time now.' On the other hand the junior elders were jealous of their greater experience and knowledge and spoke of their successors as 'youngsters who can do the work if we show them and watch them'—a typical attitude of senior elders to junior elders. At the same time the formal senior elders had become increasingly reluctant to engage in politico-jural affairs that did not directly affect them personally, and fewer attended public assemblies. They declared on many occasions that they had worked long and hard and wished now to leave responsibilities to their juniors. Already the more able of the junior elders were performing the advisory and consultative tasks which should devolve upon senior elders. The senior elders were urging the holding of their wards' formal transfer to elderhood in order to regularise the effective situation.

In discussion with older Arusha it became clear that the same kind of gradual process had occurred at this stage in previous cycles, and that a similar process occurs at other stages. After the transfer of an age-set to elderhood, the senior murran grade is left vacant until the promotion of the succeeding set from junior murranhood. In practice, however, very many of the junior murran, both by necessity and aspiration, come to occupy the vacant grade before formal promotion. By necessity, because they are then the only militant protective group of men, the only group to act as 'police' and messengers for elders' spokesmen, lineage counsellors and the chief; by aspiration, because they desire the added privileges and prestige of senior murran and no longer is there any preceding group to oppose their assumption of these. Under specific questioning, old men admit that junior murran have 'always' been able to marry before formal promotion. In early 1958, when the youngest age-set had been opened to recruitment for two and a half years only, and the first circumcision-section just about completed, about one in ten of the junior murran was already married, although none that I knew of had established his own household. Arusha fathers expressed neither surprise nor disapproval although this condition conflicts with the ideal conceptualisation of the junior murran grade.

Similarly, towards the end of the period during which circumcision is forbidden and before a new age-set is begun, the older uninitiated youths act as if they were junior murran. Such youths are more than mere boys; many are about twenty years old. They would formerly, say Arusha today, have already been out with raiding parties, and would have been reasonably competent with spear and shield. They are, despite sanctions, already involved in sexual liaisons, and some may be betrothed. They disdain herding work and occupy themselves hedonistically like murran, even sometimes wearing murran-type decoration.

This divergence between the ideal and actual allocation of roles refers to both the public and private aspects of each age-grade in the series. Maturation processes in both aspects of social life are roughly parallel. For example, a man begins to take over the actual role of junior elder in homestead and farm and in kinship matters, as he simultaneously begins to participate actively in parish assembly and lineage moot—though still for the time being remaining formally a senior murran. The two aspects of the one role, junior elder, are complementary and neither is adequately played separately. Men who have largely consolidated their marriages and who are settling down as established heads of homesteads are at the same time men who are concerned with public affairs, whose opinions carry weight, and whose participation is expected and encouraged by others. A similar complementary exists in other graded roles.

In Figure 6 an attempt is made to illustrate with model types the nature of the gradual shifting of social roles from one age-set to its successor as its members age socially as well as physically. Only three chronological points are treated in the diagram, but they are the more significant ones. The diagram, it is admitted, contains the usual weaknesses of its kind and the complexity of the real processes is over-simplified. It is, however, impossible to show all the variants in any simple way and the diagram serves to make the position clearer without further pretensions. Fundamentally it illustrates the inadequacy in reality of the ideal formulation of the way in which age-groups pass through the age-grades.

The concept of graded stages need not be dispensed with; it is necessary, however, to modify the sequence and to give due allowance for individual 'irregularities' in the light of actual behaviour and also, significantly enough, of actual expectations. In this exposition it is emphasised that the rituals which formally mark the

The Age Organisation

FIGURE 6.

Models to illustrate the developmental process in the age-set system and the divergence between formal and actual age-grade distribution.

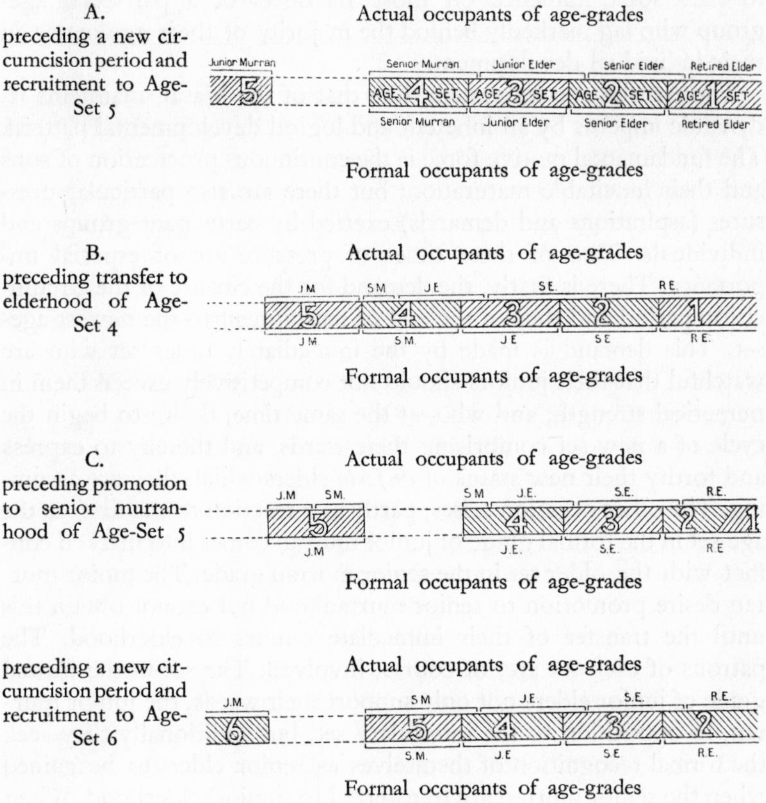

A.
preceding a new circumcision period and recruitment to Age-Set 5

B.
preceding transfer to elderhood of Age-Set 4

C.
preceding promotion to senior murranhood of Age-Set 5

D.
preceding a new circumcision period and recruitment to Age-Set 6

A, B, C and D are successive chronological points in the developmental process such that D repeats the position at A except that existing groups have all passed on one stage and a new group is about to emerge, whilst the former oldest set has died out.

The age-grades, compounded of social roles and associated mores, attitudes, etc., remain fairly constant but the occupants of each of these grades are not, in reality, members of a single age-set. Members of a single set are often distributed among two grades, and change of grade is not significantly governed by the promotion and transfer of the formal and ceremonial cycle.

These models present an over-simplified explanation for purposes of exposition and clarity.

43

transitions from age-grade to age-grade are, in practice, largely a recognition of what is already accomplished. They do not establish the necessary conditions for the adoption by groups of men of new roles in either public or private life. They may, however, serve to exert some influence on those members of a particular age-group who lag markedly behind the majority of their age-mates in their individual development.

The Arusha age-set system, like that of the Masai, maintains its dynamic impetus by an inherent and logical developmental pattern. The fundamental motive force is the continuous procreation of sons and their inevitable maturation; but there are also particular pressures (aspirations and demands) exerted by participant groups and individuals. Two of these times of pressure are of especial importance. There is firstly, the demand for the closure of the circumcision period and thus of the end of recruitment to the newest age-set. This demand is made by the immediately older set who are watchful that their juniors should not competitively exceed them in numerical strength; and who, at the same time, desire to begin the cycle of a new set comprising their wards, and thereby to express and fortify their new status of *de facto* elders which they are assuming. The other occasion arises, partly as a reaction to the first, as the age-set in the formal grade of junior murran comes into marked conflict with the older set in the senior murran grade. The junior murran desire promotion to senior murranhood but cannot obtain this until the transfer of their immediate seniors to elderhood. The patrons of each set are, of course, involved. The set in the formal grade of junior elders not only support their wards, the junior murran, in opposition to the intercalary set, but additionally they seek the formal recognition of themselves as senior elders to be gained when the senior murran are transferred to (junior) elderhood. When the senior murran are transferred to elderhood then the junior murran can be promoted to the vacant grade. Once the junior murran grade is vacant, demand begins to build up both among youths who are potential initiates and their patrons for a new circumcision period to be begun and so recruitment to a new age-set. Thus the process continues.

Although stated in general terms by reference to successive and alternately linked age-sets, these pressures are principally expressed in relations between age-groups in their separate parishes. Attitudes and actions in the various parishes are fairly closely correlated and are mutually stimulating; nevertheless it is of only secondary importance to members of age-groups in one parish what happens in another. The particular individuals who interact in cooperation or in conflict are co-members of a single parish where their roles are played and their aspirations and privileges realised in fact.

It would be a mistake to suggest that numerical pressure were an adequate explanation of the dynamics of the system. There are excellent sociological and psychological reasons for the maintenance of the cyclical progressions. Resistance to formal advancement is always weaker than the demands for it by the adjacent age-sets. It has been shown already that the notion of transfer is largely a matter of giving formal recognition to an already existing state of affairs, i.e. of role distribution, rather than creating that state. Pressures are not against a firmly closed door; rather they are against one which is ajar, but which may resist being opened wide. The pressures, arising out of men's aspirations to roles, serve as a means of assisting a fairly regular, recurrent process; and they emerge out of and are expressed through the corporate age-groups.

This tends to be disguised because of the often violent terms in which such pressures are expressed and exerted—e.g. verbal hostility, brawling and fighting, and general intractability. Most of this kind of behaviour expresses not so much the demands and resistance to demands between successive age-groups, but rather a more general inter-group hostility based on mutual exclusiveness in the chronological sequence and on competition and rivalry over, for example, song and dance forms, the nature and quality of decorations and the favours of girls. There is a structurally posited opposition—antagonism and competition—between proximate but separate groups there is the assumed superiority of the older group and the resentment it produces in the younger group; and conversely there is the developing competitive ability of the younger group and the resentment it produces in the older group. Much of the inter-group opposition and violence is conventional, and much is over exaggerated in talk. The Arusha recognise this outside of the heat of the moment. Much of it, too, is the result of, on the one hand, the older junior murran trying out their new strength, jealous of their new adult status, and, on the other hand, the reaction of a fairly small minority of senior murran (usually the younger ones) who mature later than their age-mates and who, therefore, generally resent the speeding-up process which affects them personally and, as they see it, adversely. It was notable that in 1957 and 1958 the amount of violence of any kind between the two murran age-sets, or between the senior murran and junior elders, was considerably less among the Arusha than it was among the Kisongo Masai. As far as is known there were no deaths or serious injuries among the Arusha in those years, but a number of deaths occurred from murran fights in the Kisongo country. This supports the hypothesis that these social processes are less difficult among the Arusha than among the Masai, and it suggests that over exaggerated antagonism and violence are perhaps partly imitations of the Masai pattern.

In conclusion of this section the main features may be reiterated and summarised as follows:—

1. The existence of a series of role-phases (institutionalised age-grades), though in part idealised, is important in the distribution of roles to individuals but only to a limited extent to whole units (i.e. age-groups) of men.

2. The shifts from role-phase to role-phase are earlier in time in each case for the large majority of individuals, and are rather more complex, than the ideal pattern of ritually regulated shifts by whole groups from grade to grade at set times. The ritual events[1] tend only to set a seal on an already achieved change.

3. The impetus of the cyclical progression is maintained largely because men outgrow their role-phases and seek to assume new ones. In each case this corresponds on the whole with the precisely similar needs and motives of younger successors; but, where such effective coincidence of satisfaction does not occur smoothly, active pressures are exerted by the younger men against their immediate seniors, and in this juniors are assisted by their patrons against the intercalary group.

All this means that the age-group is a less well-integrated body than it might be if all members entered a new role-phase simultaneously. The ritual recognition of formal entry into a new role-phase serves, of course, to renew consciousness and unity in terms of

---

[1] The timing of promotion and transfer ceremonies (stages 10 and 11 in Figure 4) are wholly controlled by the Kisongo Masai and emerge from Kisongo requirements. This suggests one reason for the discrepancies between formal and actual roles in Arusha, but at least a degree of discrepancy also exists in Kisongo.

common activity and co-identity; nevertheless men are not by any means entirely dependent on their age-group for their own individual progress, and commonly not all men of a single age-group are occupying the same role. That is to say, there is a basic weakness in the Arusha age-group which is never wholly overcome despite the undoubted importance of it, *qua* group, in the parish.

In the following account it will repeatedly be convenient, even necessary, to fall back on the use of ideal roles and functions. It should be clear, nevertheless, that in practice the role of, for example, 'junior elder' is not rigidly monopolised by a single age-group for a finite period. The nominal use of the formal categories is, therefore, only a means of facilitating exposition and for the same sort of practical reason which the Arusha themselves find them useful verbal concepts even though necessarily ambiguous ones. Unless specifically stated, the terms 'murran' and 'elder' and their qualified forms should be taken to refer to the role-phases through which men pass; when prefaced by the adjective 'formal', they should be taken to refer to the ideal grades, and the periods which an age-group is conceived to occupy them, between successive promotions and transfers.

Roles of Leadership and Influence

When a fairly large number of the initiates into a new circumcision-section have emerged from the seclusion following circumcision, they choose their own 'spokesman' (*olaigwenani*), with the assistance of 'the father of the wards' (cf. page 39) and the friendly interest of the patrons. This occurs within less than a year from the opening of the circumcision period or the resumption of initiation after a lull during the period. In most cases potential leaders emerge in the informal pre-initiation clusters of youths, and it becomes a matter of final choice of the outstanding individuals. Youths become prominent and are later selected as spokesmen usually for purely personal qualities of initiative, intelligence and popularity. Arusha are well aware of the abilities required—they tend to be the same as for lineage counsellors (cf. pages 103.)—and it is the 'father of the wards', with the help of his age-mates if necessary, who is chiefly responsible that the unsophisticated young men do not choose arbitrarily or on the grounds of mere popularity. Occasionally a young man is selected because his father is influential, by wealth and public reputation in the parish and the patron's group, but this is not common and on no account would an otherwise unacceptable person be agreed to by his age-mates or by the 'father of the wards'. Having such a father is only likely to favour a man when final choice has to be made between roughly equally capable persons.

In each mountain parish one spokesman should be chosen among the members of each parish-division in each circumcision-section. That is, six spokesmen should be eventually chosen within the whole age-group—two in each circumcision-section. These men are ranked according to the chronological seniority of their sections, but without regard for parish-divisions. This ranking, as well as the role of spokesmen itself, is marked by the special pieces of a carcass which are reserved to those men whenever an age-mate of their own parish division slaughters an animal for a public feast—as a judicial fine or for ritual purposes. Spokesmen are commonly referred to by the names of those portions; thus in each parish-division for each age-group there are:—

olaigwenani le ngoriong: 'spokesmen of the loins-meat'—of section 1, *Ilkikurukur.*

olaigwenani lo lngarvusha: 'spokesmen of the rib-meat'—of section 2, *Ilkereyen.*

olaigwenani le mbutua: 'spokesmen of the breast-meat'—of section 3, *Ilkirimbot.*

A spokesman's rights to the relevant portion of meat are largely symbolic of his status. Although he may have the meat sent to his homestead, there to be consumed, he normally eats most or all of it on the spot in company with his particular friends and other notables of the same circumcision-section. Unless there is plenty of meat, i.e. several animals slaughtered together, it is considered highly selfish and greedy, but even worse, presumptuous, for a spokesman not to share his meat immediately. It is a fair reflection of the actual position of the spokesman that he is scarcely able to exercise his formal privilege over against his age-mates, and I know of no case where one was able to do so when only a single beast was slaughtered.

The ideal number of spokesmen does not inevitably occur for every age-group in every parish; rather more often it does not. The senior circumcision-section frequently chooses not only its permitted two spokesmen but also one or two others who then lay claim to the next pair of spokesmen titles. This happens when members of that section have been unable to agree on only two men best suited for the positions available to it; it happens also as a conscious expression of hostility towards the younger men. If the second circumcision-section has a fair numerical strength, it will be able successfully to demand of its seniors the right to fill from its own ranks the second pair of spokesman titles; and in this it will be supported by the patrons. The senior section has to give way and finally solve its own selection problems, but fighting has sometimes broken out on such occasions. Sometimes, however, the second section is small in numbers relative to the first and its members are unable or even unwilling to exert their rightful claims, and thus the second pair of spokesman titles remain with the senior section. In many cases the second circumcision-section is too small in number to choose spokesmen even when not challenged by their seniors. In such a case the third section chooses men for the second pair of titles and it may or may not then choose others for the third titles also. Finally, if at the time of choice by the third circumcision-section there is a number of more or less equally acceptable candidates, then occasionally a fourth spokesman title may be used—*olaigwenani le ngoyo*. By the time of the unification of the age-group during its demand for promotion to senior murranhood, the number of spokesmen who eventually emerge varies between four and eight. Should a spokesman die, he may not be replaced, especially when the age-group is in elderhood, so that active groups sometimes contain only three spokesmen.

Arusha are inclined to say that the role of spokesman, though important, is not particularly coveted because of the considerable responsibility, effort and trouble it involves. It is also disliked by many because of what seems to them to be the undesirability of being elevated above and given influence over their age-mates and other men in this egalitarian society. Many men genuinely reject such elevation, many are afraid of seeming to desire it and are apprehensive of the consequences of it even when they accept the role.[1] There is a strong cultural bias towards equality and towards in-

[1] An outstanding senior elder spokesman was seriously perturbed in 1958 when, by virtue of his indigenous position, he became entitled to enroll as a voter in the national elections in Tanganyika. He was particularly concerned lest he be thought over-ambitious and presumptuous. He felt that he had to obtain his age-group's approval before he did enroll; and this he did, saying at the time that he would only vote on behalf of his age-group and in accordance with their wishes.

dividualism such that men not only resent interference in their affairs by other men but they have no desire to interfere in the affairs of those other men. Consequently men may attempt to avoid selection as spokesmen; but this they cannot easily accomplish, if their age-mates insist, on pain of ostracism and probably a fine and censure by the patrons. Of course, even in this situation, at least some men are willing and even keen to become spokesmen; but an obvious over-eagerness can deprive them of the opportunity for their age-mates are likely to resent their disapproved self-seeking. A spokesman can be dismissed and replaced by his age-mates should they agree that his behaviour or lack of zeal warrant it, though generally (at least for the groups actively operating in the years 1956-8) an inactive spokesman is tolerated so long as he is not positively inefficient or authoritarian.

The Arusha word *olaigwenani* is a verbal-noun deriving from the verbs *aigwen*, 'to advise', and *aigwena*, 'to discuss'. It is here translated as 'spokesman' for this seems to be an adequate reflection of the true meaning involved.[1] A spokesman is the mouthpiece of his age-mates in their corporate relations with other age-groups in the parish, with groups of the same set in other parishes, and with the cere-monial leader, the Kisongo ritual expert, the chief and administrative officers. He is also one of the men thought best able to speak publicly, to put an argument, to deal diplomatically with people (age-mates or others), to suggest compromises which may draw together conflicting opinion, and to be knowledgeable of custom and its pertinent application to a problem in hand. The importance of the role explains the Arusha concern to choose able men for it.

A spokesman progressively acquires these responsibilities at the same time as he gradually extends his social range of influence. At first, in junior murranhood, he acts on behalf of his own circum-cision-section, and particularly for those members of it who live in his parish-division; his influence is limited if only because his age-mates do not yet know him well enough, whilst he feels his way into his new role. Externally his main concern as representative of his coevals is in relations with the patrons' group. With promotion to senior murranhood—or, more accurately, beginning during the

[1] For clarity of exposition, *olaigwenani* of a maximal lineage is translated as 'counsellor'. That role lays more emphasis on the giving of advice and on jural responsibilities; but both spokesman and counsellor are generically similar. See pages 101ff. below.

period of preparation leading up to the formal rituals—he assumes influence in the whole age-group and becomes one of its acknowledged leaders. He gradually becomes more concerned with jural responsibilities. In elderhood his influence and leadership expand, and he becomes almost as much concerned with the parish as a whole as with his own age-group. That is to say, his role develops as his age-group develops from the self-centredness of the circumcision-section to the stage in elderhood when the corporate nature of the age-group tends to be subordinated to the wider sphere of the parish.

Spokesmen are not the only members of an age-group who are notably influential. There are *ingaminini* (s. *engaminin*), men of acknowledged talent who acquire a reputation for generosity and friendliness and a record of useful activity which causes them to be respected by their age-mates. Such men are not chosen specifically, but they emerge gradually during senior murranhood out of the mass of age-group members, and come to be recognised as 'men like spokesmen'. In elderhood men seldom have any difficulty in saying who are *ingaminini* of their age-group, and my records show two to four such men in each elders' group. In addition there are *ingobir* (s. *engobiro*). In general the term has the meaning of 'age-mate'; but it contains the conception of a man who more nearly lives up to the standards of age-mate behaviour and whose opinions and ability warrant a certain respect. To say that any member of an age-group is not *engobiro* is to insult him, and to imply that he is an ignoramus of no account who does not pay due regard to his obligations to his fellows. In actual usage, however, *engobiro* is applied consistently only to the more influential minority.

These notable men together—*ilkituak*, 'the big (important) ones'—comprise the body of influence and leadership which arises out of each age-group as it matures and its members become elders. There tends to be a gradation from the two spokesmen of the oldest circumcision-section through the more junior spokesmen, *ingaminini* and *ingobir*, to relatively uninfluential age-mates. The levels of gradation are, however, inevitably blurred and they are, above all, degrees of influence deriving from demonstrated right conduct and ability in age-group and parish affairs. These two aspects are for the Arusha necessarily closely related. The generous, helpful and friendly age-mate who shows little or no ability to speak well in public and make useful contributions to matters under discussion tends not to gain influence. But conversely the men of outstanding ability may be careless, or may become careless, of his egalitarian obligations to his age-mates, and he may incline towards authoritarian neglect of their interests or opinions; and such a man too gains or at least retains little influence.

Essentially this gradation, in so far as it exists at all clearly, is not one of levels of authority or power but one of degrees of respected influence and leadership. Neither is it a static gradation: being so closely dependent upon right conduct together with demonstrated ability, and so dependent upon the opinions of the members of the age-group and of the whole parish besides, changes may gradually appear in the relative degree of influence achieved. As already stated, the spokesmen are chosen by and from newly initiated murran largely on the basis of youthful, informal leadership before initiation. The young men, even with the supervision of their patrons, may not be good judges of the best among themselves to be chosen; in any case the outstanding persons in their late teens are not necessarily those who will in more mature age be outstanding in the qualities then required of spokesmen and leaders. The qualities required are different, and individual men may fail to live up to their expected character and ability as they grow older. Some may pointedly fail and be replaced, and others tend to cope at a tolerable, minimum level of adequacy which is rather less than outstanding. Junior spokesmen may develop more satisfactorily than some of their seniors and achieve more influence. On the other hand, both *ingaminini* and true *ingobir*, who only gradually emerge, are likely to be more genuinely adequate men in elderhood by Arusha standards and requirements, and it is usual that one or more of them have rather more influence and respect than some spokesmen. It is sufficient that one or two of the spokesmen retain influence and leadership so that they may convene assemblies, moderate discussions and represent their age-group and their parish formally. At the same time their personal influence is limited not only by the possibility of their dismissal by disapproving age-mates (a somewhat drastic and uncommon step in elderhood), but also and more importantly by the other notables whose status and opinion they cannot ignore. Few spokesmen in my experience attempt to act independently or without regard for and consultation with the other notables; indeed spokesmen habitually take care to act only in concert with them, if only to demonstrate their rejection of a desire for authority. In practice influence is largely exercised in parish assemblies or age-group meetings, for it is there where decisions are made; and they are enforced by the sanction of the whole parish or the whole age-group, not merely by the spokesmen themselves. At these times notable men of influence—as, in fact, any other men— have full opportunity to contest the opinions and suggestions of spokesmen, and it is here where the effective influence is practically exercised.

The active elders of a parish comprise, of course, members of two age-groups, so that the pattern of leadership is a product of the interaction of the notables of both, as well as of the notables of each one separately. Additionally there may be one or two members of the retired elders group, or perhaps one or two outstanding members of the group still formally in the grade of senior murran, who participate in parish leadership. The net result is that, at least from the time of later senior murranhood, the pattern of influence and leadership is fluid. The formal titleholders of spokesman may or may not retain their effective status; invariably one or two *ingaminini* surpass some spokesmen in influence and they may become no less important than many or all of the rest; true *ingobir* gain a position in which their opinion cannot be neglected. The fluidity of the pattern is often emphasised by the indiscriminate application in ordinary language of the term 'spokesman' to any particularly influential man, even though it is equally recognised that only a limited number formally hold that position.

The Parish Assembly

The internal affairs of a parish and many of the disputes between its individual members are formally dealt with in the parish assembly, *engigwana e mbalbal*. The matters that can be dealt with cover a range, in which a few examples may suffice at this point: the route of a cattle track or path and the enforcement of right of way on it; consideration of a projected anti-witchcraft campaign; the public announcement of information from the chief, a government official, or the ceremonial leader, and the formulation of parish opinion and a policy on it; discussion of a further step in the maturation of a murran age-group; responsibility for a fight, adultery or theft and the compensation to be paid; a field boundary between two neighbours farms. The assembly, that is, has both a general political function as well as a specifically judicial one.

The membership of a parish assembly is rather indefinite, and it varies from meeting to meeting. The Arusha say that it comprises the spokesmen, *ingaminini* and true *ingobir* of the age-groups in the grades of senior and junior elders, but they add that the notable members of the senior murran age-group may also attend. At particular meetings not all these spokesmen and other notables are necessarily present, whilst many other members of the three age-groups actively participate as they wish. The men who do attend are determined by the nature of the matters to be discussed, the people and the part of the parish involved, the frequency of meetings at that time and men's personal inclinations. Ordinary members of the parish, of those three age-groups that is, do not feel it incumbent upon them to attend except as and when they wish; but when they do attend they have full opportunities to take such part as they desire concomitant with their current status. On the other hand, spokesmen have an obligation to their age-mates and in general to fellow-members of the parish to attend more or less regularly, for they are selected to perform these kinds of duties because of their assessed abilities. Thus most spokesmen do attend each meeting of the assembly, and quite often all of them are present. Other age-group notables retain their positions and exercise their influence principally by attending regularly.

An assembly meeting was formerly convened when required, and usually the arrangements were made by spokesmen of the junior elders' grade. It was convened either because the spokesmen and notables wished to have some matter discussed, or because a member of the parish had specifically requested a meeting, through a spokesman or notable of his age-group, to take up a personal affair of his. To consider matters of general interest to the parish as a whole, or to discuss more serious disputes, the assembly met at a conventional spot in the parish, a conveniently central, open space; but for a more localised issue, a petty dispute or a matter involving land or land boundaries, the assembly was easily able to meet at some other site more conveniently located for the matter in hand. When news of the meeting was broadcast, other men were likely to take the opportunity to seek to bring up matters which hitherto they had not especially raised in public.

Since 1948 the parish assembly has acquired a more regular constitution as a result of being adopted as the lowest level in local
government. It has been recognised as a deliberative and consultative body to which questions can be referred for opinion, and
which may be attended by the chief or other official if necessary. Its
judicial activities are not accepted as part of the official judicial
system, and the government will not attempt to enforce its decisions;
but those activities have been stimulated by the political recognition
and by the deference given to assemblies by magistrates and chiefs.
A parish assembly should now comprise all the spokesmen of all age-
groups, and it should meet at fixed times at a single selected site.
The regular convening of meetings has been accepted in all parishes,
but the actual membership in practice remains still as it was previously. Nowadays people are aware that they can have access to the
assembly in their own parish at a particular known time and they
usually wait, therefore, until then to present a dispute or raise an
issue. Only in emergencies or when a special meeting is agreed to
(e.g. to visit the site of a disputed field and there to give a decision)
are assemblies convened at irregular times or at other locations.

Although I can give no statistical confirmation, it is clear that
affairs and disputes heard in a parish assembly are more concerned
with conflicts between men of different age-groups than between
members of the same group. In part this follows from the strong,
underlying egalitarian friendliness[1] between age-mates which helps
to minimise conflict when it does occur. There are not the incentives
to cooperation nor the inducement to toleration where men are
separated by group membership; and especially where men belong
to chronologically adjacent age-groups there exists a structurally
defined opposition, even animosity, which tends to exacerbate inter-
personal conflict rather than to reduce it. Conflict between age-
mates is often composed privately within the single age-group,
through the friendly acceptable intervention of other age-mates who
are concerned both with the reconciliation of their fellows and with
the preservation of group unity. Age-mates can, without accusation
of unwarranted interference, take it upon themselves to intervene,
and spokesmen and other notables take the lead in this. A meeting
of the whole age-group may be held, but this is uncommon; more
usually a few notables and other members who are bystanders or

[1] Cf. pp. 34-5.

neighbours or especial friends, take the initiative to seek reconciliation of the conflicting men and a resolution of their dispute. This
may, as when a fight breaks out, occur on the spot without further
delay; but in more persistent disputes a meeting may be arranged
to discuss and settle the matter. There is considerable feeling—often
specifically expressed—that the matter should not become a public
one such that members of other age-groups gain the right of interference. Usually it is only after intra-group efforts at a settlement
have failed that one or other of the disputants takes the matter to the
parish assembly.

Because matters discussed in the parish assembly are mainly
between men of different age-groups, proceedings tend to occur at
an inter-group level even in what are primarily inter-personal
conflicts. Alignment of support for each disputant is by age-group,
and to a lesser extent by stream as linked groups support one
another. A disputant expects the notables of his own group to speak
on his behalf, and to urge acceptance of his claims or denial of his
obligations on the other party. A junior murran must be represented
by a more senior member, and he looks to a leading member of his
patrons' age-group who in turn expects the support of the rest of
that group. Senior murran, though capable of speaking for themselves, welcome the assistance of their patrons. It would be incorrect to overemphasise this feature, because kinship ties may
intrude so that a disputant seeks the support of kinsmen even though
they are of a different stream. For example, a senior murran may seek
the assistance of his elder brother, or even paternal cousin, who is a
junior elder. On the other hand, if kinship ties are logically important in a particular dispute, then it is likely to be handled primarily
if not entirely at a lineage or clanship level, and does not come
directly to the attention of the parish assembly. Or, to put this in
another way, matters which do come before the parish assembly are
principally those which do not involve interests of a primarily
kinship nature.[1] Thus the 'natural' alignment of support in the
parish assembly is by age-groups.

Members of a parish assembly, though together practising judicial
function, are not themselves unprejudiced arbitrators or judges. It is
accepted that they are overtly biased in favour of the disputant who

---

[1] The connection between the settlement of disputes in the parish assembly and in
patrilineal moot is complex and is considered later in this book: See Chapter 9.

is a member of their own age-group or stream. Spokesmen and other notables act as the principal advocates of their own party. The parish assembly is thus dichotomously divided. Where disputants belong to different streams, this is virtually automatic and straightforward. Where they belong to the same stream—e.g. a senior elder and a senior murran, or two senior murran—the members of the other stream are at pains to preserve a neutral (if somewhat self-righteous) position, propounding the law and precedent relevant to the situation and intervening as conciliators.

A number of cases of this kind occurred in 1958, as senior elders brought claims against senior murran for adultery and other offences at the time when the senior murran were approaching the formal transfer to elderhood. Senior elders threatened to withhold approval of their wards' transfer until all outstanding claims were met. Such cases were brought before the parish assembly. That they were not dealt with 'privately', as disputes within a single age-group mainly are, demonstrates the relative weakness of the integrity of a stream. On these occasions the junior elders invariably acted as proponents of Arusha custom—but not as judges or arbitrators—and in this they were, of course, consciously demonstrating their developing role as new senior elders before the formal shift in grades occurred.

Essentially the proceedings of a parish assembly are marked by an attempt of two fairly distinct parties to reach a mutually acceptable agreement. Spokesmen and other notables, because of their abilities and experience, are expected to take the lead on behalf of their own side. Their diplomatic skill is applied to attempt to persuade their opponents to compromise, but at the same time to lead their own side in a shift towards their opponents' position. In a case of any difficulty, it is the two sets of notables who tend to dominate the approach to agreement and who in ultimate concord provide the result. Nevertheless, they represent their respective age-groups and especially the particular individual disputants, and they remain dependent on the concurrence of their fellows. This concurrence does not follow, in time and sequence, the agreement reached between the two sides, but rather it runs simultaneously with the procedures to reach such agreement.[1]

[1] I am concerned here only to give a general analysis of judicial processes in a parish assembly. Actual cases are described and discussed in Part 4 of this monograph.

The parish assembly is, then, a forum in which age-group unity is practically displayed, as inter-personal conflict becomes in part transformed into group conflict, whilst the approach to a settlement is sought. Further, the settlement itself is specifically sanctioned upon the individuals it particularly concerns because they are members of their age-groups which have publicly established and accepted it. A defaulter is subject to the pressures not only of the other disputant but also to those of his age-group. The person injured by a defaulter seeks the support of his own age-group against both the defaulter and the defaulter's age-group. Thus the parish assembly itself is not a decision-making and enforcing body, but only the meeting place of the effective groups within the parish. This is, however, to describe and define the reality over-rigidly, for some disputes and some differences of opinion over general affairs occur between members of the same group and yet involve members of other groups. For example, in one fairly recently established parish, the attempt to define a public cattle track was delayed by dispute between two age-mates, along whose common boundary the track ran part of its course. Such a dispute, bitterly argued, could not be left to the single age-group, for its outcome and especially its delayed settlement affected many cattle-owners of that parish. In a case of this sort, although age-group loyalties are not entirely neglected, the parish assembly tends to act more nearly as a body representative of the total community. Spokesmen and other notables still exert the chief influence, and they still seek continuous confirmation of their actions from their age-mates. Nevertheless, the interaction of these notables is here one primarily of cooperation to a common satisfaction. In other words, the common interests of the community are recognised sometimes as being superior to the interests of its component parts; although more commonly it is the interaction of the component parts in opposition which produces the settlement of conflict within the community.

A similar, twofold dichotomy operates within each age-group. There is, first, the distinction between the two principal circumcision-sections; and secondly, the distinction between members of each parish-division in a section. Although not insignificant, they inevitably weaken under the evolving emphasis on the unity of the whole age-group. Intra-group conflict may produce alignments of support on the lines of section and parish-division, but men say that they feel uneasy about this temporary denial of group solidarity, and in practice leading members lend it little reinforcement. Rather it is that all members feel equally responsible to and for the two disputants and are chiefly concerned to act as conciliators. Thus the internal structural similarity of a parish and an individual age-group does not produce similar techniques in conflict settlement. Were the parish habitually participating in decision-making assembly with other parishes, then it too might find it necessary to close its own ranks in relation to another similar unit, just as an age-group does within a parish but the case does not in fact arise among the Arusha.

In the parish it is not possible for an age-group to dominate either overtly in the parish assembly or in other ways outside of it. The age-group occupying the role of junior elders is balanced on the one hand by the senior elders, and on the other by the senior murran both jealous of their own prerogatives. These two linked groups cannot, however, prevail dominantly over the intercalary group, for both have limited potentialities by virtue of the roles of their members. The senior murran are not yet full elders and are kept conscious of their juniority; and they are inexperienced in public affairs as well as much preoccupied by their own personal concerns in the approach to marriage and family responsibilities. The senior elders are consciously giving up persistently active participation, and they are becoming fewer as age reduces their numbers; they seek mainly to act as a brake on their immediate juniors (i.e. the junior elders) rather than to usurp their position. An approximate balance is maintained which can be made practically effective when one group or another seems to seek undue power. All this must be seen not only in terms of relations and activities in the parish assembly, but also against the background of the total series of processes occurring in the age-group cycle. In this cycle, as we have seen, the age-groups operate in 'complementary opposition'[1] to one another in a pattern of pressures and counter-pressures (see pages 44-6). This complementary opposition is transferred to the parish assembly and the processes of decision-making and dispute settlement.

Another element in these processes arises out of the fact that an age-group tends to be divided within itself in a way which is more

[1] I borrow this phrase from A. H. Jacobs, in an unpublished MS, 'The Pastoral Masai'.

significant than its internal structure; that is, because members pass from one role-phase to another at different rates and different times, rather than as a corporate unit. Some of the members of the group in the formal grade of junior elders may be effectively acting as senior elders and thus have adopted the corresponding mores and attitudes of that role-phase; some of the members of the group in the formal grade of senior elder may still act as junior elders, and some may at the same time or later act as retired elders. Often, then, conflict in the parish assembly is not expressed starkly in terms of full age-groups as monolithic entities. Those members in one role-phase tend to inhibit their age-mates who are in another, and at the same time they may find some congenial alliance with some of the members of an adjacent age-group. This feature is one of the most significant results of the actual distribution of roles, as compared with that ideal pattern wherein an age-group and age-grade are neatly correlated.

Senior murran are encouraged to attend assembly meetings in order to observe procedures, to learn Arusha custom, and to become acquainted with decisions about which they will need to know as they come to acquire responsibility. Gradually they are encouraged to participate actively. Especially their spokesmen, and others who seem likely to become established notables, are deliberately given opportunities to speak. They all come to sit in the main body of the meeting, rather than around the edge; they stand up firmly when speaking. When a matter under discussion directly affects their age-group, or individual members of it, senior murran state their own case and spokesmen and notables are expected to assist their age-mates in this, as well as to join with elder notables in bringing pressure to bear on them to accept particular decisions. Senior murran—spokesmen, incipient notables and others—feel, and are made to feel, their status inferiority and their lack of experience compared with the elders; they do not participate as readily or so frequently as the elders. Nevertheless, within at least three or four years after promotion to senior murranhood they are accepted as regular members of the assembly. There has perhaps been some increase in the degree of their participation in recent times, for among them are men who have had some modern education and some experience of the modern world, which not only makes them more knowledgeable about some kinds of affairs but affords some of them a degree of self-assurance, even a feeling of superiority towards the elders.

Junior murran do not participate in an assembly unless personally involved in a dispute under discussion. They are not welcomed at meetings, and elders are sometimes offensively caustic about any who do attend. It is seldom that any of them wish to attend for their role gives them no interest in the proceedings. If a junior murran is a disputant then he should be 'represented' by a patron or by his responsible guardian who speaks on his behalf. In giving purely factual evidence and answering questions on it—the only participation permitted—he should speak in a low voice, without standing up, from the outer edge of the meeting as and when directed by elders. A junior murran who attempts to go beyond this—perhaps in explanation or justification of his actions under review—is quickly suppressed by elders of all degrees. 'He must be like a woman,' elders say, and indeed precisely the same behaviour and submissive demeanour is expected from a woman who is called to give evidence. On the other hand, junior murran (especially in the later phase of their role) can be used as servants by the assembly, and sometimes by spokesmen outside of the assembly. They may be commissioned to summon a person to the meeting, to collect firewood, to pace out field boundaries and plant markers, to clean up the assembly site and other similar tasks. Their spokesmen may be directed to see that a number of junior murran be present if it is expected that such tasks will be needed.

Following the pattern of the Arusha age-grades, the men (especially spokesmen and notables) who are most concerned with the parish assembly are the members of the age-group currently in the role of junior elders. Since 1948 each assembly has had a nominal 'chairman' (*olkitok lo lorika*, an almost literal translation) who is usually one of the two spokesmen in the senior circumcision-section of that age-group. According to his influence and ability he exercises a loose control over meetings. It is left to him with his fellow spokesmen to exert what supervision is necessary to the reasonable conduct of the meetings. One of them, preferably the chairman, starts a meeting off by calling on the proponents of the first issue to be discussed, or the plaintiff in the first dispute to be heard. Thereafter they can, if needed, determine the next person to speak, cut short verbose orators and quell noisy, angry or libellous speakers. Representing the parish as a whole, they nominally issue the agreed decision of the assembly; at least it is understood that the decision or judgment is in their name and with their concurrence, whether or not one or more of them attempt a formal statement of it. Refusal to obey the decision or injunction is treated as defiance of and an insult to the spokesmen; if, however, a fine (*sogo*) is levied for wilful contumacy it is imposed in the name of the spokesman of the offender's age-group (see below).

It is convenient that the machinery for the conduct of the parish assembly be focused on the spokesmen, the selected representatives of the age-groups of active and responsible men. But in fact—and Arusha are well aware of this—they only represent their fellows and the corporate nature of the age-group and of the parish as a whole. We have seen that there are always other acknowledged men of influence which may exceed that of many of the spokesmen themselves. Those notables do not, however, usually attempt to compete with the spokesmen in their purely formal duties. Their influence is brought to bear rather on the realities of actual discussions and decision-making, and this can be seen in the proceedings of an assembly.

First, we may note that the spokesmen rarely take any step without some consultation with the notables of their age-group—for example, the decision to convene a meeting of the assembly or to levy a fine. Decisions, even minor ones, are worthless unless they have reasonable support from the age-group, and the notables represent that support. Furthermore, spokesmen are chronically apprehensive of accusations that they are attempting to exercise too great a power. Secondly, in the actual discussions any man of elder status has the privilege of speaking; the spokesmen cannot monopolise proceedings. Most men are willing to sit quietly and accept the general opinion—unless they are personally involved—but the notables find ample opportunity to express their ideas and to press their views on the meeting. In so far as they are competently able to do this, they cannot be ignored. In effect a decision is made by the whole assembly, or at least that part of it which wishes to participate at all.

The practical limitation on an age-group spokesman and the significance of the age-group is further illustrated in the matter of a fine (*sogo*). A fine is always levied in the name of the spokesman of the offender's own age-group, but with the concurrence of the junior elder spokesman. It is, however, made clear that it is levied on behalf of the total age-group and, secondarily, of the parish assembly as a whole. A fine is usually the result of unruly behaviour in the assembly, libellous remarks against age-group notables, conduct glaringly incompatible with the norms of relations between age-mates, refusal to attend an assembly meeting when necessary to answer charges by another person or obdurate refusal to accept the agreed decision of the assembly. For lesser offences where the culprit shows reasonable contrition the fine is specified as sufficient beer to satisfy the spokesmen of his own age-group together with the spokesmen of any other group which may have been involved in the offence. The beer is served at the offender's homestead on an agreed day, but it is invariably drunk by other notables of the age-group in addition to the spokesmen. Ordinary members of the age-group are not positively denied participation but, other than chronic drinkers, few actually attend. It is clear—and Arusha pointed it out to me—that spokesmen cannot monopolise the privilege but must share it with other age-mates of influence; and secondly, that the fine accrues to the offender's age-group, although, where it is a small fine, the group is represented by its leading members.

More blatant offences, especially continued recusance, may bring a fine of a goat or even an ox. The animal is slaughtered at a meeting of the age-group (together with another group if it is directly concerned) and the meat roasted and eaten by all members. This is one of the occasions when spokesmen claim their special portions of meat but share them with their friends. Both kinds of fine are expressly conceived by the Arusha as legitimate, punitive action by the age-group against an offending member. An age-group is responsible for the proper behaviour of its members in respect to the parish assembly (i.e. public affairs of the parish) and is the rightful agent if an offence is committed. Should a man attempt to refuse to pay a fine, or thereafter refuse to accede to the decision of the assembly, including his own age-group, not only is the fine likely to be increased but the offender's property liable to seizure, either directly by his age-mates or by senior murran acting on the orders of the spokesmen of an elder's group. In such cases, deliberate harshness may be used, such as (in one case I witnessed) the ostentatious seizure and slaughter of a good heifer right in the homestead paddock of the offender. There, a display was made to the man himself, to his family and neighbours and to members of other age-groups of both the probity and the authority of his age-group.

In this account I have persisted in using the word 'influence' to describe in a shorthand way the nature and also the limitations of the role of spokesmen and other notables. I have reserved the word 'authority' to a whole age-group acting as a distinct unit. The distinction is most important, both in emphasising the actual role of spokesman and in indicating where authority does lie in the restricted use of its applications. Spokesmen are chosen, even positively impressed, to specialise in exposition, diplomacy and organisation. In elderhood they are assisted, perhaps equalled and even exceeded by a few other age-mates who have become notables. None of these men can gain authority singly. As the body of influential men of the age-group, they are respected, listened to and often heeded; but their tenure of influence is entirely in the hands of their age-mates. The spokesmen can be removed and replaced, or perhaps merely tolerated and ignored; other notables persist only by reason of their demonstration of approved qualities and abilities, and disapproval means non-recognition and the withdrawal of influence from them. Thus the appearance of what seems to be incipient authority, going beyond respected influence and beyond proper regard for age-mates' opinions and interests, means the disappearance of the only sanctions of leadership, i.e. the moral and practical approval of a man's fellows.

Nothing in the structural pattern prevents the actual playing out of practical interrelationships between particular individuals who are influential. Roles are nowhere so specifically institutionalised that they cannot be modified and manipulated by particular incumbents. In different parishes the leading influential men in public affairs vary a great deal. Sometimes one or two senior elders of outstanding ability and personality remain dominant: in one or two cases a senior murran is able to come right to the forefront because of recognised superior ability and sagacity and, sometimes nowadays, because of superior education. More usually the leading men are drawn mainly from the junior elders, with one or two from each adjacent group. The precise pattern depends also, of course, on the particular stage of the age-group cycle reached. Whilst the current junior elders are still gaining experience and confidence the senior elders tend to predominate; later on they are likely to be replaced by the junior elders, whose influence in turn carries over into their senior elderhood and is eventually similarly replaced. Just as the inter-relations of age-groups themselves and the roles of their members are never static but always slowly changing, so the pattern of leadership changes concomitantly.

The members of a parish and of its various age-groups are also members of a wide range of patrilineal descent groups, none of which are limited to the boundaries of a single parish. Disputes and differences of opinion often involve men in terms of their descent affiliations, and then these concern men who live in other parishes: such disputes are treated in a quite different context. Members of different age-groups, who are thereby distinguished from one another, may at the same time be related patrilineally, so that they are brought together. Just as the parish and age-group system provides a coherent pattern of relationships, of cooperation and differentiation, and as it provides a structure of leadership and a means of decision-making and dispute settlement, so in different terms does the patrilineal system. The two systems and their social operation are in some ways quite separate, but in other ways they necessarily interact. For convenience of exposition the parish and age-group system has so far been described as if it were entirely self-sufficient; this obviously is not so in the reality of social life, and it is acknowledged and taken into account in the final Part of this book, following a comparable account of the patrilineal system in Part 2.

APPENDIX

A note on the sizes of age-groups

THE numerical sizes of age-groups and the ratios between contemporary groups in the same parish both depend on the stage of developmental progress at the time of enumeration. It is impossible to give generalised figures unrelated to the processual events.

In this note I give figures for three separate years, at which times there were approximations to the conditions in stages A, B and C of Figure 6 (p. 43). The 1957 figures are taken from my own surveys in that year: they relate to five parishes on the mountain slopes, all of which were around the average size for all sixteen mountain parishes according to the official Census data of the same year—i.e. about 2,000 people, of whom some 460 were initiated males. Figures for 1955 and 1961 are obtained by working backwards and forwards respectively from 1957, using my genealogical and parish records plus the results of a rough estimate made during a brief visit to Arusha in May, 1961. These two sets of figures are therefore less accurate than those for 1957.

To avoid complicated tables unnecessary for present purposes, and with the sole aim of giving an indication of numerical scale and pattern, I take the liberty of assuming a hypothetical 'average' parish. (cf. Gulliver 1960, p. 5.)

		MURRAN		ELDERS			
		Junior	Senior	Junior	Senior	Retired	
A: 1955	*Age-group*	—	Meshuki	Derito	Dareto	Dwati & Dalala	
Immediately preceding a new circumcision period	% *of total men*	—	49	27	19	5	
	No. of men	—	175	97	68	18	total 358
B: 1957 during recruitment of junior murran 2 years before transfer of senior murran	*Age-group*	Kiwoni	Meshuki	Derito	Dareto	Dwati	
	% *of total men*	26	38	20	13	3	
	No. of men	120	174	92	60	14	total 460
C: 1961 preceding promotion to senior murran	*Age-group*	Kiwoni	—	Nyangusi	Derito	Dareto & Dwati	
	% *of total men*	40	—	35	16	9	
	No. of men	196	—	171	80	42	total 489

PART TWO

ROLES AND PROCESSES RESULTING

FROM PATRILINEAL DESCENT

CHAPTER FOUR

PROLEGOMENA TO THE
PATRILINEAL SYSTEM

THE Arusha determine their descent patrilineally and all 'true-Arusha' are able to trace their descent line to one of the first-settlers who came to live on the lower edge of the forest on the southwestern slopes of Mt. Meru. The origins of the various first-settlers who are now remembered in this way are traced to the people of Kikoin (Arusha Chini), the Logolala (Kwavi), or some ill-defined Masai-like group; but their genealogical connections are unknown. Where there is some knowledge, it invariably refers only to the father of a first-settler and does not effectively extend the range of the genealogy. This means that all genealogies are shallow: in many cases, in the middle of the twentieth century, the earliest ancestor was the grandfather of the oldest generation of living men, and in all other investigated cases he was the great-grandfather. Arusha say that most of the first-settlers were young men, and remembered first ancestors fathered sons in their old age.

The total of a first-settler's living patrilineal descendants now comprise the core of the maximal lineage. There are, however, a majority of present-day Arusha who cannot trace a true descent from a first-settler. These are the people who are descended from immigrants who came into the country during the second half of the nineteenth century—mainly refugees from warfare and rapacity, and also war-captives, from Meru and Chagga countries.[1]

A voluntary immigrant always sought the patronage of a 'true-Arusha', or of an earlier immigrant already attached to such a patron, in order to establish himself in a community; a war-captive was treated as a member of his captor's family. In either case the newcomer gradually assumed the attributes of a close, junior agnate, so that today the genealogical fiction of common patrilineal descent is ubiquitous. To an outsider—Arusha stranger as well as white anthropologist—it is now difficult to discover the historical truth,

[1] See the table in footnote 2, page 12.

More than that, the patrilineal descendants of immigrants have been so completely absorbed into 'true-Arusha' lineages that such truth is no longer sociologically relevant. It is not possible to distinguish 'true-Arusha' from others in respect of their status or behaviour. Therefore the historical facts may be ignored for the purposes of this book, and we shall assume that alleged patrilineal genealogies are correct.

The Family

By definition, a family is not a wholly patrilineal group. Among the Arusha it is focused on an agnatic core of a man and his children, but it contains also their wives and mothers whose patrilineal affiliations lie elsewhere. These women are not only principals in the family economy and everyday domestic life, but they are crucial intermediaries between father and son in the transmission of property rights; they also create and maintain differentiation between the sons and between the grandsons of the family head. A second point of distinction between the family and patrilineal descent groups is that the latter are all geographically dispersed groups of autonomous men, but a family is a domestic group whose members occupy a single homestead or, in its later development, a number of inter-dependent homesteads. The family is founded in and continues to be concerned mainly with domestic affairs. It is necessary, however, to give some account of the family because patrilineal descent groups are primarly associations of heads of families, and thus, indirectly, of families themselves.

There is a third distinction between a family and a patrilineal descent group which is expressed in the ideal conceptions of the people, but is also evident in actual practice. A family is characterised by a unity stemming from the authority of the family head, the husband and father, to whom all other members are subordinate; in contrast a lineage or a clanship group is characterised by the equality of its members and an absence of authoritarian control. I do not wish to make an absolute antithesis in this respect, for on the one hand established wives and especially adult sons acquire a degree of autonomy which may nearly usurp or at least ignore the authority of the family head; whilst on the other hand members of a descent group are differentiated both by generational and age-set seniority and, within a lineage, they are subject to the power of the ancestors and to certain unavoidable obligations. Nevertheless the distinction does exist, and I wish to emphasise it in the contrasting accounts of the two kinds of groups.

As in any society, Arusha families are not static units, for both their membership and their internal organisation gradually change as members grow older and as a new generation emerges. In any family which is not prematurely cut short by the early death of its head, there are two major phases:—that of the nuclear family, i.e. a man, his wives and their young children; and that of the compound family, when the original nucleus is augmented by heteronomous units, each comprising a married son with his wife and children. These major phases are themselves, of course, not static conditions; they merely identify the two main periods of the total process of a family's development.

On the death of the family head, but not until then, the family disintegrates: a number of successor nuclear families emerge, each of which is headed by a son now become an autonomous man. He and his wives and young children occupy a discrete homestead which, except in the most recently colonised areas, is usually clearly bounded by fencing, hedge or trees. The man is head of both homestead and family—both called *engang*—in his role as husband and father: but more than that, for he is the legitimate, individual owner (*olopeny*) of the 'estate' of land and livestock on which the family depends. The land, in which the homestead is situated amid banana groves and fields, is his either by outright inheritance from his father, or by right of pioneering hitherto unoccupied land, which right is confirmed at the time of inheritance. Livestock are similarly inherited, and thereafter augmented by acquisitions from bridewealth, purchase, etc. Economically the land is the more important: it is essential to subsistence and to modern cash earning, but the unity of the land and its separateness from other pieces of land typify the unity and autonomy of the family itself in this basically agricultural society.

To each wife the head allocates a portion of his estate, both land and animals, to provide both the means of subsistence for her 'house' and to designate responsibility for the management and exploitation of the family's resources. The head retains for his own purposes an unallocated portion of his estate, which is used to produce a reserve food supply as well as, nowadays, the main market supply. This portion can be drawn on to augment existing allocations or to make new ones as circumstances change and the head's personal inclinations indicate.

The Arusha lay much emphasis on the segregation of a nuclear family within its own homestead, and this is the actual practice as well as the ideal norm. There may be unavoidable dependants of the family head (mainly married sisters or daughters separated from their husbands) but without exception, to my knowledge, they live in their own houses outside the family homestead. Land is allocated to them so that they cultivate independently; and in practice, as well as conceptually, they form virtually autonomous, tenant-like units.

The wives of the family head, like their children, are jural minors and unable to own property except under his authority. In the wider society beyond the homestead, all are subordinate to the head, who is responsible for them collectively and engages in formal group relations with other family heads. Mature wives—but not young wives, young adult sons or children—participate in rituals directly concerning the family; but they do so in a minor role, subject to the guiding control of the head.

In a polygynous nuclear family—the Arusha ideal—a man's wives in his homestead are divided into two groups. Each set of co-wives is referred to as *olwashe*, pl. *ilwasheta*. The mode of establishment of *ilwasheta* has been described elsewhere[1] and it need only be said here that between linked co-wives there is marked cooperation in domestic and agricultural work. Their children are considered to be more closely related than they are to other half-siblings, and youthful gangs demonstrate this. Adult sons owe responsibility to care for their mother's linked wife should the latter have no sons of her own, and they have preferential rights in her land in that case. Especially when adult sons are making claims against the family's estate and assuming rights and responsibilities, a family becomes effectively divided into two parts—only the family head remains outside this division, in his role of overall authority. This dichotomy continues into the new lineage composed of a man's sons after his death. Similarly, the division of the original family of the founder

---

[1] Gulliver 1961a, pp. 20-23. The comparable group among the Masai is *entaloishi*, and this, like the Arusha *olwashe*, seems to be extended to refer to a dichotomous part of any social group. Unlike Arusha, the houses of the two sets of co-wives in a Masai family are arranged separately on either side of the main gateway: cf. Fosbrooke 1948, p. 43. Among the Baraguyu (Kwavi) of east-central Tanganyika, *olpahe* or *olpashe* is used to refer to one of the two groups of co-wives: cf. Beidelman 1960, p. 270.

of a maximal lineage is given as the explanation of the dichotomous structure of that descent group today.

Not all Arusha men are polygynists. In a sample of 186 elderly men who were unlikely to marry again, 59% (110 men) had two or more wives, so that their families contained *olwashe* divisions. In 41% (76) of the sample cases a mature family remained monogamous and thus without *ilwasheta*.[1] These families do not meet the norms of the Arusha, and their heads are thought to have failed in life. The ideal itself is not destroyed. Monogamous ancestors have founded 'atypical' lineages in this way; but it is significant that such a lineage usually does not achieve corporate existence but is absorbed by some closely related lineage, so that each becomes an *olwashe* of the amalgam.[2]

The development of a family enters its second phase with the marriage of a son, for this leads to the emergence of a new kind of sub-unit and to some degree of residential dispersion, as well as a new pattern of relations between father and son themselves. The married son must move out of his father's homestead. He may shift right away to pioneer a new farm in uncultivated bushland or, increasingly nowadays, to take up a tenancy anywhere available; or he may remain on his father's land, but outside the nuclear homestead. A son who remains on his father's land acquires a part of his mother's allocation of both land and livestock, to which are added such extra portions as the father can be persuaded to take from his unallocated reserve. In fact, however, the bulk of both the land and the livestock are allocated directly to the son's wife and her new house by her parents-in-law with the son as intermediary. The bulk of the sub-estate, just as the bulk of the estate of a nuclear family, is given over to wives, thus demonstrating their crucial role in family organisation.

In any event a married son becomes residentially and economically semi-autonomous both of his mother's house and of his father. The Arusha continue to refer to the total group—now a compound family—as *engang*. This usage conforms to the fact that, despite a new order of segmentation and dispersion, the family retains its unity under the persisting authority of its founder and head, who

[1] Gulliver 1961a, Figure 2, p. 22.
[2] The significance of structural bifurcation, whose prototype appears in the family, is discussed in Chapter 7.

remains the owner of the estate and retains full ritual and jural responsibility for all its members whatever their status within the group. Land and livestock obtained by a son and his wife are said to be allocations only and not outright transfers of property rights: they are said to be capable of revision as the family head sees fit and disposal of them (as against their usufruct) depends on his concurrence. The compound family perpetuates the jural unity of the preceding nuclear family, because married sons, no less then their younger siblings, are minors who must be represented by their father who is held responsible for them in society at large. They share a corporate obligation towards each other which residential separation and a degree of economic autonomy cannot destroy. The reasons for this, say the Arusha, are primarily because the father retains his ultimate rights in the total estate, and continued control over it affords continued control over his sons dependent on it. His authority is strongly reinforced by ritual necessities. A man with a living father cannot possess an ancestral shrine for that can only be established at the father's grave. The ancestors can only be approached through the dead father, the most powerful and active of them all. Whilst the father is alive, therefore, he alone conducts rituals in the ancestral cult at the shrine of his own father's grave near the nuclear homestead. Sons of whatever age and status are utterly dependent on their father's ritual prerogatives in the cult, and these effectively carry over even into non-ancestral rituals.

Thus although the family tends to become increasingly articulated internally, and decentralised residentially and economically, its primary unit remains under the enduring authority of the father. On the other hand, in practice the unity of the group tends to slacken as married sons grow older and are increasingly able to reduce their father's control. Although a father is said to be able unilaterally to alter an allocation of property, it seems never to occur; and a married son on pioneered land or a modern tenancy is little subject to economic restraint by his father. In his old age the family head may come to the position where he has allocated out practically all his estate so that his sons are severally in effective control of it. Again, although a young married son is constrained to admit his jural subordination, this is partly a function of his junior social status in the wider society. As he gains higher status in the age-grade ranking, and particularly as he becomes an elder (in about the late thirties or early forties), he acquires increasing ability to conduct his own public affairs and to participate in politico-jural proceedings.

Nevertheless people outside the family will not acknowledge the full rights of a man over the land he lives on and cultivates, or the animals he herds, whilst his father is alive. The father certainly can prevent the transfer of property rights by his son, and any important transactions such as bridewealth, loan of land or compensation payment continue to require the witnessed consent of a man's father if they are to be valid and secure. A married man cannot avoid the direct and unrestricted corporate obligations to his brothers, wherever they live, whilst the father is alive. Although he may be able to act on his own behalf in a jural assembly as an acknowledged elder, and he may bear the brunt of a dispute, yet the old father is invariably required to appear and give at least formal approval to the actions and commitments of his son. Ritually it is quite impossible to escape the father's superiority to which the whole family is subject.

Thus, although the unity of the compound family weakens and the authority of its head diminishes, neither disappear whilst he is alive. Moreoever the group retains its particular identity as a family, a group of domestic units, by the essential and continued participation of the women who are married into it. Until sons achieve elderhood status, they and the women and children are represented in society by the family head—and lineages comprise groups of such men. In later life an old father must perforce accept the competence of his sons to participate in politico-jural affairs; but always, and even in his senility, they cannot acquire complete autonomy from him.

The Lineage System

Genealogically the smallest lineage in a patrilineal society is that which comprises a man and his sons. Some anthropologists have found it convenient or even necessary to describe this as the minimal lineage in an operational sense. Among the Arusha, this patrilineage is wholly contained within the family, an essentially cognatic unit, as already described. The minimal lineage which can effectively operate outside the family and its domestic context is that comprising the sons of a man who is dead, and therefore whose family has disintegrated. The distinction is important, because for the Arusha a lineage is composed primarily of autonomous men who are heads

75

of their own, separate families. Only in a secondary sense does a lineage contain the children of those men and, by the same criterion, their wives and sons' wives also;[1] for each man represents his own family and invokes obligations on its behalf from his agnates.

The largest lineage in Arusha is that which stems from the earliest known agnatic ancestor—almost always a first-settler in the present tribal area. If the first ancestor is the grandfather of the oldest generation of living men today, this means that only two orders of lineage can exist: these are based on the grandfather and father respectively. By the nineteen-fifties probably a majority of first ancestors were the great-grandfathers of the current oldest generation: logically then three orders of lineage are possible. In practice only two orders are acknowledged by the people themselves, and demonstrated in activities, sentiments and external recognition. These I refer to as the 'maximal lineage', as already defined, and the 'inner lineage'. Ideally an inner lineage is described as a minimal lineage, but empirically this is not always so; its genealogical structure varies through time, and from lineage to lineage.

In their two orders of lineages the Arusha are distinguishing consciously between the all-inclusive and the less-inclusive groups— 'all agnates', and 'those agnates who are near'. In the maximal lineage relations are weak in action, often potential only for long periods; but in the inner lineage relations are intense, more or less continuous in action and notably corporate in quality.

An Arusha lineage of either order has no residential or territorial basis; nor does it have, as a group, more than minor rights over land or other properties. By the system of pioneering which persisted into the nineteen-fifties (i.e. until unoccupied lands disappeared), most men left their father's farm soon after marriage and went to clear an area for a new farm, there to build a new homestead. The sons of a man did not often pioneer together in a single area, nor necessarily even near to one another. Men were most inclined to pioneer alongside fellow-members of their age-group, and to cooperate with particular friends who did not need to be agnatic kin. More distant agnates felt no compulsion or even attraction to pioneer together unless they were age-mates, although there was no positive barrier against it. Sometimes a younger brother or a younger cousin followed his senior, and obtained access to a piece

[1] But on the position of women, see pp. 141-2

of land claimed but not yet cleared by the other. There has not, in recent decades, been any regular pattern or norm; although it seems probable that formerly, when the geographical range of pioneering was more restricted, agnates were likely to move at least to the same general area. The greater range of choice open since about 1930, with the beginnings of colonisation of the peripheral country off the mountain slopes, has certainly scattered men more widely; but there is no reason to believe that the essential nature of pioneering and agnatic sentiment has altered. A second phase of pioneering sometimes occurred when a man was middle aged—when, as Arusha put it, he had sons-in-law and particularly betrothed suitors of his daughters, who would undertake the labour of forest clearing and hoeing for him. At that time a man took little account of the geographical dispositions of his kinsmen; rather he sought to create a good farm where that possibility currently existed at the lower forest edge. There was no reason why his desire and his opportunity to pioneer again should coincide chronologically with that of his agnates; there was no special value to be gained by working together. A man's farm is thought to be a most personal piece of property, symbolising his autonomy as well as his means of production and livelihood. He does not wish to compromise his individual rights by close association in this particular endeavour with near agnates. There is much less danger of compromise in the company of friends and age-mates, or even relative strangers.

Members of a lineage have always tended, therefore, continuously to disperse and to find neighbours of any or even no previous connection. Dispersion could, of course, be greater or lesser and this has tended to affect the evolution of particular inner lineages. Agnates who almost fortuitously live in the same neighbourhood are able to cooperate, even merely remain in touch, more easily. Most, but not all, maximal lineages have a few neighbourhoods in which several members live fairly near together. Nowadays, as land shortage has become desperately acute for the Arusha, a greater clustering of members of inner lineages has begun, and it seems likely to intensify as inheritance becomes established as the chief source of land. This is a recent innovation however and cannot affect the already widely scattered maximal lineages.

Although in certain circumstances a lineage acts corporately in ancestral ritual, there are no lineage shrines or other group sites for this purpose. Intercessions are invariably made on behalf of a particular person in the first instance; and that person (or his family head if he is a subordinate) convenes the assembly of the group at his own homestead to perform the ritual at his ancestral shrine. A shrine is always a father's grave, or a replica of it, and there exist no shrines specifically for earlier ancestors which could have general significance for a wider group.

An inner lineage has no formal leader; all members are of equal status except for considerations of generational difference. A maximal lineage has one or more 'spokesmen' selected by members of the group, but these men are chosen for their practical abilities and are neither heads of the lineage nor the seniormost members of it. In brief, both orders of lineage are loosely organised, without defined leadership or authority and without geographical foci of importance. They are, nevertheless, units of co-activity in a wide range of social situations. In their activities they illustrate well the Arusha preoccupation with egalitarian individualism, tempered by the value of reciprocal assistance.

CHAPTER FIVE

THE INNER LINEAGE

Ideology and Practices

THE inner lineage is the smaller group of agnates who comprise an operationally effective social group. The Arusha refer to it as *engang*, and as 'the kin who are near'. Both the expressed norm and the simplest form of this group is that its principal members, heads of their own autonomous families, are the sons of one father who is now dead. When the father dies the bonds, which hitherto tied brothers together, now disappear as compulsory factors; but they are transmuted into mutually advantageous, co-operative relations. They become relations between autonomous equals, and their justification lies in their practical usefulness allied with sentiments arising out of common upbringing and common interests. Brothers no longer demand rights against one another, nor accede to obligations, through a superordinate authority; but rather they seek privileges and offer their own assistance in return. Reciprocal aid and the value of corporate action are, however, reinforced by the image of the dead father, which provides both a conceptualisation of lineage unity and, through the ancestor cult, a positive force which cannot be ignored without danger.

If the dead father had been polygynous, the members of the lineages are divided into two segments by maternal origin. Where the father had two wives, lineage dichotomy simply distinguishes the sons of each; where there were more than two wives, dichotomy follows the *olwashe* grouping.[1] The significance of this internal segmentation is discussed later, in Chapter Seven.[2]

The notion of lineage unity and continuity is expressed in the idea of the joint inheritance and ownership of the dead father's estate, *engithaka*, which continues to be thought of as a whole, although

---

[1] See above, p. 72-3
[2] Especially p. 134ff.

patently it is not for practical purposes.[1] The significance of this is tenuous and emotive rather than concrete, for each brother is jealous of his own independence and of the clear rights he enjoys in his legitimate patrimony, his allodium, and he does not willingly surrender them to the interference of the others. The idea serves, however, to mark off the lineage members from all other people, agnatic kin or not; though it can have practical significance if a brother dies without surviving sons, or if one migrates away and quits his inherited portion. Sometimes the idea of the father's *engithaka* is demonstrated by the retention of his grazing paddock (*aulo*). Men remaining on or near the father's land share the right to put their livestock there, and by cooperative labour they maintain fences and hedges and clear invading bush and weeds. The retention of an undivided paddock is often commanded by an aged father on pain of his supernatural displeasure after his death. It is probably more commonly maintained nowadays than formerly, partly because more sons remain on the father's land, and partly because with land shortage it seems a more economical method of providing a grazing area. It still is rare that a common paddock persists when the brothers reach middle age: they come to prefer full control of their own grazing along with their arable land, and men find that this kind of co-operation is liable to be productive of recurrent bickering or worse.

Of course some, perhaps most, of the land held by members of the lineage was never wholly part of the father's estate, but was pioneered or, occasionally, acquired by purchase by the sons themselves. Such pioneered land is not normally thought of as part of the father's estate, although in earlier times the bulk of the sons' lands was pioneered. This is mentioned here to illustrate from another point of view that the idea of common inheritance and ownership of the father's estate is primarily a symbolic concept not altogether rooted in reality. On the other hand there remains sufficient practical significance in it to make it a persistent and useful one.

The practical significance is demonstrated by the fact that a man's brothers are, and moreoever *should* be, his principal consultants and

[1] Originally, say Arusha, *engithaka* applied only to a piece of land acquired by a man clearing unoccupied forest or bush, and the word is still so used. Nowadays it has a number of extended usages:—the total land-holding of a man, or his estate in all kinds of property, or especially the estate of a man now dead which is divided up and owned severally by his sons or even grandsons. The similar Kikuyu word, *githaka*, has a rather narrower usage, according to Mr. H. E. Lambert in a personal communication.

witnesses in regard to his allocation of property within his family. They are his chief executives after his death of the formal dispositions of his property, and their approval is essential for the complete legitimacy of the inheritance—that is, if later dispute occurs amongst the heirs, claims shown to rest on the father's brothers' formal affirmation will be accepted unconditionally. This authority of brothers comes, say Arusha, from the fact that all the brothers' land was once their father's estate—though this is not unequivocally true, as we have seen.

During a man's lifetime, should he wish to transfer any of his property by loan, sale or pledge, his brothers are usually consulted because of the friendly assistance they are thought to be able to give. The transaction itself should be witnessed by at least some of them and thus, of course, approved by them. Except for the modern by-law requiring it in the case of all sales of land, there is no absolute requirement that this occur, but it almost invariably does. The other brothers expect so to participate, saying that they have a right to be informed and involved in the alienation of what was their father's property; they deem it a consciously unfriendly act to be denied the opportunity. They are in any case a man's closest associates, most likely to be able and to want to assist and to watch his interests. Their participation affirms the legitimacy of the transaction: firstly by confirming that the piece of property is indeed in the ownership of their brother, who has therefore a right to dispose of it if he wishes; and secondly, by tacitly accepting some joint responsibility with him for the proper fulfilment of the transaction—e.g. they are liable together with him should later intelligence show any fraudulance or unpremeditated illegitimacy. A man who attempts to act without the support of his brothers tends to be suspect in the eyes of another person with whom he is dealing. Conversely, in the event of later dispute a transaction so unsupported is immediately suspect, and it may be held void simply because of that; for example, a man may claim that a sale of land was in fact not a sale, but merely a recoverable pledge or even an uncovered loan, because his brothers did not witness and affirm the nature of the transaction. It is therefore fully in the interests of the person to whom land or livestock are transferred and for whatever purpose, to ensure the witness of the transferer's brothers.

With the sole exception of the sale of land, a man's brothers are not able to prevent the transfer of parts of his property—only can they impose such a restraint as to make the transaction troublesome and perhaps insecure. They can be required to declare the absence of legitimate reason why the transfer should not occur. Where the sale of land is concerned, they can claim the right to first preference as purchasers, although only if they are actually prepared to purchase it for roughly the price offered by someone else. Some Arusha assert that a man's brothers can prevent his selling land whether or not they wish to buy it, but this does not seem to be correct.

It is not desired to emphasise the negative or restrictive aspect of these kinds of fraternal relations. They are the obverse of the positive values of lineage membership, which are approved by the Arusha and which for them are the more important in maintaining the integrity of the group. That is, a man can obtain the support, advice and sympathy of his brothers in his transactions. More than this—for such transactions are infrequent and irregular—he can, in so far as he desires, share his experience and aspirations with them. He can seek their practical assistance in such matters as loans of plough oxen, or milch cows, or a bull. A man in the more arid peripheral lands may be able to obtain from a mountain-dwelling brother a small plot on which to plant bananas or coffee, in return for herding the other's cattle. Brothers tend to assist one another when the demand for labour is temporarily greater than one with his own family can supply, or when food shortages occur. There is to a limited extent a sharing among the brothers of money which they earn by their agriculture or labour. Although probably residentially scattered, brothers visit each other's homesteads frequently, often staying a day or two. Men feel that they can rely more on their brothers than on any other category of people, and they seek their assistance in preference to other kin or to age-mates. Not that fraternal relations are wholly amicable—for conflict may occur in the competition for scarce resources in inheritance, and that may leave unresolved animosities—yet despite this a man is inclined to trust his brothers more than other men.

To maintain a correct perspective in the light of the rather aggressive individualism of Arusha men, it should be noted that conflict is on the whole minimised by brothers' respect for each other's autonomy. There is neither right nor desire of wilful intervention in another's affairs, but rather a general readiness to give as well as to seek help when required.

The father-image and the operational unity of the group of autonomous brothers, and the significance of it to them, is well demonstrated in belief and activities in the ancestral cult. Here again is also illustrated the particular blend of cooperation and individualism which is the essence of the lineage. Every autonomous man has a large stone in the middle of the open space inside his homestead, as a memorial to his father. Just outside his homestead, typically on the mountain slopes in the adjacent banana grove and hidden from the public view, is the 'grave of the father' (*egurari e wawa*), the main shrine of ancestral ritual. This may be the actual grave if a son's homestead is next to his father's former homestead, or it may be based on a handful of earth carried from that grave to a more distant homestead. Periodic oblations of milk, beer and tobacco are made to the father at the stone inside the homestead, especially on the occasion of feasts and celebrations. These are to show a continuous memory and respect for him and to retain his good will without specific purpose in mind. Particular supplication to the ancestors, respecting some trouble affecting a person, are always made at the grave-shrine and these supplications are invariably addressed primarily to the father, even in those cases where it has been divined that some other ancestor is the cause of the misfortune. The dead father is believed to be the most powerful and active ancestor, and he is thought to be able to contact and influence all earlier ancestors, male and female, including those whose names have been forgotten by the living but who can nevertheless still affect them.

An autonomous man, possessing his own shrine, can undertake the ritual of the ancestral cult on behalf of himself and his own family. He is responsible for consultations with one or more diviners who can determine the ancestor or ancestors responsible for misfortune, and he pays their fees. He supplies the animal for sacrifice, and the additional milk, beer, tobacco and foods which are offered to the ancestors, to those living who participate in the rituals, and to those who wait aside in friendly sympathy and neighbourliness. Nevertheless all brothers are concerned with the same single dominant ancestor who, moreoever, is thought to desire the continued cooperation and unity of his sons which he commanded during his lifetime. Ritual is therefore only likely to produce satisfactory results if brothers act together on behalf of that one of their number who is directly affected. The father may ignore the supplications if they are not made corporately, and he may even take punitive action to show his displeasure. In addition to this genuine fear, a man believes also that at any time he is liable to suffer for the seemingly eccentric displeasures of the ancestors; he is therefore glad of opportunities to demonstrate his continued regard for them by participating in invocations to them through the father on occasions convened by a brother. There are, that is to say, positive inducements to cooperate with brothers in their ancestral rituals, and they reinforce the desire to assist the one currently afflicted.

Ancestral rituals are held at the grave-shrine of the family head whose own family is involved in misfortune, and thus the locus of events and assembly changes according to the location of the particular person affected. On each occasion the family head concerned is the temporary leader of the lineage in action. People who are not members of the lineage may not participate in the actual rituals, though they may share in the subsequent feast in the adjacent homestead away from the shrine. Thus the identity and exclusiveness of the lineage is demonstrated in esoteric practice, as well as in the powerful supernatural forces peculiar to the group alone.

The practical and ideal unity of the lineage is perceived by outsiders as well as by members of the group itself. Men are held to be in part responsible for the actions of their co-members, and therefore to incur the obligations which they incur. It is necessary not to exaggerate in this context. The lineage is a specific, closed group which can easily be identified by reference to its father-founder; it is not, however, a property-owning nor directly a property-controlling group, nor are members bound to consult with, even less to act with other members in important affairs affecting outsiders. The notion of corporate responsibility does *not* extend, therefore, to the idea that an injury caused by the action of one member can be made good by comparable or appropriate injury to any other member. Damages must be repaired by an offender himself. An injured Arusha should not vent himself on a close agnate of the offender nor touch the property or other rights of one of them: if he does this, he makes himself liable to a separate claim for compensation.

If a person defaults in a bridewealth transaction, or fails to repay a loan, or is proved to have stolen something, his brothers or the brothers of his family head cannot be compelled to contribute to the payments he must make. Nevertheless some jural payments, if they are to be readily met, would place an intolerable burden on the offender alone were he unable to obtain assistance from his brothers. Quite certainly he seeks their support in his defence whilst the dispute is under negotiation, and their participation in this way demonstrates their involvement—although it is almost a voluntary cooperation based on reciprocity and founded in the facts of agnatic descent. There is a moral responsibility and a practical value in material assistance, rather than a definitive obligation. Members of a judicial assembly are aware of this: often an offender's brothers are exhorted to assist him, and they may be deliberately stigmatised for failure to accept their moral duty. But in no case known to me, were brothers absolutely compelled to accept responsibility; on the other hand, in no case did I discover a man unable to obtain material assistance from his lineage members.

The inner lineage is described by Arusha as a group of family heads. In enumerating membership, usually only those men are mentioned; and this is adquate enough because each one represents and acts for his own family in collaboration with his peers. But as the sons of these family heads gain adult maturity (largely as defined in age-grade categories) they are permitted a gradually increasing degree of participation in lineage affairs, whilst their fathers grow older and less active. Some sons may begin to surpass their elders in ability, wealth and forensic skills, but they must speak with caution lest they offend the susceptibilities of their own father and his peers. The authority of a family head, gerontocratic values and the separation of the generations reinforce the prime importance of the fully autonomous members, sons of the lineage founder.

The Dynamics of the Inner Lineage

Thus far the inner lineage has been described as comprising the sons of a deceased father, so that corporate integrity and cooperation focus on the father as the past source of material resources and the present supernatural power. In this I have followed the people themselves who idealise the group in this way. But empirically it is not always like that, and it must be appreciated in order to understand the full significance of the lineage in Arusha politico-jural affairs.

When a man dies he may well be survived by some of his brothers, i.e. by members of his own inner lineage; and therefore his newly autonomous sons do not come immediately to form an independent group, but they are absorbed into the older, persisting group. This becomes obvious during the post-mortem discussions and inheritance settlement, in which members of the deceased's inner lineage play a leading part. They were most usually the witnesses of his allocations of property during his lifetime, and of his declared desires concerning the unallocated remainder. Because of their close association with him, they are the most knowledgeable about his outstanding debts and claims as they have been witnesses and associates in his transactions. And where, by procrastination or sudden death, a man had not determined the ultimate dispositions of his estate, the surviving members of his inner lineage are the appropriate persons to undertake the decisions then required. Finally, their formal public approval is essential to the legitimacy of the inheritance settlement. Where some of the sons of the dead man are still immature, and where there are widows, one or more members of the lineage may assume guardianship, and thus acquire direct responsibility for part of the deceased's estate.

Both the interest and the influence of the dead man's inner lineage are, then, immediately and significantly expressed. The dependence of the newly autonomous men on their father's close associates is made clear and its value to them is demonstrated. It remains in the interests of the younger men to retain their involvement with their older, more experienced agnates.

There is no problem for the surviving members of the old lineage, for they see only the continuance of their established group which becomes augmented by a number of younger, autonomous men in place of the single deceased member. They are still primarily concerned with their own father-based group, and retain the idealisation of their joint inheritance of the former estate of *their* father and all that implies. They continue their established relationships and readily take in the younger men. These new members, although now autonomous family heads, are not quite the equals of their father's peers, who are of superior generation. They are constrained, but generally willing, to accept the older men's greater experience and knowledge, at least in politico-jural affairs. The younger men are most likely to be less practised in ritual matters, whilst they recognise the impiety of ignoring their seniors. They do not at first establish their own father's grave-shrines, but are content to allow supplications to be made by their seniors to their father's father—i.e. to the father of the seniors. The seniors themselves place no especial significance on the powers of their dead brother, although his name is added to the list of dead agnates mentioned during ancestral rituals. Intercession on behalf of junior members of the lineage is usually, for some years, carried out at the shrine of the most senior member, or for convenience at the shrine of a senior member who lives nearby.

The lineage of the older men thus persists, although its internal structure has become more complex. In no case to my knowledge has a minimal lineage of a junior generation seceded from the older, persisting inner lineage immediately after its members acquired autonomy as family heads on their father's death. Such an incipient lineage does not achieve corporate existence nor recognition, for its members' interests are too closely bound up in the encompassing older lineage. It is not even correct to say that such a minimal lineage acts as a sub-section of the older lineage—that is, it never acts as a specific and recognised group either within the lineage itself or in relation to affairs peculiar to itself. At this level fraternal relations are purely interpersonal and dyadic, and do not aggregate into group-form.

Nevertheless as other members of the senior generation die and their restraining and integrating influence weaken, and as men of the junior generation achieve elderhood, experience and confidence, they tend increasingly to perceive themselves as differentiated by paternal origin. The father-image tends increasingly to be raised as a symbol of separation, and the ideal clustering of brothers becomes more persistent. The old inner lineage tends to become less well integrated as the necessities of cooperation diminish with the slackening influence of the senior generation. It becomes more liable to irremedial failure of cooperation and concensus; each set of brothers tend to think of themselves as more separate and more capably self-sufficient. The trend is, therefore, towards the distintegration of the old inner lineage and its replacement by a number of new lineages each based on one of the original members of it. However the developmental process is not necessarily so simple and inevitable as that: for on the one hand, some inner lineages persist in practice even after the deaths of all the original senior members, and when, therefore, the lineage becomes based on the grandfather of the oldest generation of men; and on the other hand, extended inner lineages may effectively break up whilst some of the senior members (sons of the founder) are still alive. Not only the timing of the structural reorganisation varies but also the particular pattern of operating lineages at any time.

Arusha invariably assert that brothers never become separated, although they might together combine with other agnates in a single lineage: and in all cases known this was true. Brothers might quarrel, sometimes violently, and especially over inheritance and responsibility for the unfulfilled obligations of their father. They may attempt to avoid obligations to one another or to press unduly heavy claims; persistent animosity may arise out of inter-personal friction. But ritual imperatives, jural requirements, economic privileges and the practical value of at least some cooperation are altogether too strong to allow permanent cleavage. A man, in brief, cannot afford to be without association with his brothers. Of course the degree of concensus and cooperation varies: there is no need to ignore that. It is an important factor both in the effectiveness of particular lineages, and in the development which occurs after the brothers' deaths. Nevertheless the ideal of fraternal unity is apparently never irretrievably violated. This is highly significant because the ideal lies at the core of the Arusha conception of the group of close agnates; and in concrete reality a set of brothers comprises the sole or the senior generation of men of an inner lineage in a large majority of cases.

One consequence of fraternal unity is that an inner lineage only rarely breaks up whilst some of its original members remain alive. The very few cases of this occurrence appeared to result primarily from the desires of sets of brothers to become independent of their paternal cousins, rather than a desire to ignore the old men, their fathers' brothers. And then those old men were quite senile, no longer a potent factor in the situation. Usually men wait for the death of even senile elders before seeking separation from their cousins.

Lineage persistence as a function of fraternal unity is reinforced by the pervasive importance of the acknowledged superiority of a senior generation over a junior one. Although not subject to the authority of men of senior generation (i.e. father's brothers),

Arusha are prepared to tolerate their influence and interference in a way quite unacceptable with an agnate of the same generation.

People outside the agnatic group are generally unwilling to treat solely with a man whose father's brother is still alive. A judicial body requires that the senior men be present and give at least their tacit support to the junior men; arrangements of marriage and bridewealth, or of tenancy, are strengthened by the participation of the senior man who is father's brother. Indeed Arusha say that where such arrangements are made without his participation, then one or both parties are not sure of the legitimacy of the transaction and are attempting to carry it off secretly. A man who is acting in a straightforward manner has nothing to fear from the participation of his father's brother, and much to gain. He can, if he wishes, ignore his senior's advice concerning the wisdom or practicality of the matter, for the senior man has no authority to prevent any legitimate act. The younger man may well be influenced in some degree by such opinion, just as he is by the opinion of his own brothers; and he is most likely to seek it, together with their support and, if need be, active assistance in the common course of events, for that is the main reason of the existence of the group.

The younger men do not altogether neglect their own dead father, for each son maintains his memory and reveres him at a grave-shrine at his own homestead; but they accept the leadership of their father's brothers who persist in focusing attention in the ancestral cult on *their* father who is, of course, the grandfather of the men of the junior generation. Joint ritual observances, acknowledgement and acceptance of joint ritual responsibility, economic cooperation, frequent visiting and consultation, and active support in certain matters (e.g. pressing a dispute, meeting a father-in-law to discuss bridewealth payment, etc.)—all these kinds of activities and cooperation are maintained without difficulty within an effective group wider than a single set of brothers. It must be emphasised again, to be quite clear, that an autonomous man is not subject to the authority of his father's brother, any more than he is subject to his own brothers' authority; only does he recognise the need and the value of continued, close association with both.

Thus a set of brothers, whose own father is dead, may not achieve independence as a separate inner lineage, and the ideal of the father-based group is not realised, at least temporarily. Nevertheless at a different level, in the generation of their father's brothers, the father-ideal and the unity of brothers is indeed recognised and maintained. As between adjacent generations of close agnates there is necessarily an ideological conflict, because both hold precisely the same set of values; but these are not realisable by both simultaneously. This is not a conflict in terms of authority, for the men of senior generation recognise the same autonomy for their nephews as they themselves claim as heads of their own families. The idea and practice of basic equality remains between all full members of the lineage.

Conditioned by notions of seniority and juniority embedded in the age organisation, the men of junior generation are amenable to a degree of influence. Whilst the younger men are still murran, many factors support the influential superiority of their fathers' brothers; but the older and the more senior they become in the age-set system, the more the men of junior generation are able as well as desirous to do without the interference, assistance and support of agnates of the senior generation. Potential conflict is commonly minimised, however, because concurrently with this gradual evolution there occurs a decrease in the numbers of the senior generation as 'fathers' die. Those of them who survive, begin to enter the publicly inactive age-grade of retired elders and, individually in old age, they become both less willing and less competent to continue active participation. Nevertheless it is by no means impossible that a man of junior generation is about the same age and therefore has the same age status as his father's younger brother—occasionally the nephew may even be in a senior age-set. In such a case conflict is more likely; but here the Arusha lay particular emphasis on the equality of men of the same age status, and they find it convenient to ignore the factor of generational difference. Nephew and father's brother act as if they were brothers which, in the age-set classification, they virtually are.

In a case of this kind, it was found that Ndiali had been participating in a ceremony in the ancestral cult arranged by and on behalf of Loidong, the son of Ndiali's deceased elder brother, Mabruk. During the ritual supplications chief attention was paid to Mabruk, although, on questioning, Ndiali admitted that strictly he should have been primarily concerned with his own father. He excused himself on the grounds that Mabruk had been 'dead a long time and he was like my father as he was the father of Loidong. Loidong and I are brothers. Are we not both Ilderito? (their common age-set). Are we not both elders?' In fact Mabruk had been some twenty years older than Ndiali, and no other brother survived. On their father's death Mabruk had assumed guardianship over Ndiali, then still only a boy. At the time of my inquiry Mabruk had been dead nearly fifteen years, and Ndiali felt no difficulty nor supernatural danger in participating in ritual supplications to him. Ndiali said that at his own shrine he would direct supplications both to his true father and to Mabruk; and although I was unable to verify the truth of this, it was probably correct. In other activities Ndiali, Loidong and the younger brothers of Loidong acted towards one another as if they were a single set of brothers. Indeed at first I had assumed they were and, more significantly, so did some other Arusha who, though not knowing them intimately, had had dealings with them. Thus in this case the problem was fairly easily resolved. The major consideration was the amicable and useful preservation of cooperation between Ndiali, the remaining survivor of his generation, and the sons of his brother; and to accomplish this it was convenient to emphasise the equality of age and status and to neglect generational difference.

A rather different situation arises when all the members of the senior generation have died. The persuasion, the practical incentives and the external pressures which induce men to accept continued association with their father's brothers and, through them, with already autonomous patrilateral cousins, do not necessarily apply to those cousins when the link of the senior generation disappears. Father's brothers' sons are men of the same generation who regard themselves as in no way junior agnatically, and who in terms of inheritance, mutual interests and ancestral ritual find no common link of any kind of father-image. This is the stage when the old inner lineage may distintegrate and become replaced by a number of new, smaller ones, which are differentiated in principle by paternal origin, and in practice by the kinds of continuing association which are felt to be both useful and tolerable.

In a sample of 146 inner lineages, there were 112 cases in which the encompassing maximal lineage was based on the great-grandfather, and where therefore structurally the inner lineages could be based *either* on the father or on the grandfather. In 62 cases (55%) the senior (and sometimes the only) generation of men comprised a set of patrilateral cousins. In these lineages the ideal of the father-founder was not followed at that time.

Some of these recorded cases where patrilateral cousins combined in a single inner lineage were most probably temporary associations, in that an old inner lineage had not yet divided because the death of the last original member of the fathers' generation was too recent. It seemed clear in many instances that sets of brothers in the new senior generation were feeling their distinction from one another; but so far nothing had occurred to precipitate crystalisation of their attitudes and their practical implications. This is to be expected, for there is not necessarily any immediate reason or specific occasion for segmentation, or conversely for the reiteration of continued unity, to be explicitly raised. In some societies where lineages are important, it is necessary to determine fairly quickly who is lineage head, or who has ritual leadership, when the last member of the senior generation dies; and discussion and settlement of such issues inevitably raises the question of segmentation among the succeeding generation.[1] These kinds of issues do not arise for the Arusha. If segmentation is to occur as the result of the generational shift, it comes gradually—and most probably the process will have begun earlier—as men incline to concentrate their loyalty and their interests upon their own fraternal set. Sooner or later some critical occasion occurs, when a conscious choice must be made of the practical range of co-operation. The kind of occasion varies a good deal according to particular, even accidental circumstances. It may be, for example, a performance in the ancestral cult when a set of brothers decide whether or not to attend at the father's grave-shrine of their cousin; or it may come with the denial or the acceptance of specific obligations, such as the repayment of bridewealth, loan of land or cattle, or support in a dispute. On the whole, Arusha say that they expect patrilateral cousins to separate on the lines of paternal origin; of course this is the ideal expectation, but empirically it is also in the long run the actual norm.

In some cases, however—and a statistical determination of these is scarcely possible—extended inner lineages are of long standing, and have remained intact despite the occurrence of critical issues

---

[1] E.g. among the Lugbara; cf. Middleton 1961, p. 192 ff.

which might have stimulated fission. In these instances, sometimes many years had elapsed since the father's generation had disappeared, but practical unity had been retained among their sons. In a few cases, in the sample investigated, the old inner lineage had continued to the point where a new junior generation of autonomous men had begun to emerge, following the deaths of one or more grandsons of the lineage founder. The nine recorded cases of this comprise only 8% of the total inner lineages which existed within maximal lineages founded by a great-grandfather; their significance must not be exaggerated therefore. In respect of these nine cases, I was impressed by two important features which are of more general significance. First, the members of these extended inner lineages expressed a positive unity among themselves. The persistence of their lineages intact was not merely the result of apathetic tolerance, nor yet of misguided inference by me. Secondly, and more importantly, it was pertinent that, in all these cases, the numbers of autonomous men were fairly small, and certainly no larger than the numbers of men in a more 'typical' inner lineage based on the father of the senior generation. Heuristically it is suggested, therefore, that an important empirical consideration is the optimum size of the group of nearer agnates who retain persistently close cooperation of a corporate nature.

The average number of men in Arusha inner lineages is empirically between five and ten. One with either less or more than this number tends not to be viable. For example, one containing only the two sons of a man is clearly not a viable unit; but one containing a man's five sons may well be, and those men can afford to separate from sets of patrilateral cousins. Men are aware of this, so that with a set of only one or two brothers, the men attempt to retain active relations with one or more sets of their cousins for whom it is equally advantageous to preserve a larger group. This can produce a difficult situation where one set of brothers is too small, but a related set, with whom continued relations are desired, may in the opinions of its members be strong enough to act alone. Such a problem is illustrated in Case 7, where the plaintiff (one of two brothers) in a dispute was reluctant to test the willingness to cooperate of his more numerous cousins. He preferred not to force the issue at that time— he sought instead the aid of his age-mates—in the hope that later he would be able to demonstrate the value to the cousins of ties with himself and his brother. Forcing the issue, he believed, might have irremediably split the group.[1]

On the other hand, a lineage containing a relatively large number of men tends not to be viable either, because the kind of values and ideas underlying this association of close agnates, as well as the techniques of maintaining concensus and cooperation, are such that they are not readily applicable on a large scale. Essentially the inner lineage is a small-scale group without institutionalised leadership, residential integrity or geographical focus. Thus a large group based on the father's father is doubly weak—conflicting with both ideal conception and practical viability.

For the purposes of this present account of the Arusha it is not necessary to investigate the sociological processes of lineage evolution: that requires a detailed examination of the dynamics of these small-scale groups. Here it is sufficient to make the point that the agnatic group functionally identifiable as the smaller corporate lineage has a variable genealogical structure, both through time for a single group, and for different groups. Variation in group membership is primarily important here because members are a man's principal supporters and advisers; and simultaneously they are the people who directly and intimately exert pressures on him to restrain and control his activities. Membership of this group, as of any group, both permits of more effective action through cooperation and compels a degree of constraint on each member as the price of that.

[1] See Case 7, page 191.

CHAPTER SIX

THE MAXIMAL LINEAGE

THE maximal lineage is a more easily identifiable group, but a much less active and effective one, than the inner lineage. It simply comprises the group of living people who can trace agnatic descent (or who claim they can) from the earliest known ancestor. The founding ancestors of maximal lineages are generally alleged to have been first-settlers on the slopes of Mt. Meru in the second quarter of last century—though a few were the fathers of first-settlers. Therefore these lineages have a special historical significance linked with the origins of the tribe itself; and they are all shallow in genealogical depth, for the founder is either grandfather or great-grandfather of the senior living generation of men today.

Within a maximal lineage there are, of course, a number of inner lineages, and these are divided into two sets, forming dichotomous parts of the whole. Each part is said to contain the patrilineal descendants of one *olwashe* (set of co-wives) of the original family of the founder. In many cases the names of the founder's wives are now forgotten, and even sometimes the precise maternal origin of the founder's sons within each *olwashe*; it is no longer important. The significance of this segmentation of the lineage is discussed in the following chapter.

As a corporate group, the maximal lineage is only weakly effective in Arusha social life, and therefore a brief account of it will suffice here. Rarely, in many cases never, does a maximal lineage assemble and act as a whole unit. On the other hand, because of its genealogical rationale and certain idealised co-responsibilities, members feel bound to one another so that they expect to make demands for advice, sympathy and support in jural affairs. In practice these demands are made, and acceded to, within an ill-defined section of the lineage which is roughly determined by geographical propinquity. The privileges and obligations of membership are largely confined to those agnates who live fairly near to a particular man who is in need of assistance. Arusha habitually use certain indices to identify and explain their maximal lineages—exogamy, mortuary observances, jural responsibilities and supernatural beliefs and practices—and I examine these in order to illustrate the group in conception and practice.

All Arusha agree in asserting that the maximal lineage is an exogamous group, but this has not been entirely true for at least half a century. Some inter-marriages have occurred—though not in every lineage, and always in the face of strong opposition. In reluctantly admitting these breaches, Arusha explain that nowadays their lineages have grown so large numerically and so deep genealogically that they are less well integrated than formerly. Men perceive a gradual slackening of intra-lineage ties over the last generation or so, and this is probably historically correct.

An examination of cases of intra-lineage marriages indicates that they were the result of particular idiosyncrasy where a man and girl were adamant in their mutual desire to marry despite opposition. Closer inquiry showed in the majority of cases (and perhaps all, were information adequate) that those aberrant unions were facilitated by incipient divisions within the lineages concerned, so that opposition to the marriage was not concerted. In one case recorded, one group of lineage members supported the marriage in order to show their opposition to and negligence of other members. Here Ragoyan was encouraged to force through his marriage as a show of independence of his grandfather's brothers' grandsons who, because he was exceptionally wealthy and influential, had been importuning him beyond what he and others considered to be the norms of that relatively remote link. This is the explanation given by men of both sides; and Ragoyan's distant kinsmen added that he persisted in the marriage in order to spite them.

Breaches of exogamy are still infrequent, and the Arusha assert the rule as a key criterion of agnatic kinship, and thus of the maximal lineage. Certainly the rule does touch upon some of the principle values inherent in the lineage. Affinal relations created by marriage permit a good deal of overt bargaining, and contain marked tensions and conflict, both during the period of pre-marital arrangements, and later when a wife's father and brothers press their claims to bridewealth and to material assistance in labour. A son-in-law attempts to avoid too severe obligations and to delay and reduce bridewealth payments; and he seeks to obtain assistance from his affines allegedly on behalf of his wife and her children. Agnatic kinsmen, too, may come into conflict, and they may bargain with one another over assistance sought and rendered; but the common ideal for them is one of friendly cooperation, mutual adjustment and trust. In general, agnates are constrained against too great a departure from the norms by the perceived necessities of co-membership of the lineage, and by the pressures and conciliatory intervention of other members. Affinal relationships are more frankly materialistic, and are not restrained by needs of group concensus; a man tends to seek what he can and to avoid what he can. Even after the eventual completion of bridewealth transfers—and that can seldom take less than ten years, often much longer—and when direct obligations cease, affines seldom establish well-marked, mutually fruitful relationships. In both conception and practice, therefore, agnatic and affinal relationships are of a different order. Arusha are aware of this, and they see that the introduction of affinal considerations into a maximal lineage conflicts with the ethos of that group.

In addition Arusha conceive of agnates of the same generation as 'brothers' and 'sisters', with a link between them such that relations should be modelled on those of real siblings. In a way the maximal lineage is conceived by the people as a greatly enlarged family. In consequence they express moral concern, even horror, at the idea of inter-marriage.

The second index of the maximal lineage occurs in post-mortuary observances. Within a few days of the death of a lineage member, all family heads of the group should visit his homestead, bringing beer for the mourning drinking in the adjacent paddock. Members of the deceased's inner lineage and other agnates who live fairly near to the homestead regularly observe this obligation: it would be virtually impossible for them to maintain everyday relations thereafter, were they to default. Geographically more distant agnates commonly neglect their obligations; although, if an important man dies, other inner lineages may send one of their members as representative. These more distant agnates do not engage in frequent social intercourse and, as will be shown later, they are unlikely to be expected to give support and assistance in jural affairs. Pressure to conform is, therefore, slight. Similarly, all agnates should shave their heads as a public mark of mourning; but, as Arusha readily admit, this practice (when followed at all) is limited again to the inner lineage and geographically near kin.

Two principal ideas are involved in these practices—customs which people continue to say they ought to observe, even when they are patently not doing so. First, say Arusha, it is an obligation to commiserate with the bereaved, and to act as 'one lineage' in recognising the loss of a member. The weakness of the lineage is well demonstrated in the failure of distant-living agnates to observe group requirements.[1] Secondly, they say, the supernatural power of the dead person can bring misfortune on those living agnates who are impious enough to ignore their obligations. That is to say, the field of agnatic kinship is congruent with the range of ancestral power. This is made explicit in these mortuary practices, for it is said that not only may the displeasure of the dead be visited on any member of the lineage, but the sufferer may not necessarily be the actual offender who neglects his duties.

This conception of ancestral power, and a similar limitation in actual practice, also occurs in connection with major rituals in the ancestral cult. Infrequently, and as the result of unusually severe and persistent misfortune, the head of the afflicted family initiates a special ceremony of supplication to the ancestors at the grave-shrine at his homestead. Although particular attention is given to the nearer ancestors of the afflicted persons, yet so serious a misfortune is thought to derive from other ancestors also. To make the rituals efficacious all members of the maximal lineage should attend and participate. Special pieces of a slaughtered ox[2] are offered to all the lineage dead, and parts are eaten by the living members together: thus there is not only commensality among the living, but also between them and all of their ancestors. Not only do the afflicted members seek to gain relief, but other agnates gain a measure of personal protection through showing their continued regard for the dead. The family head concerned, with the assistance of his inner lineage, does attempt to inform all members of his maximal lineage of the event and invites their attendance. This is not difficult in so

---

[1] The norm may be observed in the breach. A distant agnate may state (without intention of a blatant lie) that he and his family have shaved for a distant, dead agnate although they have not actually done so. The idea seems to be to express, even so weakly, the acknowledged obligation inherent in agnatic kinship.

[2] Lesser ancestral rituals involve the slaughter only of a goat or sheep.

small a country, and especially nowadays with the market focus of the modern township roughly in the centre. Informants told me that a man does this in order to make the rituals as efficacious as possible, and also to fulfil his obligations to the ancestors so they shall not blame him for the non-attendance of other agnates.

No case was discovered where in fact a whole lineage assembled together for these rituals. Perhaps no less importantly, men were prepared to recognise the gap between norms and practice. It is considered unfriendly, as well as dangerous supernaturally, if agnates who live fairly near to the homestead fail to attend without good reason. This flaunts both the living and the dead. But those living more than five or six miles away are not thought necessarily to be unfriendly if they fail to attend, and fears of supernatural misfortune seem not to arise then. Members of the inner lineage invariably come, wherever they live. More important elders, including the lineage counsellor, are most likely to attend even if they live rather farther off. This definition of practical cooperation and responsibility in the ancestral cult corresponds to the general limits of active, useful relations between agnates in other contexts— visiting and hospitality, exchange of news and opinion, economic assistance, mutual aid, support in conflict with non-agnates, etc. Empirically, and with certain reservations, a man's effective maximal lineage is restricted to those agnates (outside his inner lineage) with whom he can fairly easily maintain more or less continuous relations because they happen to live near enough to his homestead. Thus cooperation and mutual assistance in all social activities, which are said by Arusha to involve the whole lineage, are in reality restricted to the inner lineage together with a genealogically heterogeneous cluster of other agnates who live nearby. For each man this effective range of agnatic kin, being roughly defined geographically, tends to differ even for members of the same inner lineage. I state this briefly here, but its implications in the field of social control, and specifically in the processes of dispute settlement, will be made clearer in later chapters.

The maximal lineage has no territorial basis. Even the numerically smaller ones are all scattered, whilst the larger ones have members in parishes all over the country. This is certainly not a modern phenomenon, but since about 1930 the geographical range of settlement has been greatly increased as the result of the colonisation of the peripheral lands off the traditional mountain slopes.[1] Thus the degree of dispersion has become greater, and the infrequency of contacts between more widely separated kinsmen has increased the practical difficulties of successful corporate action by lineages on relevant occasions. Rather more important than this geographical dispersion (for still the country is not large), is the increasing genealogical depth of lineages. Geographically separated members of an inner lineage find relatively little difficulty in maintaining joint action, and Arusha express no major problems or dissatisfaction in that respect. It is also easy and still profitable to maintain continuous relations with distant agnates who live fairly near. But where both geographical and genealogical distance are combined, difficulties do appear. The weaknesses of the maximal lineage which have previously been described, are emphasised in these cases. Arusha are inclined to explain failures in exogamic rules, in ritual observances and comprehensive joint action by reference to this modern condition. This is probably too facile an explanation, however, for Arusha assertions are less convincing when it is realised that at least some cases of breach of exogamy occurred early in this century, and that even conservative old men do not really expect their genealogically distant agnates to observe head-shaving or to walk much more than about five or six miles to attend ancestral ritual.

My conclusion is that, although all maximal lineages are doubtless undergoing some loss of corporate cohesion, the gaps between norms and practices are, equally importantly, indicative of the general weakness of the agnatic link beyond the inner lineage. This weakness is almost certainly an endemic one, and must be recognised as such. It results from the fact that the social needs, rights and obligations between agnates outside the inner lineage are not imperative enough, nor well enough organised, to create and maintain a high degree of concensus and cohesion. There is no economic basis in land holding or control; there is no fixed centre of activities, no common shrine or meeting place; leadership (as described in the following section) is weak even where it is exercised; little or no cohesive quality or necessity is derived from corporate relations with like groups in the society. Were it truly the case that the integrity of maximal lineages is being undermined by modern changes, this would be a most pertinent fact to take into account,

[1] See Gulliver 1960, p. 12ff.

for it would mean that they are becoming less efficient to carry out the social tasks expected of them. In particular, in the context of this book, they would be less efficient instruments in politico-jural affairs. It is, of course, not unimportant that some Arusha feel this to be the case, or that they use this argument as a rationalisation; but I do not place much weight on this. Maximal lineages continue to change as new generations emerge within what are only shallow genealogical units; but the changes so far do not appear to be radical as older men will admit in the detailed discussion of past and present case-histories. Men continue to place as much, and as little, reliance on their maximal lineages as they have done in the past. Clearly a maximal lineage is important in marking off known agnatic kin from the rest of society, and thus marking certain limits of cooperation and responsibilities, and providing one kind of way in which members of the group are encouraged or pressured to conform to obligations and approved behaviour. No less clearly, the strength of a maximal lineage as a corporate group is severely limited; it is the local group of agnates together with the near kin of the inner lineage who comprise the effective, active grouping in the name of, but not as the specific representatives of, the maximal lineage.

The Lineage Counsellor

In each maximal lineage, one of its members is selected to be *olaigwenani le ngaji*—literally translatable as 'the spokesman of the lineage'. In order to make a clear distinction between this role and that of *olaigwenani lo lporror* ('the spokesman of the age-group')[1], it will be referred to as 'the lineage counsellor'. This gives, additionally, an informative term of reference.

At the time of field-work there were approximately one hundred lineage counsellors. In a few cases at that time, a maximal lineage contained no counsellor. Investigation showed that these were either numerically small, geographically dispersed lineages, or, more often, cases where animosities and quarrels between members have prevented a concensus in the selection of a member to fill a vacant role. Conversely, some lineages contained more than one counsellor. Arusha say that preferably each lineage should have two counsellors, one in the grade of senior elder (i.e., an experienced man) and one in the grade of junior elder (i.e. a learner who can also undertake more

[1] Cf. p. 47.

physical activity). In a small number of cases this was the case; but in those best known to me it had happened that the senior elder, feeling his age or for some other reason wishing to off-load some of his responsibilities, had requested the selection of a junior elder assistant. In other lineages, the senior elder was reluctant to agree to an assistant for he considered that the selection of one would imply that he could no longer adequately perform his duties. If, when two counsellors have been selected, the senior elder dies, another senior elder is not usually selected to take his place and the lineage continues with a single counsellor of junior elder status. As noted earlier (page 40), men in the formal grade of senior murran tend to enter *de facto* elderhood before their ceremonial transfer to that grade: recognition of this occurs in some lineages where the junior counsellor is still formally a murran. In no case known to me were there more than two counsellors in any single lineage.

A new counsellor is selected by lineage members of elder status, with the assistance and advice of counsellors and notables of other maximal lineages of the same clan. Counsellors themselves are apt to declare that only they have the right to select a new counsellor for any lineage within their clan; but in practice this means that they are consulted, and that at least one or two of them should participate in the ceremony of the installation of the chosen man. This occurs at the latter's homestead in the presence of lineage members and interested neighbours, and the new status of the selected man is affirmed by the presentation to him by an existing counsellor of his special staff of office. There is, too, a sense that the new man is accepted into the ranks of counsellors by those already occupying the role, and this is significant in view of the fact that the role of counsellor is not limited to his own lineage.

A counsellor who, it is generally agreed, is not adequately fulfilling his responsibilities can be removed and be replaced by another man. This occurs infrequently, because lineage members can afford to be tolerant of the adequacy of their counsellor where there is a second one in the group or, more commonly, where it is possible to seek the assistance of a counsellor of some other lineage within the same sub-clan. Especially as a counsellor grows old and less able and active, it is generally preferred not to raise the issue of his replacement and perhaps start faction in the lineage. Cases of removal which were known to me all involved a younger man who had consistently and openly not met demands on him because of debilitating disease, chronic drunkenness, wilful partiality, or permanent absence through migration abroad.

A man is selected to become a counsellor strictly on account of certain approved characteristics and abilities considered appropriate to the role. He must be a physically active man of manifest intelligence and initiative; he should already have shown forensic skills in public discussion and assembly; he should have a good knowledge of the people and affairs of his lineage, and of Arusha custom and precedence; he should be diplomatic and persuasive in argument, able to assess individuals and situations, and prepared to depend on patient debate without precipitately taking inflexible positions likely to hamper his work. The Arusha are quite specific about these qualities they seek and expect in their counsellors, and some of them are in marked contrast with the generally approved characteristics of a man in this culture. The ordinary man is expected to be quick to take offence against alleged insult or injury, to rush into action in his own defence as a matter of personal honour, and to resort to verbal and physical violence rather than seek strength in a reasoned moral and legal position. To a considerable extent lineage counsellors represent virtues which *prima facie* are not emphasised among other Arusha. Counsellors tend to act as men's consciences, for they act by principles which at a deeper level are both morally and practically approved. A man must, Arusha say, demonstrate his individual independence by quick reaction to anything which might suggest his personal inferiority to another man, or which might adversely affect his own interests. A counsellor, on the other hand, must take calmer and more deliberate action, if due consideration indicates not only a real infringement of a man's interests but also the possibility of effective remedial action. Thus characteristically a counsellor *qua* counsellor is set off from his fellows, and his social function is emphasised.

In my experience, the large majority of counsellors are outstanding in intelligence, knowledge and ability, although of course in part these qualities and the self-confidence to use them are stimulated by continual practice and experience in the role. It was found in the field that counsellors were generally better informants than most men, even in matters unrelated to their role. My conclusion is that Arusha do choose many of their ablest men to carry out the responsibilities entrusted to them.

At least in some cases, selection was coloured by considerations of wealth, the influence of men's fathers and, nowadays, formal education; but it is probable that in few cases were these factors dominant in determining selection, and only decisive where roughly equally acceptable men were available. So great a value is set on selection of the ablest men, and on the responsibilities which they assume, that little factionalism occurs between inner lineages or local groupings within the maximal lineage. Such conscious and conscientious efforts underline the importance which Arusha give to their counsellors.

About 20% of lineage counsellors are also age-group spokesmen. Counsellors are, of course, chosen from among junior elders—young middle-aged men—and many spokesmen are thought by their agnates at that stage not to have matured so well as some other members of their lineages. More importantly, Arusha recognise the burden of responsibilities put on their leaders: consequently men of a lineage are generally willing to accede to the request of their fellow-member who is already a spokesman that he should not be selected as counsellor. There is here an element both of being fair to their agnate in not overburdening him, and of being fair to themselves in not selecting as counsellor a man who is already committed to duties in his age-group and parish. For these reasons the degree of overlap of roles of leadership is not strongly marked. On the other hand, there is no counsellor who is not at the same time accepted as a notable in his own age-group and parish; and conversely all spokes-men are accepted as notables in their own maximal lineages. This partial overlapping serves to some extent to provide a bridge between the age-group system and the patrilineages. It is one which the people themselves certainly do not emphasise; and analytically it is relatively unimportant because of the marked differences in the total set of roles, attitudes and group alignments, social situations and practical techniques between the two systems of action in social control.

The significance of the lineage counsellor is twofold. On the one hand, his role is a product of the unity and exclusiveness of the largest group of known agnates; he often acts as a focus of group activities and group loyalties, and as its public representative to the rest of society. On the other hand, he has a key position in the politico-jural system in his co-ordinated, triple capacity of advisor and jural counsel, formal witness of social transactions, and conciliator. Here it is necessary only to give an introduction to the nature of the role, its competence and practice. The activities and influence of counsellors are complex, and will only become clear in the later description of Arusha institutions and in the context of case-histories. The role of the counsellor in the total politico-jural system is closely related to that of other well-marked roles of 'notables' of both lineages and age-groups, just as the social groups from which they are recruited are also interrelated in the whole society.

The duties and responsibilities of a lineage counsellor are many and varied, but all relate to the politico-jural system of Arusha society. In most disputes a man actively seeks the support of his counsellor, if only to keep him informed and to obtain his advice. In a matter of any importance the counsellor acts as advisor to the disputant of his own lineage; he recommends the best course of action, he consults witnesses and other people involved, he arranges a meeting for public discussion of the dispute, and he assists in the presentation of the case, the questioning of witnesses and the proposals for the resolution of the affair. In the discussion of the dispute in public meeting the counsellor also acts in the capacity of conciliator, for he takes the initiative in attempting to secure a solution, in meeting the demands of the other party and, in a successful conclusion, eventually in determining the final issue in collaboration with the counsellor of the other disputant. In an intra-lineage dispute, he acts as *primus inter pares* in the process of securing both settlement and reconciliation between fellow-agnates.

Men are generally concerned to keep their own lineage counsellor informed of transactions they undertake—e.g. betrothal, marriage and bridewealth, loans, tenancy or pledge of land—so that the counsellor is at once aware of the facts and able, then or later, to advise on them. Counsellors are most favoured witnesses of transactions—e.g. marking of field boundaries, or handing over bridewealth cattle—although they are not the only people who perform the necessary task in this mainly non-literate society. In some cases they are necessarily involved in the transactions of their agnates, not only for the benefit of individuals undertaking them, but also to prevent attempted or alleged offence. For example, nowadays a man cannot sell land without his counsellor's witness of the act (and thus implicitly his approval of its legitimacy), because formerly a number of cases occurred where men wilfully or innocently disposed of land to which they had not undisputed right. Although it is not essential that the counsellor be present at post-mortuary inheritance discussions, for these are settled within the inner lineage with the authority and witness of senior members, nevertheless in most cases, and certainly all disputed cases, he is asked to attend, and his advice and intervention are willingly accepted.

A counsellor exercises a good deal of influence, and much power of persuasion—almost authority. In his capacity as conciliator—in which he acts in consort with the counsellor of the other disputant, except in intra-lineage matters—he seldom attempts to coerce people on either side to an acceptance of his opinion. Rather he tries to influence and direct opinion; to suggest lines of argument and precedent; and to urge the kinds of resolution which, in the given circumstances, are likely to be more acceptable to the other party, and to lead to a conclusion of the dispute with a minimal concession by his own side. In joining with the counsellor of the other side in establishing a formal settlement, he affirms at least tactily that his own side is prepared to accept it and that it will be honoured. He must, therefore, consult with his own kinsman, with members of that man's inner lineage, and with other notable agnates. They too all participate in the jural assembly, expressing opinion and questioning fact and opinion of the other side; but the counsellor is chief spokesman and is recognised with approval to be so.

A settlement is ultimately and necessarily that which is acceptable to both parties in the dispute. Even in a manifestly obvious case, such as detected theft or non-payment of bridewealth, a counsellor must be careful only to join with the other counsellor eventually in an agreed decision on the nature of the settlement—however forthright he may be in his capacity as advisor and counsel. Indigenous assemblies—but not the newer formal courts—have no presiding head to whom appeal is made, and upon whom responsibility as well as authority rests. Opposing counsellors, together with their respective kinsmen, must persist in seeking a mutually acceptable settlement which in some degree is inevitably a compromise. If a dispute involves related men, e.g. two agnates, or a man and his affines, or two neighbours, counsellors have the responsibility of seeking reconciliation between men by diplomatic skill, so that the relationship may suffer minimal or no permanent injury.

Nevertheless a counsellor is not entirely powerless, and the nature of potential coercion open to him is indicative of his role. Sometimes a disputant persists in adamant refusal to accept or abide by a settlement which to almost everyone else seems to be adequate—e.g. the payment of minimal compensation, plus return of the property where theft cannot be denied nor wholly extenuating circumstances be shown. To prevent the possibly harmful continuation of the dispute, on the one hand, and to obtain some satisfaction for the injured person on the other, the counsellor of the lineage of the intransigent person may resort to positive coercion. No counsellor will take this step, however, unless he is entirely supported by general opinion, publicly declared, including opinion of most of that person's own lineage. The counsellor may administer a form of ritual curse the supernatural power of which can bring illness or death if the recalcitrant person is truly in the wrong and unless he accepts the settlement. A fine, *sogo*, of a goat or even an ox may be levied, and, if necessary, counsellors may legitimately order young men to seize the animal from the man's herd. The man's counsellor may announce his intention of refusing to act on the man's behalf in the future, and (it is said) ultimately steps may be taken to expel the man from the lineage and clan.[1] These coercive recourses are not frequently used, even in the face of sufficient contumacy such that public opinion would support them. Their use indicates, for Arusha, a failure by the counsellor and the rest of the lineage properly to persuade the recalcitrant person to accept the settlement which they themselves are willing to concede; and there is an idea of deserting a kinsman and denying him loyalty. Coercion is absolutely a last resort where all else fails, and where yet some action is essential. Not uncommonly disputes may drag on because a counsellor is unwilling to take the final, unpleasant step. In the large majority of cases the prestige and the ability of the counsellor is eventually sufficient; he can apply so powerful practical and moral persuasion that coercion is avoided. A counsellor cannot easily afford to gain a reputation of

[1] I have no knowledge that this has ever occurred and it seems to be used as a threat. Disgruntled men may change their lineage and clan affiliation, assuming pseudo-agnatic ties with men of some lineage of another clan who are willing to accept them. Usually a counsellor and fellow-agnates oppose this move strongly, but a thoroughly frustrated counsellor may pointedly refrain from opposition to it.

taking refuge in coercion; he fears injury to his reputation and to his ability in future cases; and he fears also the rupture of agnatic ties and the probable conflict within the lineage. Primarily a counsellor's task, as Arusha see it, is to act as advisor and experienced advocate on behalf of his agnates. In addition the Arusha deeply dislike the notion that one man has coercive authority over another; but they approve the notion that men, being susceptible to reason and persuasion, can be induced by their fellows to accept their opinion. A counsellor is selected by his fellow-agnates to act for them, and he is ever subject to their ultimate approval. Even the most firmly established and respected counsellors hesitate to take an authoritarian attitude for egalitarian ideals are genuinely held in this society. These ideals are conventionally illustrated and reiterated at the time of selection of a new counsellor. Even if he is willing to accept his selection—and some, at least, genuinely are reluctant—he should first refuse on the expressed grounds that he does not seek to exercise influence over his fellows. He is compelled to accede to his agnates' choice, but these men, together with counsellors and notables of other lineages, exhort him to be careful in the future lest his new influence and leadership overbalance towards dictatorial intolerance.

Because maximal lineages are geographically dispersed, some and perhaps many lineage members live at a distance from the homestead of their counsellor. For them it is not always convenient—nor, if immediate assistance is required, practicable—for a man to go to his own counsellor. At least for less important matters, it is permissible to go instead to another counsellor who lives near by. Preferably the alternative counsellor should be a member of a maximal lineage in the man's sub-clan; but if that is also difficult (as it is in some cases) then a counsellor of the same clan will suffice. This practice is not followed in the case of a major dispute, and never when the dispute lies within the man's own maximal lineage. It is considered in these cases to be not only something of an insult to his own counsellor, but reprehensibly introducing outsiders into lineage affairs. In this way a counsellor builds up a clientele composed of lineage members who live within a few miles of his homestead, and of other clansmen who live nearby but who are distant from their own counsellor. A counsellor who acquires a notable reputation tends to gather a larger clientele; and he may even be consulted by a neighbouring member of another lineage on more important issues, although he does not act on his behalf in a jural assembly without invitation from that man's own counsellor. This state of affairs is, of course, a function of the dispersion and the weak integration of maximal lineages among the Arusha; it is also a measure of the degree of cooperation and mutual trust which exists between counsellors whose lineages belong to the same sub-clan and even clan.

Where a dispute is prolonged, or if it is thought to be sufficiently serious and difficult of solution, a counsellor may invite other counsellors of his own sub-clan or clan to join him on the side of his own kinsman in the prosecution of the affair. Counsellors who acquire an unusual reputation for their forensic skill, may be frequently involved on behalf of men not of their own maximal lineage. We shall return to this point when considering jural processes more fully; here it is only necessary to point out that, during the period of field-work, although a number of counsellors were prominent in this way, none had achieved a society-wide preeminence within a single clan; and there is nothing to suggest that any have done so in this century. When outside counsellors are invited to participate in a jural assembly, they do not take the lead in advocacy on behalf of the disputant, and they cannot by themselves accept any settlement—that is primarily a matter for the disputant himself and his near agnates, for the maximal lineage and its own counsellor. More than this, people tend to grow critical of the counsellor who participates in too many cases other than those touching his own lineage. He becomes liable to be accused of undue interference—even where he is invited because of his proven skill—and of a desire to gain excessive importance. Despite their approval of their counsellors, their pride in them and dependence on them, the Arusha remain suspicious of what they feel may be the development of independent authority. 'A counsellor is not like the chief,' said one man 'because a chief gives orders.' The degree of influence of lineage counsellors is thus kept within vague but nevertheless understood boundaries.

CHAPTER SEVEN

DICHOTOMOUS PRINCIPLE AND PROCESSES

ARLIER in this book, in the accounts of the parish and of the age-group, some emphasis was given to the fact that both of these groups are segmented dichotomously, and both are themselves bisections of larger units. In the present part of the book it has been noted that an autonomous family and both types of patrilineages are normally divisible into two complementary parts, although, deliberately, little attention was given to this feature. In all these groups this kind of bifurcate segmentation exemplifies a principle of social structure which is pervasive in Arusha society, and is essential to regular social processes. It is now necessary to give it detailed consideration as it operates in the patrilineal system.

The prototype of dichotomous division for the people themselves lies in the ideal polygynous family where bifurcation arises out of the grouping of co-wives, as previously described at page 72 It will be remembered that each of the two groups of wives, together with their children, is known as *olwashe*, pl. *ilwasheta*. The adult sons of these women are categorised in accordance with their mothers' alignment, so that the subsequent lineage based on their father contains two parts, also called *ilwasheta*. The Arusha make frequent use of this word in a generic sense and they often allude metaphorically to the internal dichotomy of a family when they are concerned with bifurcate segmentation within other social groups and categories. Thus one of two segments may be referred to as 'one group of co-wives' (*ingainito nabo*), or 'one group of brothers' (*ilalasher' obo*), or simply *olwashe*. To emphasise the structural similarity, an Arusha may add that the whole in question—e.g. a pair of linked parishes, an age-group, a maximal lineage—is 'like one family' (*anaa ngang nabo*). These analogues are common, but particularly *olwashe*. Because of the absence of a suitable English synonym this Arusha word will be used throughout in the following account;

FIGURE 7.

The structure of the Arusha clanship system.

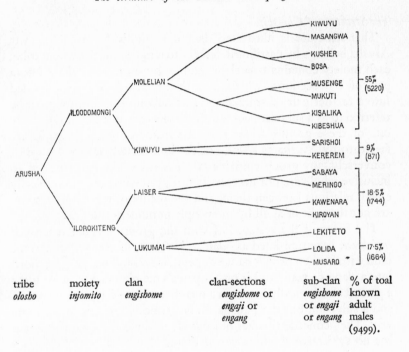

tribe	moiety	clan	clan-sections	sub-clan	% of toal
olosho	*injomito*	*engishome*	*engishome* or *engaji* or *engang*	*engishome* or *engaji* or *engang*	known adult males (9499).

Notes:

(1) Clan-sections have no proper names. They are referred to by the names of both component sub-clans, or by that one which a speaker considers more important.

(2) Figures for the numerical sizes of clans were extracted from the tax registers for 1957. Men whose clan was recorded there comprised 85% of all taxpayers.

but this will serve also to emphasise the common factor in all its occurrences in varied forms and social situations.

First an account is given of the structure of the clanship system, for there the principle of dichotomy is paramount. Following that account it will be possible to examine the social processes, particularly jural processes, which depend on the principle in the total patrilineal descent system.

The Structure of Clanship

This structure is illustrated diagrammatically in Figure 7. Any Arusha belongs by patrilineal descent to a moiety of the whole tribe; each moiety contains two clans; and each clan is subdivided into a pair of clan-sections, which may themselves each be subdivided into a further pair of segments. The smallest clanship group, to be referred to as a sub-clan, contains two sets of maximal lineages. Any one of these groups wider than the maximal lineage may be referred to by Arusha as *olwashe* of the immediately larger group; or conversely, any group contains two *ilwasheta*. The two parts of an inclusive whole are not necessarily nor even commonly numerically equal; relations between them, and the nature of the whole system, are not thought of at all by the people in numerical terms.

The focus of the system lies with the group which Arusha call *engishome*, here translated as 'clan'. There are, of course, four clans, each with its own proper name. A person is thought of as being born into a clan as a result of his or her pater's membership of it. At birth a person also logically becomes a member of a moiety, a clan-section and a sub-clan, but the Arusha do not conceive of this in the same way. They concede the fact objectively, as indeed they must, but it has no subjective significance for them. Membership of a clan is a personal attribute, although it has no supernatural or mystic quality to it—there are no clan totems, taboos or distinctive ritual practices, for example. The clan is commonly used as a means of identification among strangers to whom one's agnatic lineage is unrecognisable; but sub-clan or moiety are not so used. To know a man's clan and his age-set is to be able to place him in a significant category for the Arusha; and conversely the stranger can claim hospitality and assistance from local members of his clan (although actual practice here usually falls short of the ideal). Nowadays Arusha are adopting their clan-name as a surname in the English fashion; sub-clan names are never so used, although they would be more useful because, being more numerous, there would be avoided some of the confusion which comes from the use of only four clan-names in this connection. One of the clans, Molelian, contains over half of all the people, and its name is not therefore particularly efficient as an individual's identification device.

Associated with each clan are traditional brand-marks for cattle and donkeys, and for sheep and goats respectively—one for the ear and one for the body in each case—and for beehives. Some but not all sub-clans have particular variations of the main clan brands. These brands continue to be used in spite of the advice of the Veterinary Department, and the depreciation of the market value of hides and skins which they cause. They have not, of course, any significance as a physical and visual means of identifying animals, for the number of brands is too few; but they have a mystical value, because men feel that animals are not wholly the property of their legitimate owner unless they are branded—whether the offspring of an animal already owned, or stock received from elsewhere in a social transaction. This has no objective legal significance. Men also say that animals correctly branded are protected against disease and other dangers, simply because, like their owners, they are properly brought within the clan.

Although recruitment to a clan, and thus to other groups within the clanship system, is patrilineal there is no attempt whatever to claim genealogical connection between members who do not belong to the same maximal lineage. Nor are there remembered ancestors who are claimed to have been the founders of any such group. The original settlers on Mt. Meru are said to have brought the names of their moieties, clans and sub-clans with them. Arusha say, doubtless correctly, that moiety and clan names came from the Masai or the Kwavi, amongst whom the same names are found today, although not all Masai clan-names are present in Arusha.[1] It is likely, because of the diversity of their origins, that at least some, perhaps many, first-settlers of the same sub-clan were not agnatically related. Present-day Arusha see no importance in these matters for they seem to them to be of no significance.

The names of Arusha moieties, Ilorokiteng ('those of the black

[1] See Huntingford, 1953, pp. 119-120 for a list of Masai clan and sub-clan names. Genealogical links are not known between members of these groups in Masailand.

ox') and Iloodomongi ('those of the red oxen'), are the same as those among the Kisongo Masai.[1] The literal meaning of the names have no importance at all for the Arusha. A moiety can only be referred to generically as *injomito*, a plural form of the word for clan, *engishome*. The sub-units which are termed clan-sections in Figure 7, have no proper names, although sometimes they are referred to by the name of what a speaker considers to be the most important sub-clan in their composition. Sub-clans are all named units. Like clan-section, they may be referred to by the same term as for clan; or as *engaji* (house, a matricentral part of a polygynous family) when the emphasis is on the unit as part of a larger whole; or as *engang* (homestead, family) when emphasis is on the separateness of the unit. With two exceptions, sub-clan names, unlike those for clans, are not the same as those now existing in any part of Masailand or among the Kwavi of Central Tanganyika. Some Arusha claim to be able to equate the sub-clan names with those of the Kisongo Masai, but demonstrations of this were not always consistent and convincing.

The conceptual as well as sociological distinction between known agnates and other members of a sub-clan establishes an element of discontinuity in the total patrilineal system, between lineages and clanship groupings. Neither is it useful to regard the latter as a transmuted form of the lineage system. In another way, however, continuity is maintained, and not only because of the permeating principle of patrilineal recruitment. Each sub-clan contains a number of maximal lineages—empirically up to ten—and these are divided into two sets, *ilwasheta*, of the sub-clan. Arusha have no explanation for the linkage of maximal lineages in this way, and they merely assert that the lineage founders (i.e. the first settlers) were members of the sub-clan and of its respective *ilwasheta* when they came to the country. In one case an old man suggested to me that, 'perhaps our grandfathers were friends long ago, and so our two lineages are nearer together today'; but he was not prepared to assert this dogmatically, and it is instructive that it did not occur to him or others to attempt an explanation in terms of agnatic kinship. In two certain cases (Sabaya and Sarishoi) the sub-clan consists of a single maximal lineage, and here the sub-clan name is that of the lineage founder.

Except in those two cases, none of the groups in the clanship

[1] Cf. Fosbrooke, 1948, p. 40.

system are exogamous. Intra-marriage at all levels has been common and unremarked by the people. Usually, once it is established that no agnatic links exist between a suitor and a girl, no consideration is given to ties of clanship. In some cases, however, Arusha have said that they positively prefer their daughters or sisters to marry a clansman because, as they explain, an affine who is also a clansman may find it more difficult to avoid his obligations. How far this makes an appreciable difference it is difficult to say, and I have insufficient evidence about such marriages to provide an answer; my impression is that in fact little difference is made, even where the marriage occurs within the sub-clan. What is more important is the light that the possibility of approved intra-clan marriage throws on the nature of clanship. We saw earlier (p. 96-7) that agnatic and affinal relations are incompatible, and that this was a prime sanction in favour of lineage exogamy. The kinds of values and social relations between clansfolk and affines are not incompatible. By this I do not mean that they are the same, for clearly they are not; but only that ideas and practices of cooperation and support between clansfolk are weak enough, and are exercised relatively infrequently and in limited contexts, such that they are not seriously threatened by the introduction of affinal ties.

The counsellors of the component maximal lineages of a sub-clan and of a clan, conceive of a particular unity between themselves, and they more commonly refer to one another as 'brothers' than do other clansmen. Although the counsellors of a single sub-clan may meet irregularly and act together, a sub-clan (and a clan-section also) has no specific corporate functions, nor are there institutionalised procedures specifically requiring counsellors' cooperation in unity. It is, as will be shown later, more correct, as well as more illuminating, to regard these units as categories of people rather than as corporate groups. Although only weakly emphasised, a clan is, however, a corporate group in certain circumstances. Each clan has a fixed meeting-place, each has its own stock brands, and there are the cluster of subjective notions to which reference has already been made. In addition the clan is ideally conceived of as the unit of action and of responsibility in all cases of homicide involving one of its members (see p. 127). To deal with a homicide case and to arrange the transfer of bloodwealth, all the counsellors of a clan must meet together, perhaps several times. For this purpose, if no other, counsellors of a clan are required to act together, and because of this, though also because of the special quality of a clan in Arusha conceptions, one of their number if recognised as *primus inter pares*, and described as *olkitok*, 'the big (or senior) one'. Usually this man is the oldest active counsellor, although this is not essential: thus at the time of field-work, the leading counsellor of Lukamai clan was a junior elder who was allowed his eminence because of his recognised ability and active initiative. Ordinarily the distinction is of little importance; but when necessary this senior counsellor acts as the focus of corporate clan action. Arrangements for clan meeting are concerted through him. If the meeting involves only or mainly counsellors, it usually occurs at his homestead. He may speak first at clan assemblies, and he speaks on behalf of the clan in formal relations with another clan. It must be emphasised that this eminent counsellor is not the head of the clan—there is no such role. He is not formally appointed, nor are there insignia or other distinctions. Being an old man very often, he may be a focus of activity rather than positively exerting leadership; but the logic of certain social situations demands some such centre-point.

The corporate nature of the clan has been intensified in recent years as the local government has made use of it in the constitution of the Tribal Council. Until 1961 each clan was required to nominate two members to the Council. In 1958 each was required to nominate a member to the magisterial bench of the newly formed Land Court; this was largely instigated by the Arusha themselves, who believed that suits concerning land (of which there are many nowadays) could only be justly heard and settled if each clan had a representative participating in the process, either on behalf of a member-litigant or as a neutral arbitrator. It was convenient to make use of the clans in this way, and, as Arusha admitted, it was not feasible to use the more numerous sub-clans or maximal lineages.

Jural processes in the Patrilineal System
It is now possible to examine the total patrilineal system of the Arusha in order to understand its significance in actual social relations, and especially in the context of dispute settlement. The structure of the system is illustrated diagrammatically in Figure 8, where its essentially dichotomous constitution is clearly evident. For the moment it is convenient to ignore the structural dis-

FIGURE 8.

The formal structure of the patrilineal descent system.

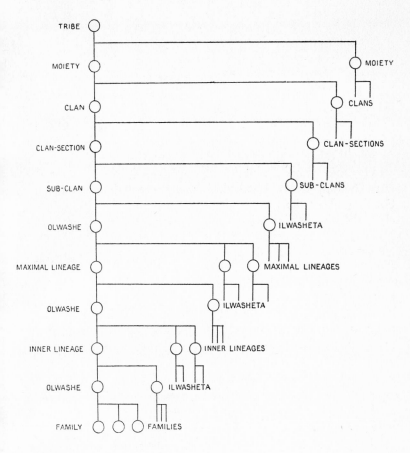

continuities at the levels of the maximal and inner lineages where segmentation is not necessarily dichotomous: consideration of this is given later.

It is useful to begin with a purely formal, ideal statement of the operation of the principle of dichotomy before examining it in action. By means of this principle the Arusha are readily able to determine their allegiance, or their exclusion from allegiance, in any situation of conflict and dispute between two people. The group or category of smallest scale of which the two disputants are both members is divisible into its two segments, or *ilwasheta*, such that each segment contains one of the disputants, and the other members of that segment are automatically his supporters. The word 'automatically' is used here because to every Arusha adult the pattern is well known; it is relatively uncomplicated, and precise alignments of supporters can easily be determined in any particular case as it occurs. Definition of alignment is invariable at the structural level identified by the patrilineal relationship of the two disputants—uncertainty is eliminated because within the minimal group so established every member must be more closely linked with one rather than the other disputant. For example, if the two disputants are related only within the same clan, then their respective supporters are the members of each *olwashe*, i.e. clan-section, of that clan; if however both men are members of a single sub-clan, then their respective supporters are the members of the sub-clan *olwashe* to which each belongs.

The primary focus of the situation lies with the individuals who initiate the dispute, because it is their formal relationship which determines the structural level at which dichotomy is actively invoked. Further, it is these men who wish to establish in the first place who are their supporters, that is those people from whom assistance of some kind can be sought in the treatment of the dispute. Secondly, and insofar as they are aware of the dispute, other people are similarly able to determine where their loyalty lies, or they can establish their neutrality because they do not belong to the minimal unit containing the disputants.

The effect of the operation of this principle is to identify a group of people from whom assistance and advocacy can be obtained by a disputant, and thus a means of dispute settlement in which outside and superior authority is absent.

Support recruited in this way varies, of course, according to the nature of the relationship between the disputant and his defined associates. A man does not expect the same degree of involvement from a fellow-member of, say, his sub-clan as he does from a member of his maximal lineage, although both may belong to the operative *olwashe* as defined in a particular issue. From members of his inner lineage a disputant looks for particularly intimate loyalty and assistance in every way. Except perhaps in the pettiest dispute, a man takes scarcely any action without consulting his near agnates and without their participation. Jural support is but a part of the total of interdependent relationships involved. To a much lesser degree, a similar kind of assistance is expected from members of the maximal lineage; but, as we have seen, a maximal lineage is generally too large and too dispersed a group for inter-personal relations to be particularly intimate and well-founded in continuous intercourse.

Within the maximal lineage a man does have some degree of permanent relationship with fellow-members, however weakly developed, arising out of the rationale of the group in agnatic kinship. At least there is the ideal that all members, wherever they live, should necessarily be involved in the actions of one of their number. A man knows and is known by all of his adult male agnates. Beyond the limits of that group there is no reason why he should know, or even know of, all the people who are linked to him by the various categories of clanship; they are widely scattered throughout the country. Conversely, there is no reason why they should all be aware that he has become involved in a dispute; or, if they are aware, that they should necessarily feel personally concerned despite, the structurally defined alignment.

This being the case, how then does the principle of structural dichotomy operate in practice? That principle has been explicitly stated in the most formal terms for the sake of initial clarity; now I go on to describe how it is pragmatically modified to fit concrete cases, whilst yet it remains as the mainspring of social action.

Unless the *olwashe* of support is smaller than the maximal lineage, an Arusha is selective in approaching those who ideally have an obligation to assist him—remembering, however, that the obligations of passive support remain with those who are not approached. Firstly, he seeks the active assistance of those in the *olwashe* who live fairly near; and secondly he looks to the lineage counsellors and other notables of that *olwashe* who are considered to have special obligations, and who have a particular value because of their experience, ability and prestige.

A disputant makes sure—it is his responsibility and in his own interests—that *olwashe* members living near know of the situation. He probably visits them for this purpose and seeks their advice, but he may send a message of information instead. Thereafter, as he sees fit, he may actively invite their participation in the subsequent negotiations. The definition of 'living near' is not precise: in the crowded mountain region it means at least living in the same parish, but other men may be involved who live within three or four miles of the man's homestead—that is, the distance a man can easily walk without special effort or loss of time. In the more thinly populated peripheral region, the range is rather wider—some six to seven miles. Thus, and speaking in rough terms only, a man tends to recognise an area around his homestead within which he normally expects the more active support of fellow-members of any *olwashe*, and to whom he acknowledges a similar, reciprocal obligation. Except for near neighbours, therefore, this means that members of any *olwashe* have more or less different areas from which to gather support—always bearing in mind that the privileges and obligations in the inner lineage transcend geographical distance. This empirical pattern may have to be modified in any case where a meeting of discussion or a judicial assembly is held at a distance from the disputant's own homestead. Where this occurs, a man does not expect that geographically near but sociologically distant members of his *olwashe* will undertake the lengthy journey. He may attempt to muster alternative support from *olwashe* members living near the place of action, though this is not easy since neighbourly reciprocity is absent.

Other considerations may be important in determining the range of persons actively involved in any particular situation. A disputant is more likely to seek the support of a member of his *olwashe* who is also linked to him in other ways. For example, a man of the disputant's own parish may well be preferred to a man of a different parish—this is not a matter of sheer physical proximity, because a fellow-member of the parish may sometimes live farther away than a member of an adjacent parish. An affine, a near maternal kinsman, or an age-mate, tend to be preferred to those not so related. A disputant tends to go farther afield to seek the support of such a person

than otherwise he might. Generally the support of younger men—
even though heads of their own families—is little sought, for the
value of it is considered to be slight, both because of such a person's
lack of experience and because of his low status. On the other hand,
such a young man (a senior murran, for example) may be useful to
carry messages or to perform other tasks, and so his obligations may
be invoked.

More importantly, a disputant seeks the support of the more
notable members of the defined *olwashe*, chief among whom are the
lineage counsellors. Here again, there are practical geographical
limits within which active participation is expected, although these
are less narrow than in the case of ordinary men. The reason is
obvious: a man is prepared to go farther afield to obtain such valued
support, and these notable men have become so at least partly
because of their willingness to undertake more than the ordinary
man's obligations. By virtue of their office, lineage counsellors accept
responsibility of this kind: other notables build up a public reputation, when they have sufficient ability and desire, primarily by voluntarily undertaking it.

When a matter in dispute comes to discussion between the conflicting parties, a man's supporters should attend with him. Discussions may be informal or formal. At informal discussions—to be
referred to as 'conclaves'—a disputant is usually accompanied only
by his nearest agnates, his lineage counsellor, and perhaps one or
two local notables of the *olwashe*. It is possible that agreement may be
reached by this procedure, and the matter concluded. If ready agreement is unobtainable—and a conclave may not be necessary to prove
this—the matter goes to a moot.[1] Nowadays it may instead be taken
to a local government court, but this possibility is ignored for the
moment and will be taken up later. At this point the dispute becomes
a public matter to be dealt with formally by institutionalised procedures.

[1] *Oxford Universal Dictionary* (3rd edition), Oxford, 1955:—'*Moot*, 1. *gen.* Meeting,
encounter—1470. 2. An assembly of people, esp. one forming a court of judicature; a
meeting, also the place where a meeting is held. *Obs.* exc. *Hist.* O.E.' Though obsolete
today, the word had a genuine significance in early English society and is used by writers
on that period. Bohannan (1957) found the term useful in his account of Tiv judicial
process. Like Bohannan, I use the word because contemporary English contains no apt
synonym. 'Meeting' or 'assembly' are too general whilst 'court' must be reserved for the
official juridical bodies established in the local government system, as described in
Chapter Eight.

It suffices here to say that a moot consists of the supporters of each disputant amongst whom the lineage counsellors are the more important single figures. When a moot is held, a man's supporters, as already defined, should attend with him; for their mere presence, even without other participation, demonstrates their loyalty not only to him and each other, but also to the other disputant and his supporters. A disputant who can muster few public supporters is thought by the Arusha to have his case weakened, as if those who should be with him at this time have found him in the wrong, or for some reason unworthy of consideration. Conversely, a weak case can in part be disguised by strong numerical support, and a disputant in that position will be assiduous in mustering his fellows. Their chorused remarks of approval of points made by the disputant or his counsellor can be most effective in encouragement, say Arusha, and even in discouragement of the other party. Support at a moot may, however, be quite passive, and it is a common sight on such occasions that numbers of attenders are obviously not actively participating. They may be engaged in some handicraft, in gossip with others, or blatantly asleep; but they are not casual spectators—who may also be present—for their allegiance is known, they tend to sit near to one another, and by their presence they demonstrate their support. At a stage in the proceedings when a disputant withdraws to one side with his active associates in order privately to consider an unexpected demand or action by the other party, these passive supporters also withdraw. Thus overt unity is demonstrated, both for those who withdraw and those who remain in the moot. It means also that the disputant and his supporters are concerned to establish a common policy and to act in the moot as a single entity.

Arusha say that they find these displays of support impressive—and my observations accord with this idea—and insofar as they do, then they are significant in the process. As far as I could ascertain, in few cases if any, is the final settlement of a dispute radically altered by considerations of numerical support, or the force of expressed unity of one party; but in many cases the details of the settlement are undoubtedly affected by it, where a man has been notably successful in mustering supporters. Perhaps more importantly, however, such details may go against the interests of the party who has been unable to muster a reasonable number of loyal supporters. In any case, the potential sizes of the groups of supporters vary a good deal, and certainly are not thought of as necessarily equal for the two disputants. People are aware who should be expected to attend the moot in support of a man, and who might also be present if extra persuasion were used. It is not a simple matter of sheer numbers triumphing over just settlements; almost never do the two sides indulge in vocal competition, nor does one group attempt to shout down speakers from the other side. Such practices are deplored, and those who attempt to make use of them may suffer because of the common interpretation given them: i.e. that they are endeavours to disguise a bad case. Rather it is that a disputant and his supporters tend to deduce from the appearance of the other group of supporters, whether or not their opponent is thought by his own side to have a good case, and one in which they will be adamant in their claims. If both parties to the dispute muster an adequate body of supporters, then the treatment of the matter can go forward from that point with little or no consideration of it. An excellent case can scarcely be spoiled by only a few supporters—although no man cares to appear without a few—and a disputant may then not bother to trouble many of those upon whom he has a right to call. But a weak case may be rendered even weaker by the lack of supporters which indicates a positive lack of faith among them.

A disputant's active supporters, both in a conclave and in a moot, are concerned to make the best of his case in the affair, and to point out the weaker points in the case of the other party. More than this, Arusha are quite frank in admitting that support should, if necessary, be given to the extent of acting in what otherwise would be regarded as disapproved, unethical ways. As a conscious obligation, men may give false evidence or suppress pertinent but damaging evidence. It is an obligation not only to show up fallacious argument or false evidence by the other disputant, but also deliberately to upset or confuse the other and his supporters by interruption, cross-questioning, twisting the argument, raising false issues or appealing to irrelevant emotion, precedence or other considerations.[1] Support, then, should transcend common morality, and Arusha perceive this as an overriding obligation. The closer the link between a man and his supporter, the greater is this obligation; but no supporter (including a counsellor) feels the necessity of an unbiased attitude.

[1] For example see p. 229, and Case 18.

The obligations of supporters are not, of course, confined only to action in a moot. A disputant looks to these men for sympathy and advice as the affair develops. Some may be able to obtain particular information which is relevant to the matter and likely to be of use to him; they may be able to sound out public opinion, or to discover where the other disputant may be prepared to give away, or to make an informal approach to the other and obtain his reactions. They carry messages on his behalf, informing others of the time and place of a meeting or a moot. They may attempt to bring pressure on supporters of the other disputant with whom they have particular contacts (e.g. as neighbours, affines, etc.).

A fairly straightforward dispute may be resolved, at least to the temporary satisfaction of both parties, by a single moot accompanied by one or more conclaves. More complicated cases, or those where agreement is less readily reached, may require two or more moots and several associated conclaves. The informal conclaves continue to be confined principally to the close agnates and the lineage counsellor of each disputant; but each successive moot tends to produce a larger group of supporters on either side. Beginning with his nearer neighbours in the determinate *olwashe*, a man tends to widen the geographical range of supporters for successive moots. This is especially the case concerning counsellors and notables, so that the more protracted a dispute the more of these important men there are likely to be drawn in. Notables of the *olwashe* who live at considerable distances away may eventually be invited in at a third or a fourth moot; so that for a smaller *olwashe*, such as a sub-clan, the ordinary members 'who live near' may be fully mobilised, and virtually all the counsellors and other notables wherever they live. A larger *olwashe*, such as a clan section, clan or moiety, may similarly be mobilised at the local level, but there is a greater selectivity of the more important men who live farther away. Other than for homicide —a special case described below—the counsellors and notables of a large *olwashe* are never, as far as I know, all assembled; nevertheless the range of involvement will in the end be geographically wide, so that counsellors of ability and prestige may become involved although they live many miles away. Such protracted disputes between men of distantly linked *ilwasheta* are uncommon, and more than two moots are rather uncommon for a single case of any kind.

Dichotomous Principle and Processes

Here for the moment we are not primarily concerned with the dispute process as such, but with the operation of the principle of dichotomy. We see that a larger *olwashe* is never fully mobilised, and that in most instances only a small part of even a smaller *olwashe* may be required to participate actively in dispute settlement. The gradual extension of participation as a dispute is prolonged, does not necessarily, if ever, precisely follow the lines of the internal segmentation of the determinate *olwashe*. For ordinary supporters residential proximity is the more important factor, not the relative proximity in terms of clanship links. The lineage counsellor of a disputant does not feel bound first to invite the assistance of counsellors of other maximal lineages of the same *olwashe* of the sub-clan, before inviting those of other lineages of the sub-clan, or those of other sub-clans. Geographical proximity again is important, but also the desire to obtain the assistance of counsellors whose prestige and particular ability is thought likely to be most helpful. Structurally near counsellors or notables who live at a distance, those who are not thought particularly able, and those who are little known at all by the disputants and his counsellor, are most likely to be ignored.

The significant point to be made here is, that social units determined by the principle of dichotomy within the patrilineal descent structure are not corporate groups, but only defined categories of people. Support and loyalty are given to an individual and not to a group; or, to rephrase this, Arusha think and speak of themselves on such occasions as the supporters of a particular disputant, and not as a specifically enduring group engaged in action. We have seen that the range of supporters varies and depends on the nature of the link between the two disputants; but they are only *potential* supporters. Whether or not they become actively involved, and also how actively, depends on other factors, of which co-membership of a parish and a rather vaguer residential proximity are the more important. Even a smaller *olwashe*—the division of a sub-clan, say—probably never assembles in its entirety, for geographically distant men may be effectively strangers. The portion of a wider *olwashe* which assembles and acts together is relatively smaller; but the particular portion varies from case to case.[1] Thus, although most Arusha can readily and objectively describe at least their own seg-

[1] Actual instances are given in connection with the cases described in Chapter 10.

ments of the total patrilineal descent system, up to the level of the moiety, nevertheless the various units so identified and named in this way have little or no coherence and functional solidarity, and, other than the clan itself, they evoke no affective loyalty. They are merely categories of persons, some of whom can be actively called upon by individual members in need of support in particular circumstances.

A number of these categories have neither specific terms of reference nor proper names, and can only be described or referred to as *ilwasheta*—i.e. dichotomous segments of a larger whole. This applies to what I have for convenience called 'clan-sections', and to the segments of sub-clans and lineages. In the case of the large Molelian clan, which contains two orders of clan-section, there is considerable difficulty in verbal identification for the Arusha. This is not, I suggest, a result of inarticulateness, but is a function of the social reality.

It should be clear that this Arusha patrilineal system differs from the segmentary lineage systems which have been described for a number of African societies. In those cases, lineage segments of whatever order act as specifically corporate groups in opposition to like segments of the encompassing whole. Where there is not a complete participation in inter-segment action by all members, at least the segment is thought of as acting as a unit through the explicit representation of it by certain members (e.g. lineage head, seniormost members, etc.). The integrity of a segment is, furthermore, persistently demonstrated in such considerations as, for example, possession or control over a shrine, land, offices, ritual prerogatives and obligations, and rationalised by a known genealogy. Among the Arusha, where there exist only structural categories of relationships, the first consideration is given to the individual support of a person involved in a dispute. Each party of supporters is, therefore, orientated to a particular person; it is only a collectivity of people which that person musters and engages on his behalf for the specific purpose at that time. Those who become engaged in this way are not thought of at all as acting for and representing the *olwashe* segment. Neither is it considered that the opposing party is or represents the second *olwashe* of the total category to which both parties belong. That is to say, a pair of patrilineal segments cannot act in opposition to each other *qua* segments; groups brought into opposition are entirely of an *ad hoc* constitution.

Essentially the operation of the *olwashe* principle in the clanship system of the Arusha comes from a desire and endeavour to obtain the widest range of useful supporters by a man involved in a dispute. He does not, on the other hand, wish to seek the assistance of anyone who is equally closely linked with his opponent, because ideally, and largely in practice too, he wants a body of supporters who are undivided in their loyalty and wholly on his side. As I have shown, he wishes to recruit to his aid both men who 'live near', and men who have special competence and prestige (i.e. counsellors and notables). It might be argued that, were the maximal lineage a better integrated and organised group, and were it not so dispersed geographically, there would be much less necessity for a man to seek supporters by these other means. Even the active and united inner lineage suffers from geographical dispersion. Through the clanship system a man is able to find assistance from certain men who live fairly near to him; and he acknowledges the obligation to give them help in their similar need. It is a mutually advantageous practice where agnatic relations are more or less inadequate.

Homicide

In the case of homicide there is some modification of the procedures utilising the dichotomously segmented, patrilineal structure, and its treatment illustrates further the operation of the system and the ideas and values involved in it.

Arusha generally state that the clan of a person who is killed is responsible for taking appropriate restitutory action, and that the killer's clan is corporately liable for his deed. Homicide, they say, requires that the killer's clan pay a set bloodwealth to the victim's clan. In practice, however, this is only a partial truth, for it over-emphasises the role of the clan—doubtless as a result of the subjective importance of that social unit. Deliberations and jural processes concerning homicide focus more directly on the moiety; and there is marked emphasis on the unity of the two clans of a moiety, whether the homicide concerns members of different moieties, of different clans of the same moiety, or even of the same clan. As explained below, in any case bloodwealth is paid by contributions from all sections of the moiety of the killer and is distributed among all sections of the moiety of the victim.

The processes begin as the victim's close agnates (inner lineage) urge their lineage counsellor to seek an assembly of counsellors, notables and other members of their clan. Counsellors send word to counsellors of the linked clan in the moiety, and a joint assembly convenes at the traditional meeting place of the victim's clan. If the alleged killer is a member of the other moiety, then a joint meeting of the two groups—mainly of counsellors and notables—is arranged afterwards. Although the counsellors of the clans of victim and killer respectively, tend to take the leading part, nevertheless counsellors of the linked clan participate fully. On the two occasions when it was possible to observe actual attendance at such moiety assemblies, I recorded that about half of all existing counsellors of each clan were present. Each time there was a larger number of counsellors from the victim's sub-tribe; but this seems to have been largely a matter of geographical proximity, and there were in any case men from all parts of the country and from all sections of the moiety. It was not possible in the circumstances to record accurately the attendance of other men, but my general impression was of a similarly representative sample. On each occasion, those present emphasised that the whole moiety was assembled as a unit. The victim's close kin, his lineage counsellor, and the senior lineage counsellor of each clan, took pains to obtain as large an assembly as possible by broadcasting the news and exhorting men to attend. Elders expressed a sense of obligation to attend and participate.

The determination of guilt for homicide is rarely any problem. Whether deliberate or accidental, Arusha do not kill by stealth, nor do they attempt to avoid responsibility. But in fact most homicide occurs as a result of fights arising out of quarrels, often drunken brawls, for men are prone in this society to resort to individual violence. Murran habitually carry swords and spears, and all men usually carry a heavy stick; and they are all inclined to use them readily. Although a fight may occur between men who have a long-standing and bitter quarrel, which is the root cause of it, I am not aware of an instance where a man has cold-bloodedly planned to kill his opponent; and in many instances the two men seem to have had little or no previous ill will. It is seldom therefore that homicide occurs without witness. Death is sometimes attributed to the witch-

craft of some other person—always a close agnate in my experience
—but this is not considered as the same kind of crime as direct
physical homicide and is not subject to public treatment.[1] There is
no jural distinction made between other kinds of homicide. Whether
the act was premeditated, in self defence, the result of accident or
uncontrolled temper, etc., is irrelevant to the settlement processes,
although people distinguish these cases from an ethical point of
view.

Self-help or vengeance is emphatically disapproved, and, should
it occur in the heat of the moment or later, it is reckoned as a separate
offence. Homicide invariably produces an inescapable liability of
indemnification and atonement through the payment of bloodwealth
cattle (*loikop*) with due ritual process. This is a jural responsibility;
but it is also a supernatural necessity which it is believed is required
by the dead person. The victim is said to resent the neglect by his
kinsmen and clansmen if bloodwealth is not obtained, and he will
send misfortune to his living agnates. The killer and his agnates
are also liable to the dead person's vengeance until bloodwealth is
paid. Amongst the living, normal relations can only be re-established
by the proper transfer of the cattle. The liability is not voided
although the killer may have served a prison sentence for murder
or manslaughter as a result of a High Court judgement; nor does a
court finding of innocence necessarily preclude an Arusha verdict
of guilty. Bloodwealth is fixed at 49 cattle irrespective of the victim,
and this is a liability primarily of the killer's moiety in favour of the
victim's moiety. Homicide within a moiety, or within any lesser unit
of it, does not remove the corporate obligation or claim of the
moiety as a whole, as described below.

The maximal lineage of the killer must produce 19 of the bloodwealth cattle, the majority of which (but no fixed proportion) are
found by his inner lineage. The remaining 30 animals are produced
by compulsory contributions from other units of the moiety. The
selection of contributors is in the hands of lineage counsellors of the
moiety. At a meeting of counsellors, agreement is reached, first, on

[1] Arusha notions of witchcraft are weakly developed, and men who are not closely
related to the alleged killer and his victim are inclined to deprecate the suggested explanation. The victim, of course, dies as a result of illness which Arusha may be able to
diagnose medically (e.g. pneumonia, heart attack). Where a near kinsman is accused of
responsibility, it appears to be the result of already existing conflict in the inner lineage
and it leads to a permanent cleavage of that group.

the allocation of numerical responsibility to each clan. Then this responsibility is distributed among the component sub-clans, apparently without reference to intervening dichotomous clan-divisions. Unfortunately it is not clear whether the sub-allocation is made by all counsellors of the moiety, or only by counsellors of each clan separately; either is possible according to my informants, but I failed to clarify this point in the field. Distribution of numerical responsibility among the various sub-clans to produce animals varies from case to case, according to the particular sub-clan which contains the killer. That sub-clan expects to find fewer animals because of the particular liability of that one of its maximal lineages containing the actual killer.

Ideally, because sub-clans are equivalent social units, each is said to have equal liability; in practice there is pressure from smaller sub-clans that larger ones should accept a bigger liability in terms of cattle contributed, and this more equitable distribution seems to be usual. In a case involving the liability of Iloodomongi moiety, there was a good deal of hard argument over the relative obligation of the huge Masangwa sub-clan which contains nearly half of the members of the moiety. This was an old argument, I was told. Masangwa men denied a larger collective obligation than any other sub-clan; whilst men of other sub-clans pointed out that there were more people in Masangwa who had not contributed to bloodwealth payments in the past than there were in other sub-clans. Masangwa men retorted that in this instance one of their maximal lineages had the liability to find the 19 cattle. Agreement is not easily reached, and certainly not at a single meeting of the counsellors. When agreement is finally obtained, then the counsellors together with other notable members of each sub-clan meet to determine which members of the unit shall provide one animal each. Arusha say that no man should pay twice whilst there remain any men who have not yet paid once; only the heads of autonomous families are, of course, liable to be chosen. Homicide is not common, and therefore a substantial number of men died without being called on to pay. Thus there arises not only the practical problem of deciding which man shall pay first and which later, with reference to estimated ability to pay; but also the more difficult task of weighing the conflicting claims of men who demand current immunity from liability on the grounds of payments in their fathers' generation. For example, Kitien asserted that two of his father's brothers (although not his own father) had paid an animal each in previous bloodwealth cases, whilst there existed some of his contemporaries in the same sub-clan whose fathers had not paid, or who had paid earlier. Kitien's argument that he and his brothers and paternal cousins had a posterior liability was accepted by the counsellors. Muringwa argued a similar immunity because his half-brother had recently paid a beast in another bloodwealth case, and he too was excused for the moment. That is, the inner lineage is used as a unit of reference in these matters, with the idea of equating liability amongst these groups. Within the inner lineage, counsellors prefer if possible to leave the final choice of payer to the members themselves, and only to intervene if difficulty arises.

The whole process is invariably protracted. All recorded cases took over a year, and some much longer, before the details were worked out. The obligated moiety has periodically to be reminded of its responsibilities by the victim's near agnates and their lineage counsellor, backed by other counsellors. Essentially the same kind of procedure occurs in the arrangement of the distribution of the animals in the victim's moiety. Nineteen cattle are allocated to the victim's maximal lineage, and the rest are taken by other members through a similar process of discussion and allocation.

Despite this method of allocation of liability to pay and right to receive, the Arusha retain the idea of the corporate liability or right of the moiety as a whole. The victim's group deals only with the killer's moiety i.e. with its counsellors, and not with the killer himself; bloodwealth is always claimed as a demand by the victim's moiety, even though the main instigation comes from his near agnates and their counsellor. Notables assist one another in deliberations within a lineage if dispute arises over the particular individuals to be chosen. The cattle are handed over in the name of the moiety, and received in the name of the other moiety.

The internal segmentation of a moiety is consciously utilised and actively demonstrated during the ceremonial proceedings associated with a bloodwealth transaction. After the liability for bloodwealth payment has been accepted by the moiety of the killer in joint assembly with the victim's moiety, a formal, public acknowledgement of this is made at a subsequent assembly of the victim's moiety. This is attended by most (ideally, all) counsellors and by a large

131

number of other members. Two (sometimes four) oxen, *ilmauda*, are provided by the killer, with the assistance perhaps of his inner lineage, for a ceremonial feast. On this occasion, the men attending assemble and sit deliberately in two separate clusters, each comprising the members of a clan, on either side of the meeting place. Each clan cluster is itself divided, so that the members of each clan-section sit together. The gathering is addressed by one or more counsellors from each clan-section, who stand and speak in the middle of their seated fellow-members. Whilst first considerations are for the homicide case in question, occasion is taken to raise other relevant subjects. At such an assembly in 1957, which I attended, a good deal of attention was given to discussion about the *olngesher* ceremony, when senior murran would be transferred to elderhood.[1] The oxen are then driven in, examined for quality, and distributed one to each clan. Senior murran of each clan are detailed to take the animals to one side and slaughter them. The carcass of each is divided into two equal parts, and senior murran of each clan-section take a half carcass to a separate spot where other murran of the section have prepared a cooking fire. A few junior elders supervise these proceedings. The rest of the clan-section reassemble at the cooking fire, where the meat is butchered and cooked, distributed by counsellors, and eaten by all present.

On these occasions the Kiwuyu group acts as a sub-clan linked to the Masangwa sub-clan, and thus in either moiety the cooking fire group consists of a pair of sub-clans when two animals are slaughtered, or a single sub-clan when there are four animals. (cf. Figure 7, page 111). As on many ceremonial occasions, the nice pattern of seating and clustering tends to be obscured by the informal and erratic ebb and flow of men engaged in casual conversation, and using the opportunity to see men whom normally they meet with only infrequently. Nevertheless the spacial separation of the cooking fires is quite distinct, and the assembled men do eventually settle down in their eating groups. There is a quite conscious and expressed awareness of the dichotomous processes which occur. As far as I know these are the only occasions when clan-sections, or sub-clans, actually assemble and act consciously as specific groups.

If homicide occurs between members of a single moiety—either

---

[1] Another example occurs in Case 24 (p. 260) where a counsellor raised the matter of a defendant who refused to come to discussion of the dispute.

of different or of the same clan—the liability as well as the right of the moiety as a whole remains undisturbed. The obligation remains for the killer's maximal lineage to find 19 of the bloodwealth cattle, as does the right of the victim's maximal lineage to receive the same number. Such cases are not rare: one occurred during the period of field-work, and informants did not consider it unusual. The determination of contributors to the remainder of the bloodwealth, and of recipients after formal transfer, follow precisely the same course as already described—with the proviso that contributors are chosen first, and these are ineligible to become recipients in respect of that particular bloodwealth. The moiety transfers compensation to itself, as it were, but with a recognition of the special positions of the two particular maximal lineages. In the case which I was able to record, the Arusha laid especial emphasis on the supernatural necessity of the bloodwealth transaction, as well as on the legal rights of the victim's lineage.

Homicide within the maximal lineage calls for essentially the same treatment: the obligations and claims of other members of the moiety remain undisturbed and the corporate responsibility persists. Where killer and victim are members of different *ilwasheta* of their lineage, then those become the units for payment and receipt respectively of the special 19 cattle. Where killer and victim are of the same *olwashe*, even perhaps the same inner lineage, the formal claim to those cattle is allowed to the victim's nearest kinsman—father or brother of an immature person, the heirs of a mature man, the husband or sons of a woman. Some of these animals are distributed to other members of the maximal lineage who have not participated in the payment. This nearest kinsman, and any others who are more closely related to the victim than to the killer, are excused from contributions; but all other members of the maximal lineage remain liable. In stating this I am relying on my informants' verbal evidence. A case was pending of a man who had killed his half-brother, but it remained unsettled when I left the country. Several counsellors, in whose company I attended the *ilmauda* ceremony (cf. page 132) in respect of this case, were certain that it would be settled in the way described. They, and others at the moiety assembly, declared that it must be settled and bloodwealth transferred because of the danger of the victim's supernatural vengeance. In addition later cases of homicide cannot be treated whilst an earlier one is outstanding; and in 1958 the agnates of another murdered man were already making strong demands to end the delay in this case which preceded their own.

In any event the joint participation of a moiety in homicide cases remains important, and pertinent use is made of the dichotomous structure of this unit during the course of the total transaction. I suggest that the reason why the principle of dichotomy operates rather differently in connection with homicide as compared with other kinds of dispute, is because homicide is held to be a super-offence. Other injuries which an Arusha may suffer are less serious, and not directly harmful supernaturally, although they are disapproved in common morality and by public opinion. The killing of a man is (or rather was) legitimately restricted to non-Arusha in warfare with the use of spears. Homicide within the tribe is a direct threat to intra-tribal peace and welfare.[1]

Lineages and Jural Processes

Dichotomous segmentation within the clanship system follows a regular pattern, varying only in the number of stages of segmentation from moiety to sub-clan. Each sub-clan similarly contains two segments or *ilwasheta*, but below that structural level the pattern becomes more complicated and in effect rather different. Each *olwashe* of a sub-clan is not itself bifurcated, but it comprises a number of maximal lineages, and commonly more than two. Each maximal lineage comprises two *ilwasheta*, but each of these contains a number of inner lineages, again usually more than two. Similarly, each inner lineage comprises two *ilwasheta*, each containing a number of autonomous men and their families.

The various orders of *olwashe* in the total patrilineal system, as already indicated, are principally categories of people rather than corporate groups; and when activated in a specific social circumstance they function in relation to a particular individual and not as persistent units. On the other hand, neither an inner nor a maximal lineage is an *olwashe*, but both are corporate groups existing in their own right outside the context of the pattern of dichotomous segmentation. In the patrilineal range narrower than the sub-clan, the principle of dichotomy and the alignments of allegiance and support

---

[1] Unlike some East African peoples, e.g. the Jie of Uganda, homicide or the threat of it is not believed directly to affect rainfall and fertility adversely—perhaps because rainfall is plentiful and regular on the Arusha mountain slopes; cf., Gulliver, 1953, p. 164.

which it governs, give way to the stronger imperatives of lineage solidarity and the interests which that serves.

Within the inner lineage, the small group of close agnates, the significance of internal dichotomy is slight. Each such lineage does comprise two parts allegedly originating in the internal division of the preceding family of the lineage founder. This appears to be largely a result of the ideal conception of this lineage as a chronological successor to the father's family. I found that men were reluctant to discuss the *ilwasheta* of their inner lineage, and some attempted even to deny their existence. All Arusha emphasised the undivided unity of the lineage, and they perceived the necessity for maintaining that unity. Clearly, any factor which would tend to diminish lineage cohesion is potentially dangerous, and is consciously minimised by members. There is little to give the *olwashe* practical importance; men of an *olwashe* have prior interests in the estate, wives and children of one another should one of them die early. Such rights are potential only, and may never be realised; they afford no real basis for group consciousness or group action.

When a dispute occurs between two members of an inner lineage other members are principally concerned with the achievement of reconciliation by some composition of the conflict, such that amity and unity may be restored. Because structural division within the group is so weakly developed, other members are able to ignore relative allegiance to the disputants—they need not take sides—and can act as supporters of both parties. In practice the number of men in an inner lineage is too small to allow of segmentation whilst yet retaining its unity.

A maximal lineage is a relatively weakly integrated group, and there is correspondingly less conscious desire to preserve unity in the face of conflict, and a stronger tendency to take sides. On the other hand, seldom and perhaps never, does a clear cut definition of allegiance occur—I was unable to discover any such case. Although members of each disputant's inner lineage must give undivided support, it is only when the disputants belong to different *ilwasheta* of the maximal lineage that the possibility of clear alignment occurs. If they belong to the same *olwashe*, but to different inner lineages, there is confusion: some members of that *olwashe* may belong to the inner lineage of neither disputant, whilst members of the other *olwashe*, who might be neutral, are involved because of the ties of agnatic kinship within the total lineage. But whether or not a particular dispute situation raises clear or confused alignment, the nature of the effective maximal lineage of each disputant is more important. Here *olwashe* differences are disregarded, for this pragmatic grouping of agnates has a marked geographical rather than genealogical basis.[1] If the two disputants live fairly near to one another, many or most of the men in their effective agnatic groups will be the same people, who, therefore, have an interest in composing the conflict in reconciliation. When the disputants live some distance apart, their effective agnatic groups will be different, but there will still be close connections between them: some individual members of each may well be close agnates of the same inner lineage, and others may be associated together in the same effective group of some other agnate. This pattern is reinforced by the influence of the lineage counsellor who has a common obligation to all members, even though he personally is more closely linked with some than with others. He represents lineage unity and concord, and directs his efforts to those ends.

If disputants belong to different *ilwasheta* of a sub-clan, then their supporters are defined in those categories just as in the wider clanship system. If, however, both men belong to the same *olwashe* of their sub-clan, but to different maximal lineages, it is likely that there will be members of other maximal lineages in that category who cannot determine a decisive allegiance. Here there is first an alignment of supporters by maximal lineage, so that the dispute becomes an inter-lineage matter; but, as in the comparable case within a single maximal lineage, uncommitted members of the single *olwashe* may be able to act as friendly conciliators. There is, of course, little conscious concern that they should do so, because they have no especial overriding unity to preserve or to give common interests and sentiments. In these circumstances, and if the conflict cannot be settled between the two principal lineages involved, counsellors and notables of the related lineages are most likely to be invited to intervene, and they are accepted as neutral but friendly. They are likely to be appealed to by one or both disputants and their counsellors. In both of these structurally similar circumstances, such friendly neutrals are in the position that they can insist on concilia-

[1] See p. 99 above.

tion, without any sense of disloyalty to either party, or of unwarranted interference in the dispute.

Disputes between agnates are by no means uncommon, and between near agnates they tend to be distinguished both by their focus on especially critical matters—e.g. inheritance, land, widows, children, bridewealth obligations—and by the intensity of feeling which they engender. The kinds of interests involved are the most important in Arusha life. Emotions are more easily aroused and less readily quelled. The very closeness of relations between brothers and between paternal cousins tends to engender a greater depth of feeling when dispute does occur; and there are more opportunities and reasons for dispute to arise because of the greater co-involvement of such people. The cultural premium which the Arusha place on individualism, and the supreme importance which they lay on the attainment and retention of autonomy as the head of a family, tend to foment dispute where resources to gain those ends are limited. Livestock have probably always been few in relation to the Masai-inspired values and uses to which Arusha wish to put them; land has become progressively scarcer for three or more decades, whilst simultaneously the demand for it has increased beyond traditional standards because of a modern desire to grow new crops and more crops for the market. But the potentialities of conflict are not confined to economic affairs, for there is to some degree an essential contradiction between the needs for lineage unity and cooperation, and the strong desires for individual autonomy.

In many instances, therefore, disputes between members of the same lineage (of either order, speaking generally) are marked by a particular emotional intransigency, a refusal to compromise where such vital interests are at stake, and a deeply felt, righteous indignation against a brother or cousin. Meetings at which the case is discussed are apt to break up in unruly bickering, or to degenerate into surly reticence. Such disputes often cannot be composed easily, and sometimes an impasse is reached which the people involved—i.e. the lineage members—cannot break. In those circumstances, in order both to settle the particular issue and to restore lineage unity, an extension of the *olwashe* is used: men are brought into the deliberations who are not structurally involved on either side, but who are linked equally to both sides, and who can therefore act as impartial conciliators. It must be emphasised that such 'outsiders' are concerned as conciliators, and not as arbitrators, for they are not allowed powers of coercion. As an impasse is reached, or when it seems likely to occur, the lineage counsellor usually takes the initiative, and approaches 'outsiders'; although he is unable to do this without the approval of lineage notables and the disputants themselves. By definition, of course, the 'outsiders' will not be agnatic kinsmen, for the maximal lineage itself marks the limit of known kin.

The tendency is, first, to invite the counsellors and other locally resident notables of other maximal lineages in the same *olwashe* of the sub-clan. If the dispute remains active and still unsettled after their intervention, then invitations to participate may be extended to similar members of other maximal lineages of that sub-clan (i.e. of the other *olwashe*). Occasionally a third extension is made, so as to include counsellors and notables of the linked sub-clan. That is, renewed attempts to solve the dispute tend to be made by widening the range of inclusiveness of participants, in accordance with the patrilineal structure. This is an oversimplification of a complicated process, which includes also many informal meetings and discussions by lineage members, or some of them, in continued efforts to obtain a working settlement. It is an oversimplification also in that the widening of the range of participating conciliators is by no means as regular as suggested. As usual, geographical considerations are important, so that a counsellor who lives at a distance may be uninvited, although he is a member of a linked maximal lineage; whilst one who lives nearby may be invited, although he is a member only of the linked sub-clan. The skill and experience of potential conciliators is important, so that a counsellor with a reputation for diplomatic ability may be asked to participate although he is distantly related. Nevertheless, despite these practical considerations, the tendency remains to expand the range of participators by the well-marked levels of the dichotomously segmented structure. A counsellor or other notable, though he live near by and hold a high reputation, is most unlikely to be invited in if he is linked only through the clan or the moiety. I state this as a result both of remarks made by the Arusha themselves, and of actual occurrences in these situations.

Although I have no statistical demonstration, it is clear that few intra-lineage disputes remain unsettled after a first moot in which invited 'outsiders' have participated. This may be attributed in part to the success of neutral conciliation. In part also it results, I think, from the fact that both the disputants themselves and their fellow agnates are brought to realise how serious and protracted the matter has become, and how dangerous it may be for the lineage. They are more inclined to a frame of mind of reconciliation and compromise, and indeed lineage members as well as outsiders tend to lay emphasis on this in the moot.

In a few cases conflict may run so deeply, in a crucial issue where emotions are high, that a first intervention of 'outsider' conciliators is unsuccessful; and in rare cases such disputes may reach the stage where the moot contains counsellors and notables of the whole clan. Nowadays this is unlikely to occur because, before that extreme stage is reached, one or other of the disputants takes the matter to a local court where it is heard and settled by a magistrate. Lineage members may be willing that this should occur, in order to relieve them of the onus of responsibility for a decision which may be unfavourable to one party. Before the local government was well established, and its courts understood and accepted by the Arusha, some intra-lineage disputes went to extreme lengths. In one remembered case about 1920, two sets of brothers, whose respective fathers were brothers, disputed over a group of fields. As the affair developed it involved wider issues, because the land in question lay in the disputed boundary area between two parishes. One set of brothers were members of an established, traditional parish which was attempting to push its boundaries up the mountain slopes, the better to control a particular perennial water source; the other set of brothers belonged to a new parish which was engaged in asserting its independence of older ones lower down the slopes. It is said that the culminating moot in this case contained counsellors and notables from both moieties of the tribe.

Although appeal to the neutral, local government court has become increasingly common in these intransigent situations—in the nineteen-fifties it had become almost a normal practice—the idea of conciliation by 'outsiders' is still accepted in the moot. Their participation may be tried first before going to court, or, more commonly, they are invited to participate in the detailed application of the court decision, either in cooperation with the magistrate at the time of decision, or afterwards in cooperation with lineage members—e.g. the precise demarcation of field boundaries, the division of close-packed coffee bushes, the allocation of animals and their offspring.

Sometimes a similar kind of impasse may occur in disputes between men who are only distantly related patrilineally, and for whom, therefore, there is a straightforward *olwashe* definition of their respective supporters at the structural level involved. It has previously been shown how the range of participants is gradually extended to the full limits of the defined *olwashe*, if the dispute persists. It was noted also that, unless the disputants were members of different moieties, there were always some people who remain neutral, being structurally uninvolved. Just as in the case of an impasse inside a lineage, so, here too, some of these neutral 'outsiders' may be invited to participate as conciliators. This occurs only infrequently, partly because such a dispute is likely now to be taken to a local court, but also because disputes between distantly related men are less likely to be so difficult of solution. The introduction of neutral conciliators is conceived of by Arusha as a virtual breakdown of normal judicial procedures. This idea of failure is not applied to the comparable intralineage situation, for Arusha are well aware of the intensity of feeling that may be aroused by conflict between agnates, and of the imperative need for reconciliation which will restore or recreate lineage unity. In that case, the invited participation of 'outsiders' provides the opportunity for experienced counsellors to intervene where otherwise only a single counsellor (i.e. of the maximal lineage involved) is concerned.

APPENDIX

I. WOMEN IN THE PATRILINEAL SYSTEM

In many strongly patrilineal societies, and especially where a significant structure of operational units is based on known agnatic ties and filiation through the father, women not only have a somewhat inferior status, but they have a divided attachment and an ambivalent loyalty. A woman is born into one set of patrilineal descent groups, but from the time of her marriage she becomes increasingly associated with another, similar set— that of her husband and her children. The difficulty is largely avoided where a woman relinquishes her membership of, and rights and responsibilities in, her natal patrilineal groups (i.e. those of her own father and brothers), and is incorporated as a full and permanent member of her husband's groups. This occurs, for instance, among the Jie of Northern Uganda as the final stage in the lengthy marriage process, and there the area of ambiguity in a wife's role and status is slight.[1] If, however, a married woman retains formal membership in her natal group, and continues in some degree to exercise rights and obligations there, whilst she is progressively involved with her husband's and sons' groups, then the area of ambiguity is larger, and the possibilities of role conflict and divided loyalties are likely to be important in their effect on her social activities. This condition has been reported fairly frequently in Africa[2] and elsewhere.

An Arusha female, like a male, is by birth automatically a member of her pater's lineages and clanship groups and, say Arusha, she never entirely loses that membership. Yet it is immediately obvious that she does not enjoy the same kind of membership as her brothers, even before marriage—or later if she is divorced and returns home. Women have no rights of inheritance of property, nor in fact can they own land or livestock. They cannot participate, at least overtly, in discussion, arrangements or contractual obligations concerning property. Girls like boys do not take part in ritual; but not until she is a well-established married woman (a vague time, but necessitating her having children and being no longer a young woman) is she permitted to participate with her agnates. Even then women do not take a leading part but, if at all, merely attend passively. Because, after marriage, they may be living at a distance from their agnates' homesteads, they may find difficulty in attending, for it is

[1] Gulliver, 1955, pp. 227-8. Cf. also Leach 1956.
[2] E.g. Fortes 1945, pp. 147-253; Mayer 1949, pp. 7-8; Southall 1952, p. 5ff.

less easy for women to move about the country than it is for men, if only because husbands disapprove of it. More importantly, however, men and also the women themselves do not feel that the attendance of female agnates is essential to the success of ritual performance, nor to the accompanying reiteration of group integration. This is a matter both of the nature of the supernatural as conceived by the Arusha, and of the progressive dissociation of a married woman from her natal groups.

Women remain permanently jural minors: they cannot themselves institute jural proceedings nor act as principals in cases which directly involve them, but must be represented by their father or brother before marriage, and thereafter by their husband or son. If they are required to give evidence in a public assembly, they must observe a markedly subordinate demeanour, speak quietly in a high-pitched voice with eyes cast down, remain at the edge of the assembly, and only speak when requested. All this is in notable contrast with the behaviour of adult men. In discussions of policy and the making of decisions, women have no public opportunity to take part. This is not at all to deny that many women, especially older ones, do in fact find opportunity to exert their opinions and to influence decisions—this they undoubtedly do. For example, many wives exercise a strong influence over their husbands insofar as they are aware of events; widows often effectively administer their youthful sons' property, and successfully resist efforts of her sons' classificatory fathers or older half-brothers to interfere. Nevertheless their advocacy is non-institutionalised and bound to be indirect, and is therefore restricted. In the face of these difficulties many women seem to be content to busy themselves in purely domestic affairs, and to leave other matters to their menfolk in the culturally approved manner.

Unlike her brother, a woman becomes deeply involved in the relations and affairs of a second set of lineages and descent groups after the time of marriage. In the homestead a wife is bounded by the socially approved authority of her husband, and, if he is still alive, her husband's father. Her residence is in his homestead; the material resources at her use are his, and they are passed on in time to her sons. Her husband's and sons' rights and obligations directly affect her welfare and her domestic economy. She persistently has more contacts with her husband's kin than with her own. Through obvious divergencies of interests and responsibilities, she is progressively separated in practical affairs and in affections from her own agnates. Her future is intimately bound up in the maturation and interests of her sons. Her own agnatic ancestors may continue to bring misfortune upon her, and also upon her children, and therefore she remains to that extent dependent on her natal lineage whose members must continue to have regard for her. If her ancestors are divined as the cause of trouble it is, however, her husband who arranges and prosecutes the matter with her agnates, and she may perhaps not even attend the rituals. But her husband's agnatic ancestors may also affect her, and in that case it is he and his inner lineage who conduct the ritual. Although I cannot substantiate the fact with sufficient concrete data, it is my distinct impression that older women are far more likely to be affected by their husbands' ancestors than by those of their natal agnatic line. The cause of troubles is discovered by divination, and it would seem that Arusha diviners are expressing the actuality of a woman's position in the social structure by finding supernatural responsibility among her husband's ancestors. In the same way a woman is liable to be attacked by supernatural forces resulting from the use of ritual oaths when either her natal or her husband's lineages are involved; but it appears that her husband's lineage is much more likely to affect her here than her natal one, for it is the former to which the Arusha normally make reference.

As a widow, she cannot inherit a part of her husband's property, although, unless she divorces and remarries, she has the legitimate right to remain in the old homestead to enjoy some part of the allocation of land and livestock made to her by her husband. This is a usufructuary right only and she has no ability to dispose of any of it. In practice, of course, a wife or widow is, within fairly narrow limits, usually able to sell or barter her surplus food stuffs or occasionally a goat for the personal advantage of herself and her young children; but this occurs with at least the tacit approval of her husband or son, and ultimate right is never hers.

In brief, then, a female has fewer and rather weaker rights and also responsibilities than a male; but more than this, these rights and responsibilities are not clearly located in one set of patrilineal groups. She relinquishes most of her slighter membership commitments in her natal groups, and yet remains still a member; and conversely, whilst gradually acquiring many interests and rights in her husband's groups, she never becomes a full member of them. It is, no doubt, easy for a male observer to accept too readily the cultural norms relating to women as they are expressed by men in such a dominantly male-orientated and patrilineal society; but it cannot be doubted that a woman's status, and her access to authority, influence and property is inferior to men's, and this inferiority is increased because of the persistent ambiguity of her status.

Unlike some dominantly patrilineal societies in Africa, a woman's influence in the role of mother towards her sons is limited. The matri-centred sub-unit of the Arusha family is weakly developed in the face of the sons' concentration on achieving independence of one another, whilst the nature of initiation and the norms of murranhood effectively separate mother and sons. Filial affection and concern for a mother is by no means absent among the Arusha, but it is not culturally emphasised. As we have seen, lineages are not differentiated according to maternal origins, but strictly according to paternity. There is tremendous emphasis laid on the father-founder of an inner lineage—or a transference of that ideal to the grandfather when the effective inner lineage is of a two generational depth—and the founder of a maximal lineage is always a male first-settler, whose wife or wives are commonly no longer remembered by name. The dichotomous division of either kind of lineage, though originating in the grouping of wives in the family, is primarily a grouping of half-brothers, and maternal origins as such are of little consequence.

Finally, Arusha women are not normally effective in their intercalary position, as they sometimes are in African societies. Male affinal relations tend to become involved in conflict, expressed in bargaining and attempts to extort and to avoid extortion; but wives are unable to act as intermediaries or conciliators, although they may be used as pawns by their menfolk. At least on some occasions, her natal group and her marital group become ranged in opposition to one another (remembering that the maximal lineage is generally exogamous); but here again, women are powerless to intervene and are sometimes assailed by the conflict on either side. It is true that some women of unusual character and initiative are able to exercise some influence, but even then they have frustrating experiences which tend only to underline their social limitations.

In general Arusha men, and women too, tend to speak of their lineages and clan-groups, and to act in social situations connected with these bodies, as if they were almost entirely, and certainly principally, composed of males—indeed, of mature adult males. In public assemblies and other places where affairs are discussed and decisions taken, women are excluded; even in private discussion a man often meets with other men in his own house in the homestead, or at one side during the course of male gatherings (e.g. beer-drinks, feasts, etc.). A man is quite confident of his affiliations and his loyalties, but a woman cannot easily gain that degree of certainty, and particularly not until she is an older person. Marital separations and divorce do occur, and women know that their connection with their husbands' groups can be radically weakened or even entirely severed.

II. A NOTE ON SOCIOLOGICAL DICHOTOMY
AND SYMBOLISM

AMONG the Arusha the principle of dichotomous segmentation is a sociological one by which social groups and categories of persons may be divided and re-divided, or alternatively amalgamated and re-amalgamated, to produce alignments of loyalty and support, and allocation of rights and obligations in particular situations. In the preceding chapter I have attempted to show how this works in the patrilineal descent system, and it will be further demonstrated in later chapters by reference to specific case material. Earlier I indicated a similar structure in the territorial system, which however no longer has much, if any, practical significance. In the age-organisation, not only are there two streams of adult males, but each stream contains two principal age-sets—senior elders and senior murran, or junior elders and junior murran, with the retired elders largely ineffective. Each age-group has three possible segments— the circumcision-sections—but in practice in most (but not all) cases only two are effective in social action. Furthermore, the people recognise the common factor in all these phenomena by commonly using the word *olwashe* to refer to any one of the two parts of a whole.

To a degree not yet made clear in the published information available on the Masai, those people too have a comparable principle of dichotomy in their social system, and there it is associated with an integrated symbolic pattern. In view of this, and of the comparative and theoretical attention given to symbolic dualism in the work of Hertz and Needham,[1] it is pertinent to note that the Arusha do not possess and use a symbolic system in connection with their sociological dichotomy.

Among the Masai there is a pervasive notion of 'right hand' and 'left hand', the former being in someway senior or superior. By direct questioning, I found that the Arusha knew of the Masai usage, though they do not make it themselves. For example, the two sets of wives of a polygynous man are not so designated, nor are they distinguished in status; neither are their houses physically segregated on either side of the homestead entrance. Similarly, there are not right and left hand segments of an age-set, nor are the patrilineal moieties so described and given status ascription. The Kisongo Masai correlation of black, right hand and senior, and red, left hand and junior in their moieties finds no place in Arusha. The latter do use the appelations red and black for their moieties[2] but it has no particular significance for them and is, perhaps, only a convenient term of reference copied from Kisongo. More usually a moiety is referred to by the name of one constituent clan (or both) and, as far as I am aware, there is no notion of relative seniority. The major points of the compass are not conceptualised by the Arusha, nor associated symbolically with sociological categories; although, among the Masai, north and east are

---

[1] Hertz 1960; Needham 1958 and 1960.
[2] See p. 114 above.

connected with black and senior, and south and west with red and junior.[1]

There are a number of dual categories in Arusha cosmology, each of which is significant in itself: for example, the living and the ancestors, the mountain and the lowlands, uphill and downhill, wet and dry seasons, earth and water, etc. But these are not combined into any common conceptual system. 'Uphill' (*usuku*) is in one sense associated with the high-god, Engai, whose name refers to 'the sky' and 'above'; but *usuku* has no ritual or symbolic connotation otherwise, and 'downhill' has only its everyday mundane meaning.

It can be admitted that, during field-work, I did not specifically enquire into this aspect of Arusha symbolism; thus the finer points may well have escaped proper attention. On the other hand, I do not believe that it could have gone entirely unremarked during other investigations, had it been of real importance; and I did take pains to enquire about 'right hand' and 'left hand', and about the significance of the colours attached to moiety names. Therefore I conclude that the Arusha do not have a conceptual, symbolic system associated with their sociological dichotomy, despite the great importance that has in their social system. Because of failure to investigate the matter thoroughly, however, I do not intend to advance any explanation of what appears *prima facie* to be an unexpected anomaly.

[1] Information on this aspect of Masai society is poor, and I am indebted to Mr. A. H. Jacobs for personal information. But see Fosbrooke 1948, pp. 25, 40-41, and 43; and Huntingford 1953, pp. 117-8 and 120.

1. The Mountain (Mt. Meru, 14,979 ft.) viewed from the lower slopes.

2 (*a*). A homestead on the mountain slopes.

2 (*b*). Homesteads in the open country of the peripheral region.

3. Girls and women on a ceremonial occasion.

4. A young wife.

5. A notable of a senior elder age-group.

6 (a). Junior murran spokesmen leading their age-mates and girl-friends in singing and dancing.

6 (b). The senior elder notables of a parish in ceremonial procession: their leading spokesman (right-centre) carries his staff of office.

7. A parish assembly in progress in the peripheral region.

8. Warriors of a large tribal group, drawn up to await the conference to decide on the peaceful settlement of a dispute. The lower edge of the mountain forest is

PART THREE

ROLES AND PROCESSES RESULTING

FROM ORGANISED GOVERNMENT

CHAPTER EIGHT

THE MODERN LOCAL GOVERNMENT

Historical Introduction

IN pre-European times the political system of the Arusha was contained within the institutional complexes relating to the parish age-groups and patrilineal descent groups. In keeping with the dominant Masai ethos, there were no specialised political or administrative roles of authority which could be described by the terms 'chief', 'headman', etc. Particular roles such as those of age-group spokesman or lineage counsellor were, as they still are, inherently ones of influence rather than authority; and although it was not altogether impossible for men in these roles to resort to coercive sanctions to achieve their public end, this was uncommon and was disapproved by the men themselves and by the members of the groups which supported them.[1] Such infrequently-used sanctions were a final recourse in the face of utter intransigence, and were exerted only with general, explicit public approval. By conscious intent, spokesmen and counsellors were specifically selected by their fellows because of outstanding abilities. They acted as foci of discussion and action in which their fellows participated. Insofar as they were leaders, they merely guided opinion by virtue of their greater experience and aptitude in handling men and affairs. They were, however, continuously aware of opinion as it tended to emerge and crystallise in formal and informal discussion, and they were unable to act in contravention of a coherent expression of it. Intractable differences of opinion amongst members of their groups could render these leaders impotent. Thus, although their influence was marked, especially in view of their personal abilities, if it tended to develop into authority it began to lose its efficacy, because there was no established basis for the effective maintenance of authority. In discussing and attempting to decide and administer such typical issues as a bridewealth dispute, an offensive raid, the direction of new pioneering expansion, the development of irrigation works, or a

[1] Cf. pages 107-8.

ritual performance, the men of influence varied according to both the kind of issue and the groups of people involved in it. In any issue these men could not enforce decisions against the adamant opposition of their opponents, but could seek only a mutually acceptable compromise of some kind. But there was no centralisation of decision-making except in the most indirect fashion. Most deliberations and decisions were of a more or less local kind—at the parish level—or they involved a scattered selection of people, patrilineally related, amongst whom (except for the closest agnatic ties) geographical contiguity was an important feature. A *cause celebre* might, in its long drawn-out proceedings, come to involve men and particularly lineage counsellors from a wide geographical as well as patrilineal range; but these were most infrequent, and led to no permanent, large-scale centralisation of politico-jural authority or action.

Deliberations and action on a wide scale regularly occurred in only two specific connections:—concerning the major stages of the age-set cycle, and warfare. The importance to tribal integration of the age-set events has been indicated earlier in Chapter Three; and although they were, as they still are, important, nevertheless they did not produce continuous and deliberate centralisation of action, much less persisting authority roles. *Ad hoc* meetings of interested parties were quite adequate for that purpose. The ceremonial leader (*olaunoni*) acted as a focus of deliberation, and he had ritual prerogatives; but his influence in action was less than that of his leading coevals—age-group spokesmen and notables—for, unlike them, he attained his position by inheritance rather than by selection for ability.

Warfare and raiding were not carried out on a tribal basis. Raiding parties were frequently recruited and directed from a linked pair of adjacent parishes, or by two linked pairs, and were never in any sense the fighting force of the Arusha, centrally directed. In any case, the Arusha only began sustained offensive warfare in the eighteen-eighties. This development produced the first indigenous attempt at a larger scale administration—at least in retrospect that implication can scarcely be avoided. By that period the two sub-tribes of the Arusha had begun to emerge as significant units, based on geographical exclusiveness and a greater degree of cooperation in age-set rituals and in warfare.

In that decade, as well as can be estimated by age-set chronology, there was selected in each sub-tribe a 'great-spokesman' (*olaigwenani kitok*). In each case he was one of the spokesmen of the age-set then in the formal grade of murranhood. A second, but inferior, great-spokesman was also selected from that half of the sub-tribe to which the superior one did not belong. The earliest great-spokesmen to be so chosen were members of the Dalala age-set, which became the only set in the murran grade when their immediate predecessors (Laimer set) were transferred to elderhood in about 1886. Dalala were promoted to formal senior murranhood about a year later.[1]

An earlier man, named Meoli, of the Nyangusi set (the patrons of Dalala) is said to have been an earlier great-spokesman, before the separation of the two sub-tribes; but, as far as can be ascertained, he was more probably an outstanding man of his era, and seems to have acquired his reputation as an elder. There is no tradition that the Laimer-set, chronologically between Nyangusi and Dalala, produced a great-spokesman.

The great-spokesmen were military leaders. Through them raids were mounted on a sub-tribal basis, probably for the first time in Arusha history. Old men in the mid-twentieth century, including a son of one of these leaders, were agreed that they had no civil authority, and that politico-jural functions were, as since then, reserved to elders' spokesmen and lineage counsellors in parish assembly and patrilineal moot respectively. The great-spokesmen led their coevals who, in the grade of senior murran, were the experienced fighting men. The two men holding these positions at the time of the German conquest, each led his sub-tribe in pitched battle against the invaders advancing from Chagga country. After German victory in the two separately fought engagements, the great-spokesmen (who were assumed by the Germans to be chiefs) were seized and executed. In modern Arusha tradition, they have become linked with both the brief golden age of successful raiding and the armed opposition to the Europeans.

The subordinate great spokesmen in each sub-tribe were appointed as chiefs by the German administration, and were given the title of *mangi*, the Chagga word for 'chief'. They were, of course, given non-military responsibilities, and, as the Arusha came to appreciate something of the new regime, they realised that a man of junior

[1] Cf. Figure 5, p. 33.

elder rather than senior murran status should hold the office. This accorded with German requirements, for mature men were needed. The Dalala age-set was transferred to elderhood in about 1905, and the appointed chiefs were able to continue in office to the mutual satisfaction of both conquerors and conquered. Since then it has become the general rule that a chief is in the age-grade of junior elder, and there has been indigenous pressure on an incumbent to retire when his set is promoted to senior elderhood.

The title of 'great spokesman' quickly died out of general use in favour of the alien term *mangi*. At some later time the Arusha word *olkarsis* began to be used, and by about 1940 the term *mangi* was used only by the older and more conservative people. *Olkarsis* means literally 'wealthy man' (*karsis*, 'wealthy'). Although it is true that chiefs have tended to become affluent because of their salaries, perquisites and doceurs, yet they have never been the only or even the most wealthy men in terms of livestock and wives and children, the traditional forms of wealth. The word has, however, come now to be applied almost exclusively to the chief.

The British took over the local administrative regime as established by the Germans. The chiefs were given formal magisterial powers thereafter, and, supported both deliberately and indirectly by the colonial government, the authority of the chiefs gradually increased. The history of local government has been primarily concerned with the status and powers of the chiefs, and with the particular men holding office. Contention in these matters has been common, and at times bitter to the point of civil strife. Conflict has arisen as Arusha showed resentment against the developing authority of the chief and his widening area of competence, which have increased at the expense of the autonomy of parish assemblies and lineage counsellors. In addition, Arusha are convinced that an incumbent of the chief's office has always favoured his own clan and his own parish in subordinate appointments, perquisites and influence. There is some reason to accept their opinion. Because of this, it has always been important to the Arusha not only what powers a chief has, but who precisely the chief is. On the other hand, chiefship has become an accepted institution, even if only a necessary evil.

A latter-day re-emphasis has arisen in respect of the traditional role of the great spokesman. This is most marked among the younger mature men—junior elders and senior murran—who claim that those earlier leaders were indeed chiefs, and that the Arusha have 'always' (*sic*) had chiefs. Their assertions would be convincing, so concerted and vocal have they become, were it not that neither the concensus of accounts of pre-European culture nor the older men support them. Men of the Dwati age-set, who formally became retired elders in 1948, had been junior murran when the German invasion occurred and they had participated in tribal raiding immediately before that, as well as in the battles against the invaders. Without significant disagreement, all those retired elders with whom the matter was discussed were certain that the powers of the great spokesmen were strictly limited to military affairs. This is what might be expected from a knowledge of Arusha social organisation and cultural heritage. But it accords with a modern ideology to make a claim to traditional chiefship, for younger men have seen the road to chauvinistic progress through chiefship. The absence of chiefs among the Masai (as compared with, for example, the Chagga) is associated with backwardness and inferiority. This has been a common presumption in post-war Tanganyika, but the rise of the nationalist political party[1] and the development of self-government has seriously undermined it recently.

A new and formal local government constitution was introduced in 1948, when the whole Arusha country was amalgamated into a single chiefdom, and a partial separation of the executive from the judicial side of government was made. As a result of the increasingly obvious inability of the constitution to meet modern political and administrative needs, but also because of a vociferous and threatening opposition against the incumbent chief, a modified constitution was introduced in 1958-9.[2] This was after my period of field-work, and no observation of its operation was made. In this Chapter and elsewhere in the book, therefore, the system of local government is described as it worked between 1948 and 1958, and the ethnographic present refers to that period. In many ways, particularly in judicial matters in the local government courts, but also in basic ideas concerning the chiefship and authority, there has been a

---

[1] I.e. the Tanganyika African National Union.
[2] In 1957 I sat with a committee of twelve Arusha chosen by the Tribal Council, and with the administrative officer-in-charge, to recommend changes in the constitution.

continuum from earlier decades to the post-1958 constitution. Fundamental attitudes and principles have persisted after 1958 as they began well before 1948. In any case, I am only concerned to describe and analyse a working system of social control, and my account is not invalidated merely because it no longer works in quite the same way.

The Chief

In 1948 the two independent chiefdoms, based on the sub-tribes, were combined under a single chief. The first new chief was selected by the newly formed Tribal Council, and approved and formally appointed by the Territorial Government. Tenure of office is indefinite; but clearly on both sides there is a notion that it is dependent on continued ability to undertake the responsibilities involved and to retain an ill-defined, general popularity. For the Government this primarily means an ability to maintain executive efficiency; but for the Arusha the personal popularity of the chief is equally important, and this is not altogether commensurate with his efficiency. Although not necessarily decisive, the Arusha have a notion that the chief ought to be in the age-grade of junior elder—the 'executive' grade in the indigenous system, in contrast with the more consultative and deliberative ('elder statesman') status of senior elders.

In 1952 the chief resigned: he had been chief of the old Boru sub-tribal chiefdom before 1948, and was a popular choice in that year for the new unified chiefship. The chiefship was, however, incurring a good deal of the ill feeling resulting from rapidly intensifying land shortage, the dissatisfaction arising out of a rather inadequate control of land allocation in the peripheral regions, and general anti-Government attitudes amongst people who found it highly convenient to make the Government a scapegoat for its modern difficulties, especially the ineluctable necessity for radical social change.[1]

The tribal Council selected the deputy chief for the vacant chiefship. This was immediately shown to be unpopular to the people at large: opposition was led by a group called the Arusha Citizens' Union, based on the small minority of educated and Christian men connected with the Lutheran Church. It was agreed, therefore, after

[1] See my 'Land Shortage, social change and social conflict in East Africa'; Gulliver 1961b, pp. 23-25.

a temporary impasse, to acknowledge openly the principle of popular selection of a chief by holding an election by secret ballot in which all taxpayers (i.e. adult males) were eligible to vote. The leader (a Lutheran schoolteacher) of the Citizens' Union was elected by a substantial majority, and accepted by the Government. Again no period of tenure was laid down; and in fact during the 1957-8 constitutional discussions the refusal to accept a specified period, but reservation of the popular right to call for the resignation of the chief at any time, was a major decision of the Tribal Council, against Government recommendation. The proposal was strongly rejected to institute a four year term of office, such that an incumbent chief would have to obtain a reiteration of public approval; but it was made clear by Arusha in the Tribal Council and elsewhere that, though indefinite, the tenure of his office depended on his continued approval by the people.

This historical note is given in order to make clear the people's notion about the chief—they are comparable to their notions concerning a lineage counsellor. That is, the chief must retain the general approval and support of the people, and may well forfeit his office if he loses this.

For the Central Government, the chief is primarily an executive officer whose main responsibility is to administer the local government of the area as efficiently as possible. But what is, for the Government, efficiency in tax collection, enforcement of law, regulations and administrative planning, may for the Arusha establish the unpopularity of the chief. They themselves see a principal responsibility in his duty to put forward the complaints, desires and opinions of the people to the Government, and to attempt to prevent the prosecution of measures thought inimical to their welfare. In an important way the chief represents the tribe to the alien Government. Although this is desired by both the Arusha and Government officials, it produces the familiar conflict in the chief's role. His loyalties, or at least his obligations, may be divided, for simultaneously he should represent the Government to the people. The District Commissioner, for example, expects him to pass on and administer some order or policy; but the people frequently treat the directive and its enforcement as the chief's own policy—or at least one in which he concurs. This kind of conflict has been noted in many colonial situations—and not there only—and it calls for no particular comment here because it lies on the periphery of our interests.

In the nineteen-fifties the Arusha had come to accept the chief-ship[1] as differing from its incumbent at any one time: and in addition to expecting the chief to represent them, they look for more positive and immediate satisfactions from him. They expect him to listen to complaints and problems which it is thought have not been ade-quately met by other procedures—in the local courts, or in moot or parish assembly—to have them reviewed and, if injustice be shown, to reprimand whoever is responsible. They expect the chief to explain the procedures available to them under the modern govern-mental regime, and to find loopholes for them sometimes. They seek to obtain exemption from tax or court fee, or the agreement to overlook past defections. They seek his help and advice in their dealings with foreigners—e.g. Government officials, European and Asian employers, farmers and shopkeepers. As an ex-chief put it: 'People came to me when they had troubles, difficulties; not when all was well.' But the point is rather that they come when other procedures seem to have failed, or when they do not know what means to use at all. The offices of the local government are fairly central for the bulk of the population, and the chief is therefore easy to reach: generally a number of petitioners and complainants hover near his office seeking interviews.

Not a few people believe that the chief, perhaps with some material inducement, can be persuaded to upset a judicial decision, influence a case which is *sub judice*, or take some other extra-legal action on their behalf. This is, of course, an expression of Arusha evaluation of the potential power of the chief, which is thought to be, and rightly, superior to all other powers in the country, except when the community as a whole or some substantial part of it acts against him. Although he is ultimately subject to general public approval, yet he is also significantly backed by the Central Government. In addition, he is less subject to the day-to-day scrutiny by the people which influences and limits counsellors and spokesmen. Individual Arusha are inclined to think that whatever the general sanctions on the chief, yet in their particular case he is powerful enough to do as

---

[1] By 1961, under the influence of national self-government and democratic repre-sentation, the Arusha, or a vocal majority, rejected the chiefship in favour of an elected head of the Tribal Council.

he and they wish. This is indeed often the case, but continuously compounded, such actions lead to a situation in which he lays himself open to popular resentment and official reprimand. On the other hand, the chief has a real responsibility to attend to the complaints which seem legitimate, and to advise people who are ignorant of their rights and obligations.

The chief obtains both moral authority and coercive powers by virtue of his approval and support by the Government. Because of this supra-authority gained from outside the tribal society, he may legitimately (from the viewpoint of the Government, that is) be able to enforce laws and rules, and to bring pressures to bear, which are nowise derived from indigenous sources. And because the people are not always sure of the precise limits of the chief's power, and of his authoritarian support by the Government, they are inclined to allow him to expand his power when doubt exists. To take a single example of great importance in the post-war era: in the matter of pioneering, land allocation and administration, and often in the settlement of the many disputes arising in the newly colonised, peripheral region, the chief has been able to exercise new authority and to enforce regulations never existing before—often to the disadvantage of indigenous leaders and procedures. In this crucial matter the chief has increased his range of power tremendously; further, he has been able to intervene directly into one of the major fields of Arusha conflict and disputes, in a quasi-judicial but authoritarian way.

Before 1948, a chief was also the only magistrate in his area: he held regular court sessions for criminal and civil hearings. Such a court, and the procedures and judgements connected with it were originally a complete novelty too in Arusha country, and they have become closely associated with the chiefship *per se*. In 1948 a number of separate courts were established,[1] and an appeal court; but until 1954 the chief retained magisterial competence so that he could take appeals from the appeal court and hear the more serious cases in the first instance. Since then he has had no right to hear any case or to interfere in judicial matters; but quite clearly the earlier tradition lingers, so that both the people and the magistrates, as well as the chief, accept the possibility of his interference. Thus the chief remains in a position where he can significantly affect judicial processes

[1] See p. 163ff. below.

and decisions, even though he no longer personally appears in court. Litigants still seek his counsel and assistance, and as a minimum he advises on procedures to be followed by them. Often he considers a dispute *in toto* by a conclave in his office, at which plaintiff and defendant with two or three supporters appear before him. Although he can scarcely issue an enforceable judgement, nevertheless his opinion carries much weight—not only with the two parties, but with any other judicial assembly (court, moot, parish assembly) which may later consider the issue.

As part of his routine duties the chief must supervise the whole of the activities of the local government, such as tax collection, Treasury budgets and expenditure, schools, clinics, some roads, markets and trading centres, and other services provided. He should, but sometimes does not, frequently tour all the parts of the chiefdom and investigate local problems as they arise. He therefore usually has an excellent knowledge of affairs, even the details of particular disputes, conflicts and discussions which are in progress. More than any other single person he is, or can be, in touch with all that goes on, and can exert influence if he wishes. A magistrate or court clerk who is uncertain, for example, what judgement to give in a difficult case, or what the law is as required by the Government, or whether to refer a dispute back to the lineage counsellors, tends to seek the chief's opinion and to act on it. The parish headman, whose people are slow to pay their taxes or to turn out to clear parish tracks and roads, or whose people become involved with the Forest Department, a foreign estate owner or trader, similarly seeks the chief's advice and support. He may also be stirred to particular action by the chief's uninvited intervention.

Age-group spokesmen or lineage counsellors may appeal to the chief for guidance because he has, or is thought to have, the authority to overcome delays and intractable situations. Even where any of these people see no reason for absolute acceptance of the chief's advice or interference, yet they are often glad to try and put on him the responsibility of a difficult decision. He cannot easily refuse without loss of standing, for he is believed to be able to do these things if he wishes. Indeed he frequently welcomes the opportunities to intervene, for they serve to extend his influence and authority. Because indigenous judicial processes are not officially recognised by the Government, the chief has no formal power to intervene there; he cannot as of right do so continuously, and spokesmen and counsellors are not prepared to accept that he should. Nevertheless the modern alternative to indigenous processes is the official court system, the believed tool of the chief; because of this alternative, subject at least to his influence, he is able to exert influence over parish assemblies and moots.

The chief is assisted by a staff which he formally appoints—the deputy chief; clerks and messengers in his office; magistrates, clerks, assessors, and messengers of the local courts; technical supervisors and temporary employees. Although he is subject to the wishes of the District Commissioner, nevertheless this is not altogether understood by the people, including the appointees themselves. In any case he is in an excellent position to nominate men of his own choice and to press their case. The employees of the local government, therefore, feel themselves beholden to the chief for their continued employment and for promotion or salary increase. The weakness of the Tribal Council in supervisory matters, and the inability of indigenous leaders to intervene, affords the chief an autocratic position in some ways. It is an autocracy which is in part forced upon him by the Central Government's desires for efficiency, but there is relatively little indigenously to prevent it. Even where some degree of public opinion is expressed, the chief can often afford to ignore it and may be compelled to do so. Whether he wishes or not, the chief is bound to intervene in matters touching upon vital Arusha interests. This has been especially significant in relation to the allocation of land at a time when it was becoming acutely scarce. But the Arusha have no tradition of autocracy, nor was there a conscious desire for it by the Central Government's officers. The logic of the situation compelled it. Because of resentment about this by the people, the office of chief is an unstable one; and it remains without firm roots in the society as a whole.

Parish Headman

In each of the twenty-eight parishes there is a headman (*jumbe*) who is selected by the parish assembly, subject to the approval of the chief and District Commissioner. The chief's influence on the selection is generally slight, partly because he prefers not to challenge parish xenophobia, but also because headmen are commonly ineffective executives. Most headmen are well content to permit the chief to take responsibility in local government affairs in order that they themselves may be rid of it, especially in tax collection. Should conflict occur between a headman and the chief, the latter, in any official matter, can generally rely on his superior position and the support of the Government. In practice most headmen do little, or as little as possible, and allow the chief to intervene as he will. They explain to their people in the parish that they collect tax or impose some unpopular regulation only because the chief and the Government compel them to do so.

With only a few exceptions (where a man has been both able and willing to continue in office for a long period) headmen are members of the age-group in the formal grade of senior murran. Arusha argue that this is properly so, for a headman is the local servant of the chief and the Government, just as senior murran in general are expected to undertake tasks and obey orders from elders in their parish or lineage. Apart from his official duties, which in practice are slight, a headman plays a role in the parish which his age-mates do not and are not expected to do. The reason for this lies partly, of course, in his official paid position; but rather more important is the fact that he is consciously chosen by his community—largely by the elders—specifically as its representative. A headman is expected to be continuously available to people of the parish in order quickly to take action where other processes are cumbersome. He should make himself acquainted with any strangers who come to the parish, so that information about them is available if necessary and a curb may be put on any undesirable activities. More importantly he should act on behalf of parish members as difficulties arise. For example, a wife who is beaten by her husband, or men involved in a brawl, or a farmer whose field is invaded by neighbour's cattle, can immediately appeal to the headman. They seek not so much to obtain his judgement on the issue in order to achieve a settlement of it, but rather it is desired that he shall intervene to stop the continuation of the alleged offence, pending a proper hearing in due course. People seek to make the facts known publicly, and perhaps to engage the headman as a valuable witness. Relations and neighbours may serve this purpose, and often do, but the headman is thought to be a valuable, neutral witness. To some extent, too, he serves as an outlet for enraged feelings.

The headman is expected to be able to act quickly in a way which spokesmen and counsellors cannot. The ill-treated wife, for instance, is able in due course to bring a suit against her husband or to leave home and go to her father's or brother's homestead; but immediately she requires protection, so that her husband shall not molest her further, and she wishes to show the headman her torn clothing or physical weals, as well as the emotional upset, caused by her husband's deed. If she appeals to a neighbouring spokesman, she is likely to be told to attend the next parish assembly meeting and present her complaint there, for a spokesman, *qua* spokesman, is rarely willing to act on his own. He does not conceive it as his duty, and prefers to act only in cooperation with fellow notables. A lineage counsellor is even less likely to take immediate action, for the arrangement of a conclave or moot takes time because of the dispersed nature of lineages; and he, like a spokesman, is unwilling to act on his own in what might appear an authoritarian way.

Occasionally a headman, particularly one who has come to enjoy sustained popularity and support, may attempt to settle the conflict by hearing the arguments of the people concerned, and in effect giving a judgement, or at least recommending a form of settlement. He cannot enforce any decision, except insofar as he represents public opinion and the voice of reason. He may, however, be able to censure the drunken husband who assaults his wife, and the rebuke may be at least tacitly accepted and some immediate amends made to the wife. Where serious issues separate the married pair such that the physical violence is merely a symptom of these, the headman's opinion is unlikely to be acceptable; indeed the headman rarely attempts to do more than protect the woman for the moment and, no more than any other man, does not seek to interfere in any affairs of people who are not his kin. Later, in an assembly, moot or court, the headman's witness is important and his opinion may well carry weight.

The headman therefore performs a useful local function, and earns the continued support and respect of the parish insofar as he is successful. Many, but not all, headmen play an active part in the parish assembly and even in moots convened in his parish. Some fail signally to do this. Whether they do or not depends largely on the character and ability of the headman. Usually a senior murran of demonstrable ability is selected for the office, because of the generally perceived value he provides; but sometimes, where the main emphasis is currently laid on his official, local government duties, a man is selected who is unlikely to be efficient in improving tax collection or the enforcement of Government regulations. It occurs also that a reaction sets in against a headman who is too successful, to the point where he seems to challenge the influence of his parish spokesman and other notables. An incumbent headman can be removed on appeal to the chief, and a successor selected by the parish assembly, although this is not common. Parish leaders prefer to avoid the entanglement with external authority, and choose to bring informal pressures against the over-powerful headman. They may censure him in the parish assembly, and actively deprecate his influence. As a murran, the headman is particularly susceptible to this kind of action by men of elders' status, and seldom does a headman seriously attempt even to challenge them.

The headman may represent his community in extra-parish affairs. He may be called upon by the chief or a government official to report on his parish—the state of the roads, tax collection, people's opinions on some matter—and he is responsible for summoning people to a meeting requested by such a person in authority. Arusha often prefer to be accompanied by their headman when they go to seek the advice or assistance of the chief or an official, or when they go to court. Sometimes this may be required in order to establish the *bona fides* of a petitioner; but a man may be apprehensive, unable to speak Swahili properly, or merely inarticulate. A person seeking this kind of assistance from his headman, gives a small present of cash or beer, or he becomes indebted to the headman and his supporters on future occasions.

Like the role of chief, that of headman is not of indigenous origin, but was created by the colonial government for its own administrative purposes. It is nowadays ubiquitously accepted by the Arusha because of the useful way in which it augments the indigenous organisation of a parish. In 1957-8 there was considerable opposition to the administrative policy of reducing the twenty-eight headmanships to fourteen, each new headman having wider territorial and executive competence. In part, this opposition arose from the opinion that the amalgamation of headman's areas was a threat to the autonomy and prestige of each separate parish, which no longer would have its own selected headman. No less importantly, the people appreciated the value of the work of their headman in the parish in what were essentially matters unrelated to the formal requirements of the local government. Although the policy of amalgamations was eventually accepted at an administrative level, such that two or three parishes were grouped under a 'senior headman' (*oloitoshul*); at the insistence of the people, an 'assistant headman' (*olaretoni*) was appointed for each separate parish, and he continues in the role of the old-style headman.

The Tribal Council

This body (*Engilata o losho*) was first established in 1948. It comprises one representative from each parish, two from each clan, and nine nominated members. The parish and clan representatives are not necessarily, or even usually, spokesmen or counsellors respectively, because it is felt generally that men should be chosen who have some knowledge of Swahili and of the outside world. The indigenous leaders are, however, unwilling to compromise their local influence in the interests of inadequately understood tribal government. Because of this and because neither the procedures nor the responsibilities of the Council are appreciated, it has achieved little influence. The dominant position of the chief has inhibited it, and its members have little competence or experience in local government matters, such as the local tax rate, water development projects, or market regulation. It was hoped by the Government that the Council would be both a legislative and consultative body; insofar as it serves a useful governmental service, it is as a sounding-board (of unknown fidelity) for ideas and plans put to it. To some extent, in its more informal sessions, it provides a form for the exchange of news and views at a tribal level; but for most Arusha it has little significance of any kind. It does not diminish the power of the chief, nor have influence in judicial affairs. Significantly enough, the opposition to the chief himself, and to certain aspects of the chiefship in general, and the deep disquiet over the critical shortage of land and certain features of maladministration in land affairs, have not been expressed through the Tribal Council, but instead largely by extra-constitutional methods and through the spokesmen, counsellors and headmen.

The Local Courts

In 1948 the two sub-tribal chiefs' courts were replaced by a number of separate official courts of first-instance (*ilbaraza*), dispersed through the country. Three salaried, Arusha magistrates have charge of two courts each, holding hearings on alternate days in each one, or as current needs require. Magistrates are appointed by the chief, but they must be confirmed and given their warrants by the Central Government, which, through the District Commissioner, is able to exercise the main influence. They must at least be able to read and write Swahili, and should be men of some integrity. Each magistrate is assisted by a court clerk who is responsible for the registering of charges and plaints, the issue of summons, the recording of cases, and other clerical tasks. Although the magistrate holds prime responsibility for his courts and the judgements there, he tends to regard his clerk as a junior partner rather than a subordinate. He commonly consults him, and is susceptible to his opinions. Both magistrates and clerks are necessarily drawn from the small educated class of Arusha, almost always Lutheran Christians. Being educated, they are therefore usually younger men with little indigenous seniority. Because of this they are not representative members of what is still a mainly pagan, non-literate 'and conservative people, and they are inclined to be dissociated from the standards and the values of the people with whose disputes they deal.

Each court is housed in its own permanent building, which contains both the large, open-sided court-room with a low platform at one end where the magistrate and clerk sit when in session, and also a small lock-up office where other business is transacted and records kept. Hours are usually from mid-morning to mid-afternoon, but the magistrate may adjourn the court to a temporary location in order, for example, to inspect disputed land and hear evidence there, or to take evidence from a sick person. A small fee (minimum two shillings) is payable when a suit is registered by the court clerk, who is also responsible for collecting fines. Although most of the proceedings of a court are held in the Arusha language, all records are in Swahili, and summaries of evidence by disputants and witnesses are read back to them in Swahili for their affirmation. Many technical terms (e.g. words for 'court', 'fee', 'magistrate', 'plaintiff', 'appeal', etc.), now in common usage by all Arusha in these courts, are taken directly from Swahili. Procedures are more formal than those the people follow in their indigenous practices.

In a number of ways, therefore, the courts are differentiated from the judicial bodies of the Arusha themselves.

Magistrates (with their clerks) have a quite different judicial role from that of lineage counsellors and age-group spokesmen (with their associated notables). A magistrate has a position of delegated authority, deriving from a centralised government, whilst those indigenous leaders have only an acquired influence which is limited by the necessity of the continuous support and approval of their fellows in their lineages and parishes respectively. A magistrate exercises an authority which has no foundation in the society itself but is sanctioned entirely from the outside.[1] Supervision of the courts' work, including opportunities for appeal and regular inspections of court records, is directed wholly by the Central Government. The geographical areas of jurisdiction of a court are ill-defined, but they are unrelated to indigenous areas, and always contain several parishes or parts of them. In brief, these courts are an arm of the Central Government, but locally staffed.

An Arusha magistrate is by no means neglectful of the virtues of conciliation and the social advantages of dispute settlements which are mutually acceptable to both parties, as these are pursued by indigenous procedures: but a magistrate is obliged to give a specific judgement in every registered case which comes before him, and to give it as a third party who is not overtly aligned with either of the disputants. Cases cannot be unduly delayed once they are registered by plaintiffs, because the supervisory, Central Government officer will not permit it. It is not possible to hold a succession of hearings at which gradual attempts are made to reduce the differences between disputants, as commonly happens by indigenous procedures. A man before the court must be found innocent or guilty, or as having failed to meet his legitimate obligations or not. Considerations of the relations between disputants, and the wider context of the dispute are given less weight than they are by indigenous bodies, and some-

---

[1] In contrasting authority and influence, here and elsewhere in this book, I do not mean to imply that authority does not have some basis in the consent of the persons over whom it is exercised. A consideration of this qualification would take me beyond the scope of this present work, for the situation here described was such that, at that time, the coercive power was so great that only vast and overwhelming dissatisfaction could raise the question of consent. To some extent this question has been raised in Tanganyika by demands for self-government; but an independent government still maintains essentially the same superimposed local courts in the Arusha chiefdom.

times none at all. Free of partisanship and personal commitment, a magistrate is often able to reach a decision more easily and quickly, and to determine the extent of compensation payment, fine or other award. Unlike counsellors, spokesmen and notables, the magistrate has not the onus of justification outside his court in everyday life, nor the responsibility of enforcing his decision in practical terms. Deliberate flouting of his juridical orders can be punished in his own court, or a higher one, by contempt-of-court proceedings, and enforcement is, if necessary, left to the chief and to the police. Finally a magistrate has no direct responsibility for the future of relations between disputants, and between their groups of associates.

The law which a magistrate administers is not altogether the same as that with which parish assemblies and moots are concerned. It has long been the policy of the Tanganyika Government that local courts shall administer the local customary law of the region in which they are situated, where 'it is not repugnant to natural justice or morality or is not, in principle, in conflict with the provisions of any law in force in the Territory'.[1] Customary law, where it is allowable, is augmented by ordinances, orders and decrees of the Central Government and by local government by-laws. Court law in Arusha is, therefore, in part different in both scope and content from 'customary law'. Parish assemblies and moots are seldom concerned with Government laws and regulations, but on the other hand they may (unlike a court) concern themselves with, for example, accusations of witchcraft or the powers of the ancestors. Even where similar matters are dealt with by both courts and indigenous bodies, the law may differ. For instance, theft is normally punishable by imprisonment, if guilt is proved to a magistrate; but invariably an agreed compensation payment is the result of a hearing in a parish assembly or moot, and the size of the compensation depends on the relations between property owner and thief and between their respective groups. In another kind of case, a magistrate (with official endorsement) imposed a fine, and ordered an economic compensation to be paid, by a cattle-owner to the Lutheran Mission in whose field his animals had strayed; but the Arusha themselves continue to put the onus of responsibility on the owner of a field to prevent livestock entering. Even where both kinds of judicial body administer the same law, as stated in objective terms—e.g. concerning

[1] *Local Courts Ordinance*, Tanganyika, 1951, section 15 (a).

bridewealth or inheritance—a moot, by its essential nature, administers it with a much wider tolerance than a court, because the ultimate agreed settlement (as against an imposed settlement) necessarily requires some compromise in relation to the total social context. For example, a court is most likely to order that the full number of the appropriate animals be transferred to complete a legitimately claimed bridewealth; a moot, on the other hand, may well reach a compromise, where perhaps a goat is handed over in lieu of the outstanding cow, or where a witnessed promise is made that the wife's father shall have an interest in the bridewealth which will be received at the marriage of his daughter's eldest daughter. In another instance, a pioneer may claim all the land he has cleared and brought into use, and his suit to evict an agnatic tenant-helper is allowable in court: a moot would doubtless acknowledge the landowner's right, but it would be most unlikely to agree to an eviction which transgresses general kinship obligations and lineage unity. The court might well express the moral sentiment that the tenant should be permitted to remain, but a moot places that sentiment before the ideal land rights of the pioneer-owner.

It is necessary, therefore, to identify a court not only in terms of its possession of authority, delegated by an outside government, but also in terms of both the procedural and substantive law, and the kinds of decisions it administers. Arusha have been slow to accept the courts' jurisdiction, where they have not been compelled to do so in cases of offences against Government laws. They do now accept it, with reservations, as an alternative to their own jural procedures, in certain situations where it seems to offer advantages to them. Particularly is it resorted to as an 'appeal' against disapproved decisions of indigenous bodies, or where such bodies' competence is weak. This feature is discussed in Chapter Nine.[1]

An attempt has been made to bridge the gap between the local courts and the society in which they compulsorily operate, and also to curb the ignorance and peremptoriness of magistrates and clerks. Each court has a number of 'court elders' who are appointed from among the more notable men who live fairly near the court. They are usually junior elders, often spokesmen, and sometimes counsellors. Three or four of these men should attend court (and are paid a daily allowance) to advise the magistrate on points of Arusha law.

[1] Pages 204ff. below.

Usually at least one or two are present—but not invariably—and they can be useful to a young magistrate, and also to litigants who are timid or inarticulate. In the opinion of most Arusha, with which I must concur, the 'court elders' have, on the whole, relatively little influence on final decisions. They do not always properly appreciate the official procedures of a court, nor the responsibilities a magistrate has to his superiors; and they have no training of any kind. They, unlike the magistrate and clerk, are seldom subject to criticism or censure by Government officials or the chief, and they are, not unnaturally, prone to avoid responsibility for the necessary clear-cut decisions in difficult cases.

Appeal from a local court is always possible to the Arusha Appeal Court, headed by another salaried magistrate, with his own clerk and 'court elders'. He is generally the magistrate of greatest experience. He has rather wider powers of competence than the lower magistrate, and therefore also hears the more serious cases in the first instance. Fees are payable when an appeal is lodged, although there is discretion to waive them. Although an appeal court, with the record of the first hearing before it, cases are generally heard *de novo*. There is, however, little significant difference between the Appeal Court and the local court in procedures, kinds of decisions and general principles. Because the Appeal Court is held in the same building as the chief's offices, some Arusha say that the chief's influence here is greater; and in this they are likely to be right.

Further appeal is possible to the District Court, administered by the District Commissioner, who is assisted by 'court elders' to advise him on customary law. Appeals at this level are heard within a set of rules which arise from a mixture of the experience and sense of equity of the colonial administrator, and the ideal statements of Arusha custom provided by the court elders. Judgements at this level seldom establish precedents which are thereafter followed by Arusha magistrates in the lower courts, except insofar as an administrative order to those courts may be afterwards based on an appeal decision. Like the Central Government, and administrative officer himself, the District Court is conceived by Arusha as a powerful but alien force; the orders of all (they are virtually the same to Arusha) are not easily avoided in particular matters, but they seldom make much impression in similar matters between the people themselves.

In addition to their formal duties as a judge in open court, magistrates conduct unofficial hearings on disputes in their offices. A plaintiff wishing to register a dispute for official hearing and judgement, explains his case to the court clerk and magistrate. It may be decided to register it forthwith, to collect the registration fee, and assign a time for the hearing. If a plaintiff is adamant he can scarcely be refused, for fear he may complain to the chief or to an administrative officer, who will reprimand the magistrate and order registration to be made. Where the defendant is unrelated to the plaintiff, and if there is a *prima facie* case, registration is virtually automatic. A trivial plaint may be rejected or referred to the parish headman or spokesmen. Where the disputants are related, especially if they are close kin, the magistrate may urge that their case be taken up by their respective counsellors, or that it be referred back to them if they have already been involved. In doing this, or in attempting an act of reconciliation himself, the magistrate may request that the disputants, with one or two of their closer associates, meet in his office to discuss the issues. Here he acts as a neutral third party. He may, as a result of the meeting, suggest a compromise solution, urge acceptance of the previous decision of spokesman or counsellors, or propose a course of procedure through indigenous institutions which it is hoped will lead to a settlement. Thus a magistrate's private hearing may lead to an acceptable solution of the case (or even agreement to drop it altogether), or it may lead to it being taken up by or reverting to appropriate indigenous procedures, with perhaps recommendations for its solution. That is to say, the magistrate's private hearing may be an end in itself, or it may become a stage in the total process of reaching a settlement. Even if the dispute is thereafter officially registered and heard in court, the private hearing serves a useful purpose both in clarifying the issues and providing a pre-view of the magistrate's judgement. The advantage of the private hearing lies in the fact that, as a third party, the magistrate can act both as a conciliator and as a means of emotional release for frustrated disputants. Men may welcome the opportunity to put their case to a third person who may be able to influence the final solution, even when it is acknowledged that eventually the decision of a moot will have to be accepted. Although the private hearing is entirely unofficial, it has become a recognised procedure of some value. The extent to which it is used depends a great deal on the personal inclinations of individual magistrates and their clerks.

PART FOUR

PROCESSES OF DISPUTE SETTLEMENT

CHAPTER NINE

THE LOCUS OF DISPUTE PROCEDURE

THE preceding parts of this book have dealt in turn with three major sub-systems of Arusha society—the parish and age-group system, the patrilineal descent system, and the modern local government. Although these are not the only coherent sub-systems which can be analytically isolated, they are essential to the study of almost any particular field of action and belief among the Arusha. Their especial importance for present purposes lies in three intimately inter-connected features. Firstly, two of them provide a set of corporate groups or established categories of people, which largely determine both the kind and the strength of support and constraint to which men are subject when disputes occur and settlement of them is attempted. Secondly, each of these sub-systems identifies a number of particular roles of influence and leadership, the occupants of which, *inter alia*, play a permanent part in the arrangement for and the carrying out of dispute procedures as advisors, advocates and conciliators. Thirdly, each sub-system provides regularised means for dealing with overt conflict and dispute between individuals. These means are of two kinds:—a public assembly, at which disputants present their cases before a joint congress of their respective supporters in formal meetings, at which attendance is open to any who care to be present; and a conclave, which comprises either the members of a basic, nuclear group to which both disputants belong, or a few of their closest associates where the disputants are members of different nuclear groups.

For convenience of exposition, these three sub-systems have been described separately, almost in isolation from each other. It is now necessary to consider them in conjunction in order to give an articulate account of dispute procedures among the Arusha. Before attempting this, a summary recapitulation of each, in respect of these three principal features, may help to clarify understanding.

The age-group system is largely confined to a single parish. The nuclear unit is the age-group itself, but also there are the segments of the group—circumcision-sections—and the combinations of groups—the streams. The men of influence are the age-group spokesmen, together with the other notables, of each age-group. Regularised means of dispute settlement are provided by the public parish assembly; or by conclaves which comprise either the members of a single age-group, or—where disputants belong to different age-groups—they comprise some of the age-mates of each man, together with relevant men of influence.

In the patrilineal descent system, the nuclear group is the inner lineage, i.e. near agnates. Beyond that are the maximal lineage, and the various levels of patrilineal *olwashe* from the dichotomous segments of a lineage to tribal moiety. Roles of influence and leadership are played by the counsellors selected in each maximal lineage,

FIGURE 9.

The Elements of Three Sub-Systems of Arusha Society

Sub-System	Parish/Age-Group	Patrilineal Descent	Local Government
Groups and Categories	Parish-division Parish Circumcision-section AGE-GROUP Stream	INNER LINEAGE Maximal lineage *Olwashe* segments	
Roles of Influence and Leadership	SPOKESMEN Age-group notables	COUNSELLORS Lineage notables	MAGISTRATES Court clerks Chief Headmen
Public Assembly	PARISH ASSEMBLY	MOOT—INTERNAL —EXTERNAL	LOCAL COURT Appeal courts
Conclave	Single age-group With spokesmen	Single inner lineage With counsellor(s)	With magistrate With chief With headman

and by certain ill-defined, but readily identified, notable members of each lineage. In respect of this sub-system, the public assembly is the moot. This may be an external moot, where a dispute concerns members of different maximal lineages, so that the assembly comprises members of each *olwashe* of the disputants within the smallest descent category to which both belong; or it may be an internal moot, where the disputants belong to a single maximal lineage, and the assembly is confined (at least initially) to lineage members. A conclave comprises either the members of a single inner lineage, or—where disputants belong to different inner lineages—it comprises a few close agnates of each man, together with their respective counsellors.

The local government system precipitates no corporate groups or categories of importance which are not of indigenous origin in the other sub-systems. The particular roles of influence here are those of chief, magistrate, court clerk and parish headman. The public assembly is the local court, beyond which are the appeal courts; each is controlled by a magistrate. Conclaves occur under the aegis of a magistrate, the chief, or a headman.

This summary is set out in tabular form in Figure 9.

The principal indigenous roles of influence are specifically named: here they are translated as age-group 'spokesman', and lineage 'counsellor'. They are not the only important roles, however, as I have shown. For convenience in the following account of Arusha judicial procedures, the term 'notable' will be used generically to refer to all roles of influence and leadership, including spokesmen and counsellors. Government officials, and sometimes Arusha themselves, loosely use the word 'elder', or the Swahili equivalent, *mzee*, for such men in those positions. In this monograph the word 'elder' is used to refer only to the occupants of a particular age-grade— formally, a man whose age-group has been transferred from murran-hood—and in that sense not all elders are notables.

The Arusha have no specific term for a public assembly or a conclave, either generically or for particular kinds. The only technical word they use is *engigwana*, which literally means 'a discussion' (a noun derivative of *aigwena*, 'to discuss'), but which most usually refers to 'a matter in discussion', or what I describe as 'a dispute'. Arusha say that a plaintiff 'has *engigwana*' (*eeta ngigwana*), and they mean, as we might put it, 'he has a matter to be discussed', or 'he has a dispute'. Plaintiff and defendant are not verbally distinguished; both 'have *engigwana*'.[1] The spokesmen and notables in a parish assembly, or the counsellors and notables in a moot, who are leading the consideration of a dispute, also 'have *engigwana*'; and they or the whole of either assembly may be referred to directly as *engigwana*. If it is wished to distinguish different kinds of assembly, they can speak of *engigwana e mbalbal* (parish assembly) *engigwana e ngaji* (internal moot), and *engigwana e ngishome* (external moot). Arusha might be a little puzzled by my translations since, for example, *engigwana e mbalbal* really means 'a (matter in) discussion in the parish'. The parish assembly is often referred to simply as 'the parish', *embalbal*, which indeed is accurate enough because the assembly is in fact the corporate meeting of the parish in action, or at least of those of its members considered qualified to participate on its behalf. A similar reference is applied to a moot.

There is no direct way of distinguishing a conclave from an assembly. A conclave is *engigwana* in the extended meaning of that word; it is also 'the age-group', 'the parish', 'the lineage' or 'the clanship group', as the case may be, but without specific delimitation. Nevertheless, both empirically and in the understanding of the people, a counsellor's conclave, for instance, is different from an internal moot in its composition, its procedure and its scope. This will be made clear in this and the following chapter. Both are *engaji* (maximal lineage), both are (or alternately, have) *engigwana:* but the conclave is a small, private meeting of a few agnates in the homestead—often the house—of one of them, whilst the moot is a larger, public meeting of many—ideally, all autonomous male—agnates in an open place, usually a grazing paddock.

A court is usually referred to as *olbaraza* (from the Swahili word), although it too is sometimes referred to as *engigwana*, as is the matter under discussion—the dispute—there. A chief's and a headman's conclave is *engigwana*, with the appropriate qualification; a magistrate's conclave may similarly be referred to or it may be described simply as *olbaraza*.

Although the various kinds of public assembly and conclave are properly defined in terms of the sub-system in which they emerge, nevertheless it can happen that any one of them may involve men

[1] The Swahili words *mdai* and *mdaiwa* are sometimes used for plaintiff and defendant respectively, deriving from the official usage in courts.

who are not, strictly speaking, members of it. A man may participate because he has special evidence to give which it is desired to make use of. An example of this is given in a later case (No. 16, page 210): an internal moot convened to deal with a land dispute between paternal cousins, was attended by a counsellor of a linked maximal lineage; this counsellor lived fairly near the plaintiff, and had previously been concerned with the piece of land in question as well as other matters in that lineage. A disputant may wish to have the strongly supporting evidence of a particularly close friend or a neighbour. Whilst such additional participants do not attend merely as witnesses in the objective, information-giving sense of a western court of law, their part in the proceedings tends to be smaller than that of full members. A conclave, but seldom a public assembly, is generally willing to forego the attendance of a really neutral witness, and to accept his evidence at second hand. It is not desired to have present in a conclave someone who has little or no relationship with the disputants, for such a meeting is pre-eminently the occasion for private discussion.

The roles and relationships of one sub-system may intrude in the procedures pertaining to another. Thus at a parish assembly, a bona fide parish member may also be a lineage counsellor. He cannot dissociate his two roles, and, if his agnate is a disputant, he speaks as and is accepted by others as a counsellor as well as a member of the age-group. It sometimes occurs that a parish assembly is virtually taken out of the hands of the spokesmen by parish members who, as counsellors and lineage notables, are connected with particular disputants. Conversely, a member of a moot may be given particular attention because he is also an age-group spokesman. A magistrate or the chief normally summons to a conclave either the spokesmen or counsellors of the disputants—both if necessary.

It would be an error, then, to define too rigidly the membership and functions of members in a juridical meeting. On the other hand, having made this allowance, it must not disguise the principle features of definition which refer to the particular sub-system concerned. This would not only deny the practical reality of the different kinds of procedures, but it fails to distinguish the kinds of roles, relations and processes which are involved in each, and which are fundamental to its operation.

The various kinds of public assembly and conclave are available to all Arusha in the event that they are involved in a dispute. Any single one of them may be able to produce an adequate settlement of the matter, such that it goes no further and both parties are satisfied, at least for the time being, and perhaps permanently. But any one of them may become—often by conscious intent—only a single stage in a total process of several stages during the attempt to reach an acceptable and practicable solution. In such a process any two of the assemblies or conclaves may be linked together successively, and any one may be repeated as a further stage at any point. An Arusha seeks to make use of that assembly or conclave which seems most likely to suit his purpose, taking into consideration the nature of the relationship between himself and the other disputant, the nature of the matter in dispute, and the advice, support and constraint he receives from his close associates. The procedural rules which govern a disputant's choice and the reaction of his opponent are extremely flexible, but there are certain limitations. Arusha themselves are inclined to over-simplify the rules, and thereby both distort and over-formalise them, by saying that a parish assembly takes disputes between members of the same parish; that a moot takes disputes which, pertaining to kinship relations, are more critical, such as those concerning inheritance, land, marriage, bridewealth and the like; and that a court takes disputes in which a settlement seems impossible or at least highly difficult by indigenous procedures, and where then the coercive authority of the magistrate becomes paramount. The reality is by no means as simple as that, even when the possibilities of conclaves are ignored. Partly, this is because disputants may be related both patrilineally and by membership of the same parish, and therefore an element of uncertainty and choice arises. Partly, it is because there is generally no essential compulsion to follow one kind of procedure rather than another, and a man tries to choose that which is most advantageous for him, and which his opponent does not or cannot easily reject. As a general rule, other than in petty cases, a final settlement is the end-product of a chain of two or more kinds of procedures each of which takes the treatment of it a step further.

Initiative in the choice of the particular procedure may lie with either disputant. Generally the man who seeks redress of an alleged injury, and therefore desires positive action in his favour, is the one who instigates a stage in the total process; but the defendant may himself take the initiative in attempted self defence. Neither disputant has an entirely free choice, for each is subject to the constraint imposed on him by the need for support from his associates, and thus by their opinions. Except in the heat of the moment, a man invariably consults with his near agnates, members of his inner lineage, for these men are the ones most likely to be of assistance, and most nearly involved in his actions. The choice of procedure commonly results from discussions in the inner lineage and a decision to take joint action. It may happen that members of this lineage are scattered and not immediately easy of access; and perhaps too they are, or seem likely to be rather unhelpful. Then a man may instead, or additionally, consult with those of his age-mates who live nearby or with whom he is especially friendly. Further, he must approach one or more of the men occupying a role of influence relevant both to his own position in the social structure and the nature of the matter in dispute. This he does both because of the specialist advice which they can give him, and because he requires the active agency of one or more of them actually to put into operation the procedure decided upon. A moot or patrilineal conclave can only be convened through the agency of a lineage counsellor. A man cannot permanently be denied the opportunity to register a plaint in a court, but he must at least make a *prima facie* case to the magistrate or court clerk. Formerly a man required the agency of a spokesman to gain a consideration of his case by a meeting of the parish assembly; nowadays, with regular meetings in all parishes, he cannot be denied access to the assembly, but a sympathetic hearing is more likely if he comes with the initial support of one or more spokesmen. Consultation with one or more of these notable men— including also, perhaps, the chief and parish headman—leads to a decision of the course of procedure to be followed.

The defendant in a dispute does not inevitably have to submit to the initiative of the plaintiff, though in some circumstances he may be compelled to do so. Once a plaint is formally registered at a court, the defendant must appear when called, on pain both of contempt of court action and of the possibility of the case being judged in his absence. If a spokesman agrees to promote a plaintiff's case in the parish assembly, the defendant makes himself liable to a fine if he refuses to appear and answer the charge made against him. On the other hand, he may attempt to shift the venue by suggesting an alternative procedure before the hearing is made, or even during the course of it. Both a magistrate and a spokesman may be willing to allow the matter to be further discussed, and perhaps settled 'out of court', if that seems more satisfactory, and if both disputants agree. The proposal for a moot may be rejected by a defendant, but once his own counsellor becomes involved in the matter this is not easy, for the counsellor has obligations also, both to other members of his maximal lineage and to fellow counsellors, which induce him not to countenance undue delays in convening a moot. This is more fully discussed later, and all that need be said here is that if the plaintiff and his counsellor remain adamant, and unless an acceptable alternative is agreed to, the defendant may become subject to coercion by his counsellor and by his patrilineal supporters to accede. Fear of intimating that his case is a poor one, thus weakening himself in the eyes of his supporters, his opponents and general public opinion, is a main sanction here; but counsellors may impose a fine or use some other compulsion should the need arise. One of the objectives of a conclave may be to reach agreement on the mutually acceptable procedure to be followed; although it may itself bring a settlement, or at least advance the discussions towards that end. On the whole, defendants do not attempt to refuse to accept the choice of procedure made by the plaintiff.

The kind of close associates with whom a potential plaintiff consults, and the men of influence he approaches, are themselves in some degree a matter of choice which often leads logically to the further choice of the particular procedure to be used. Even where this does not occur, the two connected decisions are both subject to two considerations:—the nature of the matter in dispute, and the nature of relationships between the disputants.[1] Neither of these considerations is an absolute determinant, as will be illustrated, but at least they provide guiding lines for the individuals concerned, and heuristic indicators for analytic understanding. Thus whilst it is not possible to assert dogmatically that, given the kind of dispute then the procedures open to a plaintiff are such-and-such; on the other hand, it is possible to suggest which are the more likely procedures

[1] It will be remembered that any two Arusha must be related at some point in the patrilineal descent structure. Ideally any two Arusha are also related in some definable way in both the age-set and territorial systems, but outside the single parish and its own set of age-groups the relationship is unimportant in jural processes.

from which a plaintiff will choose. This is most readily done by stating the following general principles which derive both from the statements of the Arusha themselves and from empirically observed action. These principles follow logically from the nature of the three sub-systems of Arusha society which have already been described. In stating these principles, illustrations are given not only of their actual manifestation, but also of significant instances when they fail to to be observed. Ultimately it can be fairly said that the choice and prosecution of a particular procedure, or chain of procedures, depends on the unique circumstances of each new dispute and the individual men involved in it.

A parish assembly, or conclave with spokesmen, deals only with disputes between members of the same parish. The reason for this is obvious: the authority of corporate age-groups and the influence of age-group notables are restricted to a single parish, and therefore spokesmen and notables are unwilling to consider the plaint of a member of another parish. A plaintiff feels, with good reason, that he is un-- likely to receive equitable treatment from men who are not linked to him by age-group and stream. These considerations apply irrespective of the kind of matter in dispute.

Nevertheless it may sometimes be to the advantage of the plaintiff —or so it may seem to him at the time—to take the matter to a meeting of the parish assembly of the defendant.[1] This is not because he expects to gain an acceptable, final settlement there, but rather because he hopes to compel the defendant publicly to acknowledge the existence of the dispute, and to make at least some answer to the charge. If he has a good case, the plaintiff may be able to suggest to the defendant's age-mates or patrons that their associate has acted wrongly and is tending to bring disrepute upon them. If he is able to accomplish this purpose with some success, it may then be easier to obtain the defendant's acceptance of a conclave or moot. That is to say, the parish assembly is utilised not as an end, but as a means towards the end. The parish assembly might be able to suggest an acceptable settlement, but this is highly unlikely and I have no verified instance of it in my records. Spokesmen, with whom I discussed the matter, said that they would not attempt to suggest a

---

[1] A parish assembly never deals with a dispute between people neither of whom are members of that parish, even where the alleged offence concerns the parish in some way, e.g. a fight occurring within the parish boundaries between men of another parish.

settlement in detail, although they might state the general norms appropriate to the dispute.

Case 1: Lerombe alleged that he had loaned Meitan (of an adjacent parish) a goat, to be slaughtered in order to provide meat following the birth of a child to Meitan's wife. This happened some years previously and Meitan now refused to acknowledge the loan, and denied any obligation to pay a goat to Lerombe. The counsellor of Lerombe suggested that he should attend a meeting of the parish assembly in Meitan's parish, and there state his allegations and demand for repayment. This Lerombe did. He persuaded a maternal kinsman, Weto, living in Meitan's parish to accompany him so that he should not have to sit alone in the assembly, and Weto informed the 'chairman' (the seniormost spokesman of the junior elders) that he (i.e. Weto) wished to raise a matter during the meeting. When Weto was called on, he merely introduced Lerombe without comment. Before Lerombe could speak, one or two notables objected: 'Who is this man?' 'He is not one of us. We do not know him here.' 'Let him go to his counsellor if he has a matter (to discuss).'

Weto stood up again and said that, although Lerombe was from another parish, 'Is he not an Arusha? Has he not the right to speak, to bring a matter? Let us listen to his words. We all know Lerombe, He lives over there (indicating the opposite side of a stream about a quarter of a mile away) beyond the Ngarenarok.'

After some discussion, it was agreed that Lerombe should be allowed to speak, and he proceeded to state his allegations. When he had finished, the 'chairman' asked where Meitan was. On hearing that he was at his homestead about half a mile away, a murran was dispatched to summon him, and the assembly began meanwhile to deal with another matter. Sometime later Meitan appeared, and, after the conclusion of the subject under discussion in the assembly, he was called on to speak.

First a spokesman of Meitan's age-group briefly summarised Lerombe's statement. Meitan denied knowledge of the alleged debt at first, and grumbled about being summoned unexpectedly when he was occupied in his fields. The same spokesman asked him if he truly knew nothing about the matter: 'Does Lerombe come here with lies and bad words to make trouble in Kidinga (Meitan's Parish)? Do you know why he does this?' A murmur of approval went up from several of the men present. Meitan then began to answer the allegation; he agreed that he knew of Lerombe's demand because Lerombe had been to his homestead some days previously. He eventually (after questioning by the spokesman) gave his version, which was that, although he had received a goat from Lerombe, it was a purchase for money. At the end of his statement, Meitan sat down and there was a silence.

Eventually, and without standing up (as all speakers should in the assembly), a notable said, 'What do we know of this? Truly debts should be paid; but is there a debt?'

Weto then stood up and said, 'I do not want trouble in this parish. I am not bringing this matter here. How do we know the truth? Who knows about this payment for the goat? Can we not ask?'

A spokesman rose and turned to another man sitting in the meeting. 'Palalet, you are the father (actually father's younger brother) of Meitan, what do you know? Surely kinsmen know these things.'

Palalet rose and agreed that he knew of the matter, and that Meitan was in the right. 'We can show we are right,' he said, 'But we are not all here today. We did not know these words would come today.' He said that his sons were witnesses of the money payment, and that he knew from them the truth of the matter. These sons were not present and no one knew where they were at the time. Palalet declared that his sons, and others who knew, could if necessary give evidence, but not at that time. A spokesman of Palalet's age-group thereupon suggested that Lerombe and Meitan should meet together with their supporters and witnesses to discuss the matter. This brought a general chorus of assent, and was accepted by Lerombe immediately. Meitan stood up and demurred, saying that there was no need for such a meeting for he had done nothing wrong and owed no man anything. After some further questioning of both Meitan and Palalet, they eventually agreed to arrange a meeting with Lerombe, but no mention was made of the nature of the meeting—that is, moot or conclave. Finally a spokesman of Palalet's age-group reiterated the agreement, and discoursed briefly on the evil of false accusation and on the trouble caused when men refused to discuss disputes between them. He also said that debts should be repayed if they really existed, and when the creditor needed repayment.

My inquiries afterwards revealed that, according to his own statement, Lerombe had accomplished what he had intended. Further, the dispute was in fact known to at least some of the men in that parish assembly, and one of the participating spokesmen told me that he believed Lerombe to be in the right, although not altogether so. He said, and the subsequent moot bore him out, that Lerombe had received some money but not the full price of a goat. 'We could not make Lerombe agree to lower his demands,' the spokesman said, 'Because his is not a neighbour (i.e. a parish member) of ours. His age-group is different.' In fact no attempt was made to bring pressure to bear on Lerombe; but it is doubtful if he would have been susceptible to it in any case. At least he told me he would not, for he feared they would be biased in favour of Meitan.

Disputes between age-mates should be dealt with by a conclave of the age-group. The principles involved here have already been discussed in the account of the age organisation. Briefly, the notion is that affairs between age-mates (co-members of one age-group) are no concern of other age-groups, i.e. in a parish assembly; but also a solution to a dispute is thought more likely to be found through the friendly conciliation of fellow age-mates. There is the idea, also, that public disputation between men of one age-group spoils its reputation, and its external unity in the eyes of other age-groups of the parish. Therefore members of the disputants' age-group make strong efforts to persuade them to accept the intervention and assistance of their fellows, and to prevent the intervention of men of other age-groups. Spokesmen and notables take the lead in this. If, however, the dispute is not fairly readily resolvable, the plaintiff may perhaps take it to the public parish assembly, where it is hoped that the combined influence of the parish's leading men would be available on his behalf. This is especially the case if the disputants are murran, so that the plaintiff seeks the assistance of his patrons' age-group.

Age-mates other than the disputants tend to be as much concerned with reconciliation as with justice, because their interest is the unity of the age-group and the desire to avoid outside intervention:[1] at least plaintiffs feel this to be a danger, and I have heard it said in a parish assembly by a plaintiff that he fears being coerced to cede his equity on behalf of group solidarity. He may, of course, be prepared and be persuaded to make this concession if he feels but slightly aggrieved, or if his plaint is shown to be weak or ill-founded. But should he feel a marked sense of injustice, then personal advantage may be sought over group loyalty. Should a plaintiff perceive a lack of sympathy in the parish assembly, he may decide to seek a counsellor's conclave rather than press for a solution in the parish. Nevertheless, having indicated the possible exceptions to the general principle under discussion, it must be noted that almost every dispute between age-mates is at least initially dealt with by age-group conclave, and many are successfully concluded by that procedure.

The principal may be illustrated by three disputes resulting from fights breaking out among junior elders at beer-drinks. The larger beer-drinks may become occasions for drunken brawling, and men

[1] The question of reconciliation is discussed at pp. 277-9.

of junior elder status tend to participate more frequently in such drinks than other men.

Cases 2, 3 and 4: On one occasion a man accused an age-mate of assaulting him and causing bruises and slight cuts. The plaintiff appealed to the spokesman of his parish-division to assist him in obtaining a goat as compensation. The spokesman, who had been present at the beer-drink, deprecated the whole matter; but at the plaintiff's insistence he arranged for a conclave of the age-group at the defendant's homestead. I was told that informal discussions among spokesmen and notables, preceding the conclave, brought a general agreement that the plaintiff's injuries were slight, and that he himself was at least partly to blame that the fight occurred. This opinion was pressed on the plaintiff, whilst the defendant was censured for his behaviour. By this time, three days after the fight, the plaintiff's injuries were less troublesome, and he was prepared to be mollified. Fairly quickly the matter was settled without any further demand for compensation by the plaintiff, and the conclave ended in congenially consuming beer provided by the defendant, in recognition of the balance of the fault being against him.

In another similar case, the injury to the plaintiff was more severe. He had been hit so hard with a stick that he was unable to use his arm because of severe bruising of the shoulder and upper arm, and he had a cut on the head. He claimed a large male sheep in compensation, and also a calf because of the slander against him, by the defendant, which had precipitated the fight. According to the plaintiff, his Chagga ancestry had been referred to, with the suggestion that he was not a proper Arusha. At the age-group conclave, the plaintiff's allegations were quickly established, for several age-mates had witnessed the affair and had, in fact, stopped the fight by their intervention. The defendant attempted to minimise the seriousness of the matter; but in addition he counter-claimed that the plaintiff had not invited him to a recent meat-feast, and thus had shown unfriendliness. Several age-mates pointed out that the two men were chronically inimical, and the general feeling of the conclave began to emerge that fault was not all on one side. A spokesman suggested that the defendant pay the sheep for the injuries, but that the calf for slander was unwarranted. The plaintiff promptly refused this, saying that his age-mates were against him. Discussion continued but no agreement reached.

Eventually, and apparently in anger, the plaintiff began to rail against his age-mates that they would not support his legitimate demands. He went on to say that he would go to the parish assembly, and to his lineage counsellor, and no longer depend on his group's spokesmen who showed so little concern for him. 'You are all against me because my father was a Chagga,' he stated, 'But he came here as a youth and married here, and I was born here. Am I not an Arusha? Should the spokesmen not help me? You are not spokesmen, you are just old men. Why do you not help? I will go to Sabaya (his lineage counsellor) and to the chief. They will help. They are big men. There are no big men here.'

Here the plaintiff put himself in the wrong by insulting the spokesmen, and he was cut off in his shouted speech. One spokesmen suggested that he should be fined, but no one took this up. The spokesman of the plaintiff's parish-division and circumcision-section (a near neighbour) then spoke, reminding his hearers that they were age-mates and should settle their differences in amity, not with fines and angry words. 'Are we not all Derito (the name of their age-group)? Are we not friends? One parish, one age-group. What is this, that we do not help? It is our duty to help. We are one, we must remain one. Do we want those Dareto (senior elders) here? No! Let us discuss this and finish it properly. We know what to do, we know the customs of the Arusha.'

In effect he made an appeal to group loyalty, only a small part of which I have reproduced here. His appeal was well taken by his hearers for there were choruses of 'Eseva!' ('truly'), 'Tokul!' ('absolutely'), 'Eee-ee!', and Ndiyo!' (Swahili: 'that is so'), after each brief statement. Men turned to the plaintiff and sought his approval. Eventually the spokesman concluded by reiterating the agreement for payment of the sheep as compensation for the physical injuries, and suggesting that the defendant present the plaintiff with four *debe* (a four gallon can) of beer as an expression of regret for the slander. The plaintiff was unwilling to accept this reduction of his claims, but after further persuasion he finally did. The defendant took no part and his silence was taken as a token of his assent. Finally the plaintiff agreed. He said later that he had been compelled to accept less than his rights because of the appeals of his age-mates. Both he and other Arusha were of the opinion that had the matter gone to the parish assembly or a moot, the plaintiff would have obtained at least a goat or a sheep for the slander claim.

In the third case, the fight occurred between two age-mates who were already in conflict. Olkeru's old father was the owner of land which Kiteng occupied as tenant. By plying the old man with beer, Kiteng had obtained his witnessed permission to build a store in semi-permanent materials and to plant coffee bushes on the land. There had been a lengthy but desultory dispute over this tenancy, as Olkeru contested the legitimacy of Kiteng's improvements and sought to evict him from the land. The end of this seemed most likely to be that Kiteng could not be evicted until he was paid full compensation for the improvements; and, since these were costly and beyond Olkeru's means, it appeared that Kiteng had effectively gained secure tenure. Olkeru much resented this, and declared his feelings on several occasions. At a beer-drink he became intoxicated and began to insult and taunt Kiteng who, also affected by the drink, retaliated verbally. According to age-mate witnesses later, Olkeru left the scene at dusk and lay in wait as Kiteng walked home. He confronted Kiteng with more insults and the fight followed, during which Kiteng's clothing was torn and he himself suffered head and chest wounds.

This was a serious matter, the culmination of increasing animosity between two fellow-members of the age-group. Next day two spokesmen of the group in that parish-division arranged for a conclave of their age-mates, and this was held on the following day. Because of the ill-feeling between Olkeru and Kiteng, the conclave met in the grazing paddock of one of the spokesmen—i.e. on neutral ground. It was attended by the two spokesmen and one other, two *ingaminini*, and about 25 other age-mates, most but not all, of whom lived in the same parish-division. Kiteng demanded the replacement of his spoiled clothing and a compensation payment of a young ewe. The facts of the case were straightforward and well attested, and the notables and age-mates were inclined to support Kiteng. But they agreed in suggesting the substitution of a male sheep for the young ewe, to be accepted by Kiteng as a show of willingness for reconciliation—this was explicitly stated by one spokesman. Olkeru was ready to accede, but Kiteng firmly refused. The reason he made clear: he declared that the fight was the result of the earlier and persisting land dispute, and he demanded that Olkeru should acknowledge the legitimacy and security of his (Kiteng's) tenancy rights. 'I want no peace without my land,' he said bluntly. In the event it appeared that Kiteng was not prepared to be satisfied with anything that the conclave could give him, for later he refused even the young ewe unless he also obtained Olkeru's endorsement of the tenancy. The conclave broke up after he said that he wished to raise the matter in the full parish assembly.

A few days later Kiteng stated his case in the parish assembly and asked that Olkeru and the assembly declare his security of tenancy. Before the assembly meeting Kiteng had been persuaded by his two spokesmen to claim only a male sheep as compensation. He had agreed on the understanding that they would give him some support in the assembly; whilst they were able to show Olkeru their efforts on his behalf. Thus the compensation claim was quickly settled because, as one senior elder spokesman pointed out, both Olkeru and his age-mates (notables and others) were willing to accept it. The parish assembly then began to consider the land dispute; but two members of Olkeru's maximal lineage (senior elder and senior murran respectively) pointed out that this was a matter for the lineage and their counsellor. Olkeru's aged father agreed (he was verging on senility) and this therefore bound Kiteng—as perhaps Olkeru had planned. The real dispute which lay behind the fight was therefore advanced little if at all, but the attempt by Kiteng to accomplish this had moved him decisively to refuse his age-mates' efforts at conciliation.

There is a major exception to the principle that an age-group conclave deals with disputes between age-mates. This applies where the two men are kin—especially if they are agnates, but often also when they are related by any link of known kinship. In such cases the following principle is the norm.

Disputes between kinsfolk should be dealt with by a moot or by a conclave with counsellors. Here Arusha are primarily distinguishing between agnatic kin from those between non-kinsmen. It is considered not merely impractical, but wrong to take agnatic affairs to a body not connected with the lineage, and composed of a heterogeneous congregation. Conflict between lineage members should be dealt with by an internal moot, or a conclave with their common counsellor. Between nearer agnates of a single inner lineage, a conclave of lineage members is preferable. The smallness of this group and the difficulties of resolving such vital conflict as often arises over inheritance and demands for repeated and lavish assistance, as well as the fact that often the counsellor is a member of another inner lineage, tend to result in such disputes being taken to an internal moot. This is the norm for disputes between agnates of different inner lineages. Men say that they dislike becoming involved in the affairs of another maximal lineage, just as that group itself desires to have no external interference. A lineage counsellor seldom, if ever, is prepared to agree to such interference; partly because it appears to reflect on his abilities, but mainly because he has responsibilities for both disputants, and is instrumental in bringing them together for discussion. Moreoever, disputes between agnates are likely, directly or indirectly to concern some of the more important aspects of Arusha life—inheritance, land, marriage and children, agnatic rights and obligations—and therefore a potential plaintiff goes to his counsellor, who is already well informed in these matters relating to his own lineage, rather than to a notable of his age-group. Even although the two disputants themselves may live in the same parish, it is fairly certain that at least some of their nearer agnates do not; and they, of course, are unwilling to appear before a 'strange' parish assembly.

Although Arusha stress the agnatic sector of kinship in this connection, much the same principle applies to maternal and affinal kin, and for similar reasons. Further, it applies not only to disputes specifically concerning kinship relations as such, but also to any kind of dispute between kin: that is, not only, for example, the rights and obligations of a mother's brother, or the question of bridewealth payments between affines, which arise directly out of the particular relationship, but also disputes in affairs which might occur between any two people.

Case 5: For example, Kamian had been invited to the initiation celebrations for the son of Teronge, his mother's patrilateral cousin who lived a short distance away in the same parish. It is usual, though not absolutely obligatory, that men who are specially invited (kinsmen, age-mates, neighbours, friends) by the initiate's father should make a gift of an animal. This establishes a debt to be repaid on a similar occasion at the donor's homestead. On this occasion, Kamian presented Teronge with a male calf. When several years later, Kamian's only son was circumcised, Teronge failed either to attend the celebrations or to send the reciprocal gift. He claimed afterwards that he was absent visiting a kinsman many miles away, and he promised to make the return gift on the next occasion. Because Kamian had no other son to be initiated, he demanded the animal immediately; and further he accused Teronge of deliberately absenting himself. Kamian consulted with his lineage counsellor, and both went to see Teronge's counsellor to urge a conclave to discuss the matter. Kamian told me that parish spokesmen would be of no assistance to him, and he also said that he did not want to cause trouble between his own age-group (junior elders) and that of Teronge (senior elders). It so happened that Teronge's counsellor was the half-brother of Kamian's mother (i.e. he belonged to her natal inner lineage), and therefore Kamian could appeal to kinship sentiment in seeking that counsellor's agreement to a conclave. I do not think that this latter feature was crucial to the procedure chosen, for other Arusha commented on the rightness of the decision of Kamian and his counsellor in acting as they did. 'Kinsmen' (*ilderegeni*) should not quarrel before the parish assembly,' one spokesman in that parish told me, when we discussed this case.

It is this principle of jural procedure which inclines Arusha to state over-simply, that moots take disputes between kinsfolk, and parish assemblies take other disputes. This is not correct in one way which has previously been discussed (disputes between members of different parishes); and is not altogether true even of disputes between members of the same parish. Neither is it entirely true that kinsmen, even close agnates occasionally, never raise disputes in a parish assembly. For much the same reason which persuades a non-member of the parish to use the parish assembly, so a parish member may raise a dispute with a fellow-member who is a kinsman—i.e. to make the dispute public, to try to compel the defendant to make some answer, and to gauge public opinion. Both the plaintiff's agnates and his lineage counsellor tend to disapprove of the stratagem. But they can do little to prevent it, other than by making efforts to pursue the matter more strongly by another procedure; and that also may be the intention of the plaintiff.

Case 6: In a temporary pause during the proceedings of a parish assembly, a man suddenly stood up, without invitation or warning, and began to accuse his patrilineal cousin of encroaching on his land. The two men owned adjacent fields, and they had for about five years bickered desultorily over the alignment of their mutual boundary—which lay in uncultivated land in area about 75 yards long and 2 yards wide. The matter came to a head when the defendant hoed up and planted a portion of the unused land. The plaintiff obtained little sympathy from the only member of his inner lineage (a half brother) who lived near, because, his agnate said, he had plenty of land, whilst their cousin had little. Factually this was true. The parish assembly met next day in the normal course, and the plaintiff (as he explained to me) resolved to raise the matter there. This he did in what seemed a highly indignant, self-righteous manner.

Perhaps because he was himself a spokesman (junior elder), his unexpected outburst was not interrupted. When he had finished, he was censured directly by other spokesmen and indirectly (by their failure to support him) by his half-brother and a counsellor of a linked maximal lineage. It was quickly agreed that the plaintiff had acted with impropriety in raising the dispute there. 'Go to Namuka! (the plaintiff's lineage counsellor). Do not bring the shame of brothers (i.e. agnates) quarrelling here. We know nothing of all this,' said one spokesman. The plaintiff became incensed at the lack of sympathy, and in his emotion began to upbraid the men present. He was quickly cut short this time and, after a short discussion, it was agreed to levy a fine (*sogo*) of beer on him for his contumely. After this announcement, the plaintiff's half-brother stood up and said that they must both go to the counsellor and discuss the matter. This brought approving remarks from the assembly, together with an admonition to the defendant (who was not present) to be prepared to accept the counsellor's intervention, and to discuss the matter peacefully with his agnate, the plaintiff. One spokesman made a short speech about the modern difficulties of land shortage, and of the need to demarcate boundaries once and for all, making them clear with trees, sisal plants or other markers in order to avoid dispute. He expressed disapproval of the defendant's action in hoeing up the disputed strip of land before a settlement had been made; but he said that the plaintiff was not short of land, and had not acted as a 'brother' should. The plaintiff should, said the spokesman, have been ready to help his 'brother'. 'Brothers ought not to quarrel over two paces (the width of the strip of disputed land). That is bad. They must discuss the matter in peace.' No one else got up to speak when this spokesman sat down, and his speech therefore represented the general view of the meeting, i.e. of public opinion.

The plaintiff said later that by his action he had achieved the aim he desired. This was correct in that an internal moot was held soon afterwards at which he obtained the support of members of his inner lineage. He had, however, incurred a fine because of his intemperate behaviour; and it appeared that, contrary to his intention, he had alienated public opinion. The moot agreed that the defendant had acted imprudently in hoeing up the land, but in the end he was allowed to retain the disputed strip. Clearly the plaintiff's nearer agnates (brothers and nephews) felt less sympathy for him than they might, had he not brought the dispute to the parish assembly and there spoken so wildly. The half-brother, who had been present at the parish assembly, reported what had occurred, and his implied censure was not gainsaid by his listeners. Thus the plaintiff may well have chosen the wrong procedure, despite his assertion to the contrary, and at least he had pursued it clumsily.[1]

A plaintiff may choose to take his dispute to the parish assembly, rather than to a moot or a counsellors' conclave, if he considers that he is likely to obtain more support there, particularly if he is unsure of the degree of support he may obtain from his inner lineage. In the following case, the plaintiff chose the parish assembly rather than impose a strain on already brittle relations with his patrilateral cousins.

Case 7: Two brothers, the only surviving sons of their deceased father, were concerned to maintain and if possible strengthen their ties with their father's brother's sons and autonomous grandsons, because they feared to be left alone as a non-viable lineage. Their cousins were capable of acting independently of them, being numerous enough to make a viable group. One of the two brothers, Karime (see the genealogy), became the plaintiff in a dispute concerning the repayment of bridewealth. His second wife had deserted him for another man, and now requested a divorce. Karime agreed to the divorce, and demanded the return of a number of animals

---

[1] The conclusion of this case is referred to again at p. 278.

and a sum of money he claimed to have paid to her father, Teronge, as the early instalments of bridewealth. Teronge agreed to this. Two matters caused dispute:—the amount of bridewealth which had been paid, and the fee for the woman's virginity. This kind of case normally is dealt with by a moot or a counsellors' conclave, and a conclave had been held at which the only result was to isolate the points of disagreement. At the conclave, Karime was supported by his elder brother (C in the genealogy), and by one of their cousins (B) who lived in the adjacent parish. The other agnates lived farther away, and Karime had contented himself with informing them of the dispute and of the arrangements for the conclave: they did not attend it.

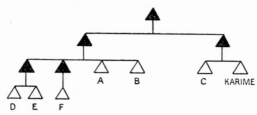

Following the failure of the conclave, Karime had to decide what procedure next to follow. A moot would compel him to request the participation of all his cousins, some of whom might refuse, thus perhaps breaking up the lineage. Even if they did attend, he was not, he said, sure of the degree of support they would give him. It so happened that Teronge, the father-in-law, lived in the same parish as Karime; and Teronge was a senior elder whilst Karime was a junior elder. Thus Karime could go before the parish assembly, and he could look for the support of his age-mates against Teronge and his age-mates. Furthermore, it was to Karime's advantage that at this time (1958) his age-mates, formally in the junior elder grade, were beginning effectively to act as senior elders; that is, they were engaged in replacing the next senior age-group, that of Teronge. Inter-group opposition was stimulated by inter-stream conflict. The formal senior murran were preparing for promotion to elderhood, supported by the formal senior elders, and the two murran age-groups were engaged in bickering and quarrelling, each looking to its patrons to support it. Karime was able therefore to make use of this sociological situation for his own purposes. His age-mates tended to regard the dispute as another example of the perfidy of the men of the other stream, and they desired to demonstrate their own strength by Karime's success. Karime was therefore able to avoid the problem of the danger to his own inner lineage, and also to recruit the stronger body of supporters in the circumstances. The counsellor of his own maximal lineage lived several miles away, and Karime was accustomed to consult a locally resident counsellor of his sub-clan. This counsellor was also an age-mate and a spokesman, and so his assistance could be expected in either a moot or the parish assembly.

It is, of course, impossible to say whether Karime's choice was the right one—the eventual compromise settlement was slightly in his favour with reference to the conflicting claims he and Teronge had made at the earlier conclave. In any event, it might seem that Karime was merely avoiding the issue concerning his fragile inner lineage. I suggested to him that members of his lineage, on whom he could not depend for support in an instance like this, were of little use to him. He would not accept this evaluation, for he said that he had been able to avoid an act which might have precipitated fission. His contention was that so long as the lineage remained intact, relations might improve. His cousins might need the assistance of him and his elder brother, and would thus incur an obligation to reciprocate.

This example is given because the issues which determined the plaintiff's choice of procedure were perfectly clear to him. Every fresh dispute is in some way unique according to the total context in which it occurs, and I can only attempt to illustrate the kind of choice-situations which may arise. Karime might have chosen differently had his father-in-law been dead, and had he, therefore, been disputing with his wife's brother. Had the two disputants lived in different parishes, the possibility of access to the parish assembly would have been denied. He might then have chosen to go to a magistrate's court, or to appeal to the chief; or he might have thought a moot to be preferable.

Disputes between members of a single parish who are not kinsfolk should not be dealt with by moot or conclave with counsellors, but by intra-parish procedures. This is the reverse of the preceding general principle, but it is more commonly ignored. Arusha say that neighbours (*elatia*), i.e. co-members of a parish, should settle their affairs, through the agency of fellow-neighbours in the parish assembly, or in a conclave with spokesmen and notables. This has the advantage not only that parish affairs do not go beyond the parish—as they must if a moot is convened—but more pertinently, that it is easier and generally quicker to use intra-parish procedures. Nowadays a parish assembly meets regularly at known times at a central spot, and formerly a man could readily approach a nearby spokesman and seek a meeting. Living fairly near together, unlike agnates or clansmen, members of the parish assembly can meet within a day or two without much difficulty.

Case 8: Kasenje accused Tomas of the same parish of stealing, killing and eating one of his goats. Kasenje claimed that a near neighbour had seen Tomas drive off the animal, which had strayed from Kasenje's paddock into the fields one evening. Kasenje went to Tomas' homestead and angrily denounced him, but Tomas and his wife denied the matter. Kasenje then went to a counsellor of his clan who lived in the parish—his own counsellor lived several miles away. The counsellor advised Kasenje to complain before the parish assembly in a few days time, and this he did. Kasenje and Tomas were related only within the common moiety; Kasenje was a junior elder, and Tomas a senior murran, and therefore Kasenje obtained the support and assistance of his age-mates in the parish assembly. This case was fairly straightforward because a second witness had seen Tomas with the goat, and an immediate neighbour of Tomas related that he had seen a new goat skin in the house of Tomas' wife for which no satisfactory explanation was given. Tomas' age-group spokesmen fairly readily acceded to his guilt, and concentrated on urging a light compensation.

As Kasenje explained later, there was no need to take the trouble in this case of going a distance to his own lineage counsellor, and of asking his agnates to meet at Tomas' homestead. That might have taken many days to arrange; whereas the parish assembly successfully settled the matter within a few days. One of the spokesmen of Kasenje's age-group told me that Kasenje had acted properly. 'We must watch these Ilmeshuki (the senior murran, the age-group of Tomas),' the spokesman said, 'They are bad. They thieve and lie and bring bad words upon us here.' He was thinking of the dispute in an age-group context, as a feature of the opposition between adjacent groups. It was to Kasenje's advantage to make use of this, for the support he obtained from his age-mates was clear and firm.

This was not a difficult dispute to settle. The facts were well substantiated: no real defence was put forward, nor were any mitigating features found acceptable. Tomas accepted the decision of the parish assembly, and the compensation was in fact handed over to Kasenje the following day in the presence of spokesmen of both men. There might have been a number of factors which could have produced a different procedure. Had Tomas' guilt not been well established; or had he made a good case for extenuating circumstances (for instance, that Kasenje owed him a goat and refused to give him it); or had the parish assembly been unable to reach a decision easily (perhaps by the senior elders supporting their wards and refusing to accept the conclusions of the junior elders);[1] or had Kasenje and Tomas belonged to the same age-group—in any of these circumstances, Kasenje might have considered it more advantageous to ignore the parish assembly and to attempt to convene a moot or patrilineal conclave. Alternatively, in the light of the difficulty of acceptable decision in the parish assembly, he might afterwards have sought another procedure thought more likely to satisfy his demands. A man cannot be compelled to accept the decision of a parish assembly, unless that decision is so unanimous that the spokesmen of his own age-group are affronted by his refusal to accept it, and they impose a fine on him and threaten further coercion. In that event, apart from the coercion, he is not likely to gain a more advantageous settlement by any other procedure. Thus in practice Tomas had no alternative other than to accede.

If the dispute between co-members of the parish is of a more important kind, then the plaintiff may well decide to ignore the parish assembly altogether, and instead seek the support of his agnates and others in a moot.

Case 9: Ndasiken alleged that Malenda, his immediate neighbour, was cultivating a field which had been originally loaned to Malenda's father by Ndasiken's father. Ndasiken now demanded that Malenda give back the field so that Ndasiken's newly married son could have the use of it. Malenda denied Ndasiken's allegation, saying that Ndasiken's father had merely allowed his own father to take an adjacent piece of untouched forest, which Malenda's father himself had cleared by his efforts as a pioneer. If Malenda's account was correct, then Ndasiken had no claim at all. This dispute arose in a mountain parish where the density of population was about 1000 people per square mile. Land was therefore acutely scarce, and the matter of a field of about one acre was of major importance to both parties.

As far as I could ascertain, neither Ndasiken nor Malenda considered an approach to their age-group notables, of senior elder and senior murran

---

[1] In the actual case the senior elders took little part. One of their notables accepted Tomas' guilt and tacitly agreed that there were no mitigating factors. Another briefly suggested a lighter compensation than the junior elders' spokesman demanded, but he did not attempt to pursue this.

status respectively. The conflicting contentions were not new; but it was not until the marriage of his son that a specific demand was made by Ndasiken. Both men visited their respective lineage counsellors, and an external moot was convened. The case was complicated by the lapse of time since the original occupation of the piece of land by Malenda's father some thirty five to forty years previously, and the deaths of the better witnesses; and also by personal animosity between the two disputants which induced each of them to raise a number of side-issues. The patri-lineal descent group of smallest size to which both belonged was a clan-section, but the first moot involved only a small portion of each man's potential supporters in their respective sub-clans. There were three moots and a number of conclaves before the dispute was settled.

At no stage was the parish assembly involved. An attempt by the senior elder spokesman of Ndasiken's age-group to convene a conclave with the spokesmen of Malenda's age-group came to nothing. Ndasiken said to me at that time: 'Will these men (of his own age-group) help me as my brothers will? No! Why should they? They are not of my maximal lineage. And Lokwaya (one of the spokesmen) is he big like Kirika (his own counsellor)? Lokwaya says that we must have peace here, that Malenda is our ward; but why should I care about that? I want my land. It is mine. Was it not (part of) my father's estate? My brothers know this, and Kirika knows it; and they will help me. Olmulaka knows too, and he will help.' Olmulaka was a counsellor in another lineage of the same sub-clan as Ndasiken, and he lived in a nearby parish. I was not able to record Malenda's thoughts or declared motives; but in any event he did not attempt to avoid the moot. Clearly Ndasiken believed that his strongest support lay with his agnates, most of whom lived elsewhere, and he was encouraged by the warm support he gained from Olmulaka, the other counsellor. He considered that he could not expect such unequivocal support from his age-mates or other parish members.

In cases of this kind, which Arusha consider to involve interests of great importance such that the support of agnates is mandatory, although the real intention of a plaintiff may be to convene a moot, he may nevertheless make use of the parish assembly. An example was given earlier (Case 6, p. 190), where in doing this the plaintiff's desire was to make his dispute a public matter, and to stimulate his agnates to action where they seemed to him to be apathetic. An alternative intention in going to the parish assembly may be to attempt to convince those men of his own *olwashe* segment, who live in his parish, that his case is good, so that their attendance at the subsequent moot is more readily gained. It may be useful also for a plaintiff to hear the kind of defence his opponent will bring to the moot, and what witnesses, by putting the onus of explanation on him in the parish assembly. Of course, a defendant should be aware of the plaintiff's stratagem, but he may be unable to avoid its results altogether if the spokesmen require him to answer the allegations. A refusal to answer may damage his own case; but he may perhaps be so moved by emotion (anger, fear of loss, etc.) that he commits himself more deeply than intended. A lineage counsellor may advise the plaintiff to go to the parish assembly for these reasons, in the hope of making his task of advocacy easier in the subsequent moot. But apart from such calculated design, a plaintiff may merely seek to make his case before anyone who will listen, and the parish assembly is an excellent and ready forum for that purpose. Despite the degree of skill with which many counsellors advise their agnates, it would be incorrect to suggest that men invariably assess available procedures cooly and objectively. Although seeking that which seems to afford most advantage, they often act unwisely, without forethought, and under the pressure of poorly controlled emotions.

A conclave is preferred to a moot, and sometimes to a parish assembly, when the dispute is of a minor kind, or where speedy settlement is important. Conclaves are also convened to deal with an impasse arising in a public assembly, or to execute the details of a settlement in an assembly, or to establish an injunction pending an assembly hearing. A conclave is essentially a small private meeting between the disputants and their associates—age-mates or nearer agnates. Here intimate discussion, bargaining and counter-bargaining can occur, without direct attention to other people, and without the need for some degree of rhetoric and self-justification. A conclave with a headman, or with one or two notables related to each disputant, is the easiest jural procedure to invoke, and therefore resort to it is common for petty affairs. Sometimes the initiative is taken by the headman or spokesmen themselves in an attempt to end the dispute speedily, before it can go further; although many spokesmen do not conceive it their responsibility to take such action without a request by an age-mate. Both kinds of conclave, and especially that with the parish headman, are sought also by complainants who seek the equivalent of an injunction against an offender—for example, the wife who fears further assault by her husband; the man who finds his cattle being harried by another man's herdsboys at the watering point; the cultivator who objects to a new path being made across his field of growing crops; the storekeeper who fears the brawling of murran in his store. Such complainants may be satisfied with a cessation of the annoyance, and they may be able to gain some small compensation for damages—a shilling or so, a gift of beer. If more serious injury is claimed, it is, of course, always possible to go later to the parish assembly or to seek a moot. Thus the assaulted wife, who initially desires free access to her house and fields (having fled to her father's homestead) may, through her father, later claim a heifer and beer as compensation before she will return; or she may perhaps sue for a divorce.

A conclave, under the aegis of their counsellors, is the common result of a less serious dispute between kin. Again, a major advantage is the relative ease and speed with which it can be arranged. Although a man may wish to obtain his rights against a kinsman, he does not necessarily desire to air their dispute in public. Not that the results of a conclave can be kept altogether secret, but rather a man feels more able to speak freely in private.

Case 10: A typical example of this was the dispute between Nkoyia and his estranged wife who had been living with her father, Sanya, for several months. The reasons for this situation are irrelevant here. Nkoyia wished to have his wife return, and had sent his full-brother earlier to invite her back. She and her father refused, and demanded first a suitable acknowledgement of his ill behaviour by Nkoyia, and a payment of compensation. A conclave was agreed to at Sanya's homestead. Nkoyia came accompanied by his two brothers, a paternal cousin, their lineage counsellor and two notables of the maximal lineage who lived near to him. Sanya had with him four members of his inner-lineage, his counsellor and a counsellor of a linked lineage who lived nearby. After a meeting of some two hours, an agreed settlement was achieved, including the promise of Sanya that his daughter would return to Nkoyia's homestead. This was a straightforward case, since Nkoyia did not attempt to deny his actions which had driven his wife away; and he badly wanted her back, as he admitted.

In other similar cases, agreement is not reached either because the husband refuses the minimum compensation demand by his father-in-law, or because the wife refuses to consider returning. A moot may then be convened by either the husband or the father in an attempt to settle the matter of compensation, or to establish divorce; although often the situation of stalemate is accepted for a period until either party resumes negotiations by, perhaps, another conclave.

Conclaves, and especially those between kin and involving counsellors, are almost inevitable concomitants of the hearing of a dispute in a public assembly. My notes indicate that most moots were preceded by a conclave which failed to produce agreement. Many public assemblies reach a deadlock over some aspect of the matter in discussion—the facts of the matter, the size of a compensation payment, the period within which payment should be made, associated arrangements, etc.—and the discussion is adjourned. There may be a positive agreement to meet privately, or the situation is left fluid. One party, probably at the advice of his counsellor, later convenes a conclave to discuss the particular points of dissension. This can result in a final settlement, or it may open the way to a resumed public discussion in a fresh moot or at the parish assembly.

Case 11: A man accused of adultery in the parish assembly, insistently denied his guilt and refused to discuss compensation. His age-group spokesmen were not prepared (so one said afterwards) to refuse to support the defendant against the plaintiff, a member of the next senior age-group. The discussion in the assembly became deflected from the particular issue to mutual recriminations between members of the two streams; and eventually, in some disorder, the assembly broke up. It was clear to the defendant's spokesman that he was in fact guilty of the charge, and the cuckolded husband persisted in declaring that he would raise the matter again. He talked of seeking to convene a moot. A private meeting of the defendant with some of his age-mates, including several notables, made it obvious that they believed him guilty and would only support him further if he confessed and allowed discussion of compensation to go forward. The defendant acceded to these pressures, and agreed to meet in conclave with the plaintiff. The conclave was held at the plaintiff's homestead. It comprised, on the plaintiff's side, two spokesmen, two notables and his elder full-brother;[1] and on the defendant's side, three spokesmen and three notables. The defendant's admission of guilt was declared, and the plaintiff agreed to resume the public discussion at the next meeting of the parish assembly, and to stop negotiations for a moot. Subsequently at the parish assembly, discussion concentrated entirely on the nature of the adultery compensation, without overt mention of the defendant's admission. His age-mates spoke strongly on his behalf and urged a small

[1] In fact the brother was of a senior age-group, so that this was not purely an age-group conclave. He attended primarily as a supporter of his younger brother but also because he might, as a patron, be able to influence the defendant who was a member of his wards' age-group.

compensation; and their patrons interceded to persuade the plaintiff and his age-mates to agree to reduce their demands.

After a generalised decision has been reached in a public assembly, it may be deliberately left to a subsequent conclave to determine the final details and to execute them; or this may be performed by the assembly leaders themselves. Much depends on the nature of the matter in dispute and the degree of genuine, mutual agreement between the two parties.

Cases 12 and 13: In two essentially similar disputes over tenancies, different procedures were followed. Both involved the claim of the legitimate owner to evict his tenant, who was his father's sister's son. At the moot in each case the eventual agreement was that the tenant should be allowed to remain on part of the land. In one case, however, there was little if any animosity between the land owner and his tenant; they were age-mates and friendly, and the land owner had frequently in the past received assistance of various kinds from his tenant. Primarily, the owner in this case wished to secure a public affirmation of his ultimate title to the land, and to acquire the actual use of an area sufficient to make a coffee plot. The tenant was persuaded to accede to this, on the understanding that he would remain secure on the rest of the land; and he also received permission to plant coffee there.[1] The land owner was not suffering a severe land shortage, and he valued the association with his kinsman-tenant. In this case the moot did not discuss in detail the precise alignment of the new boundary. This was established a day or two later by the two men, witnessed by some of the near agnates of each, the tenant's counsellor and two notables of the owner's maximal lineage.

In the second case there was a long history of quarrelling between the owner and tenant, which may have been causally connected with the acute shortage of land at the actual use of the owner, who therefore resented the privation whilst some of his land was occupied by his tenant. Whatever the cause of the ill-feeling, the owner declared his determination similarily to evict the tenant. After two successive moots, a magistrate's private hearing[2] and two or three conclaves, the owner was persuaded to leave the tenant on part of the land (as in the previous case). He remained resentful of the tenant, and declared the latter to be stealing his

---

[1] This is important, because if coffee is planted or other improvements made with the land owner's permission, the tenant cannot be evicted until full compensation is made for those items. In effect this commonly means that he can never be evicted, because the compensation is too high: in 1957-8 compensation was five shillings per coffee tree.

[2] The magistrate advised against the dispute coming to open court, and returned it to the lineage counsellors.

land. He quarrelled with the members of his inner lineage (brother, father's brother, three patrilateral cousins) as they gradually came to advocate the compromise solution to him. The lineage was a tight-knit group, unafraid of segmentation whilst the father's brother (still only middle aged and a strong personality) was alive, and it was the constraint of these men which finally caused the land owner to accept the solution. In view of the animosity between the disputants, and the strains already imposed on the inner lineage, it was suggested that the demarcation of the new boundary be carried out by the two men's counsellors and other notable agnates together. They, it was believed, could take the responsibility more easily. The second moot, therefore, adjourned to the land in question, established the new boundary, and directed murran to plant shoots of *dracaena* bush at points along it. Any future attempts to ignore these markers would, it was declared by the tenant's counsellor, be construed as an act of contempt against himself and the owner's counsellor. Thus no final conclave was necessary.

It may be considered necessary by a plaintiff and his associates to seek an immediate injunction on the defendant's actions until a full consideration of the dispute is possible in a parish assembly or a moot. Some examples of this, in connection with a headman's conclave, were given earlier (pages 16off.); a chief's or a magistrate's conclave may act similarly. It is not always the intention of the plaintiff to gain this end—he may well be seeking a complete settlement of the dispute—but he may accept the temporary decision until he can take the issue elsewhere. Although typical of conclaves of chief, magistrate, and headman, this kind of procedure is not limited to these alone, as the following example shows.

Case 14: Mbavaani, a tenant on Kito's land, was accused by Kito of planting coffee without permission. When Kito remonstrated personally with Mbavaani, the latter declared that he had been given permission earlier, and that now Kito was attempting to deny this in order to avoid compensation claims (i.e. for the coffee already planted) by Mbavaani in case of eviction. Mbavaani continued the next day to put in more coffee seedlings. Kito went to see his counsellor, Lorowan, who lived in the same parish, and with him he visited Mbavaani's patrilateral cousin and another of his agnates who lived near. These latter men, of the same clan-division as Kito, had sometimes sought Lorowan's assistance in the past, because their own counsellor lived several miles away. Lorowan's request for a conclave to discuss the coffee planting was agreed to, and it was held three days later at Kito's homestead. Kito was supported by his brother and a cousin, and by a neighbour (also the father-in-law of Kito's daughter), a spokesman of his age-group (senior elders) and the counsellor, Lorowan. Mbavaani was supported by his cousin and the other agnate, and by a notable and a spokesman of his age-group (senior murran) who were his near neighbours. This was a mixed conclave: the counsellor was the leading figure in it, but it was accepted that the neighbours could contribute.

The discussion first turned to the conflicting claims concerning the legitimacy of Mbavaani's acts in planting coffee. Neither party produced evidence which satisfied the other. Mbavaani said that Kito had given permission, but that the only witness, a suitor of Mbavaani's daughter was away travelling and could not be immediately contacted. Mbavaani's age-mate neighbours supported him, saying that Kito had not objected to the planting of some coffee the previous year—i.e. the inference was that since Kito had not objected then, although he must have known of it, he at least tacitly approved. Kito denied ever giving permission, and said he had not known of the previous year's planting. This could hardly have been true. Kito's affinal neighbour said that he had heard Kito refuse permission to Mbavaani to plant trees on the land; and that Kito had protested immediately when Mbavaani had begun planting coffee this year. He denied knowledge of happenings the previous year. Kito's brother and cousin completely supported Kito's assertions. Lorowan, the counsellor, said he knew nothing of all this, and demanded to know why he had not been informed if Kito had permitted planting the previous year (for his own benefit a man normally keeps his counsellor informed of such matters). Mbavaani's age-group spokesmen suggested that in any case Kito ought to permit the planting as an act of friendliness. Kito rejected this angrily, and the discussion began to become acrimonious on both sides. Lorowan, the counsellor, suggested suspending further consideration until Mbavaani's own counsellor could attend—it seemed to me and my Arusha assistants that Lorowan felt uncomfortable, in that he had some obligation to Mbavaani and his local agnates although his main obligations and his sympathy lay with Kito. He suggested a moot should be held as soon as Mbavaani's witness (the absent suitor) returned. The spokesman of Kito's age-group disagreed, and suggested that the dispute be taken to the parish assembly since it was confined to members of the parish. Either alternative was possible, but Kito did not commit himself to one or the other at that time. He reverted to the fresh plantings that Mbavaani had made two days earlier, and demanded that no more be made. All of Kito's supporters immediately backed him up, and both Lorowan and the spokesmen told Mbavaani that he was not to plant any more seedlings until the dispute was settled. The spokesmen appealed to the spokesmen and notables of Mbavaani's age-group to support this and they agreed after some hesitation. Thus if Mbavaani attempted any further planting he would make himself liable to contempt of both the spokesmen and the counsellor. On this apparently interim agreement, the conclave broke up.

The dispute was not renewed afterwards—at least not during the following year before I left the country. No further plantings were made by Mbavaani, and Kito appeared prepared to accept the *fait accompli*, either because it was really legitimate, or because he did not wish to continue in conflict with his tenant, and had achieved his limited intention. Other Arusha suggested that the dispute would be raised again later, because Kito's eldest son (not involved in the conclave) had said elsewhere that he would evict Mbavaani in order to get the land for his own use. Thus the conclave may have produced a settlement of the dispute, or it may have provided only an injunction against Mbavaani planting more coffee. I did not know Kito well enough to be able to discuss the matter adequately or to learn his intentions; but it is probable that he was of two minds in the matter. In any case, at least the limited results of the conclave were clear to all concerned.

Courts deal with cases which involve offences against ordinances, orders and laws issued by the central or local government: for example, failure to pay local taxes or to pay school fees, failure to obey a legitimate order of the chief or his representative, damage to government property, etc. These are not strictly disputes between Arusha, and most men feel no obligation to support the superimposed laws and authority. Such cases are, however, brought to court by the chief and his representative, or by a parish headman, as part of their official duties; and the defendant has no choice but to accede to the judicial procedure. Nevertheless even here there is sometimes an alternative procedure available, as illustrated in the following case.

Case 15: As usual each year an order from the chief was sent to parish headmen to arrange for the clearing and improving of all motor tracks in their parishes, after the rainy season was ended. This order was announced by the headmen at the next parish assembly meeting in X parish, and arrangements were made that all murran should attend on alternate days the next week, to give their free labour until the task was completed. On the first of these days about a fifth of the murran did not attend. As soon as the morning's work was completed, an emergency meeting of the parish assembly was held at which the names of absentees were announced by the headmen. Some absentees were found to be justifiably excused on the grounds of illness, employment obligations, or absence on a journey which began before the chief's order was announced. Several alleged cases of malingering were discussed in detail before an absentee was either excused or declared an offender. Finally the spokesmen of both age-groups of elders together enjoined the two murran age-groups separately to punish their defaulting age-mates. Absentees were ordered to pay a fine of one goat or sheep each on the next working day. It happened that one absentee junior murran appeared during the course of the assembly meeting, and protested against the compulsory road labour. He said he would pay no goat, nor would he appear for work on the next occasion. The spokesmen of his patrons' age-group (who were already effectively acting as senior elders) quickly silenced the young man, and ordered their wards to go immediately and seize one of his cows, and to slaughter and consume it on the spot. The offence of the murran was taken as an offence against both his own age-group and that of his patrons, and members of both participated in eating the meat shortly afterwards. As far as I know, no report of the offences of the absentees was made either to the chief or a magistrate; certainly there was no need for it. The turn-out on the next working day was practically a complete one.

This was an example of indigenous institutions working to meet modern needs; but whilst parish members may be stirred to corporate action in a matter which directly affects them in a very obvious way, they have never taken a similar action against the tax defaulter. In the latter case public opinion merely sympathises with the offender. Similarly, offences against, for example, local government by-laws dealing with butchers' shops and with trading centres never come to an indigenous public assembly.

Courts deal with disputes between men who are distantly linked patrilineally, and who live more than a few miles apart. Such men, having no access to a common parish assembly, often have great difficulty in convening a patrilineal moot or conclave. If they are linked at the level of the clan-section or more distantly, they and their respective supporters may be virtual strangers to one another. It is not always easy for the plaintiff to persuade his geographically near supporters to journey with him to the defendant's distant homestead. Unless the dispute is exceptionally critical—and it seldom is between men living far apart—a moot is scarcely considered. The plaintiff may choose to take one or two near agnates and a counsellor to a conclave at his opponent's home. Before there were courts, and indeed until the courts were accepted as juridical alternatives to indigenous procedures, this was the only practicable procedure. Nowadays many Arusha find it simpler to register a plaint at court. Then it becomes the magistrate's responsibility to summon the defendant and witnesses to appear on a specific day which is set for the hearing. There is the disadvantage of payment of a fee—but this is recoverable from the defendant if the plaintiff's case is upheld—and also the disadvantage of the intervention of an unknown quantity in the magistrate and his clerk. Most frequently in such cases, these disadvantages are outweighed. A plaintiff will not, of course, go to a court whose magistrate or clerk are known to be fairly nearly related to the defendant. Most Arusha would not expect an equitable hearing in these circumstances.

As in the great majority of disputes, the plaintiff attempts to make an assessment of the relative advantages. Evidence which he fears might be unacceptable by the more formal rules of court procedure will perhaps be accepted in a conclave. An agnate, willing to go to the distant conclave, may be considered so experienced and skilful a proponent of the case that his value exceeds that of a more or less neutral third party, the magistrate. Arusha feel that there is always an incalculable risk in going to court; they are unconvinced of the impartiality of court justice. Courts are on the whole only appealed to when indigenous procedures seem unhelpful, as will be described more fully later.

According to older informants, it was sometimes (I can give no quantitative assessment) impossible formerly to obtain a settlement in a dispute with a distant person. The chances of this were doubtless reduced by the fact that agnatic and wider patrilineal kin have always been scattered; and thus there are sometimes one or two living near the defendant who will then be able to assist the plaintiff readily. Formerly, before the colonisation of the peripheral lands, the Arusha settled area was small—roughly eight miles by five miles in extent—and therefore few disputants lived far apart; and those who did had little or no contact. Nowadays men meeting in the township or at the local government headquarters, for example, may come from homesteads twenty miles apart. Nevertheless, still the contacts between distant men are not of the kind to produce a serious dispute unless they are related in some way which makes them more susceptible to indigenous procedures.

The kinds of disputes involving men living far apart, which plaintiffs choose to take to a court are of the following type:—injuries from a fight occurring at a market or a beer club; the seduction of a girl by a murran; theft; damage to property; obusive behaviour, especially to a local notable. They may be slight matters, but even if they have some importance (e.g. quite serious injuries resulting from a fight) they are not, by Arusha standards, of the same degree of significance as matters concerning land, marriage, children, or kinship obligations.

Courts and conclaves with magistrates or chief deal with disputes which indigenous procedures have failed to settle: or in which the men of influence wish to avoid responsibility for advocating a solution. Just as courts provide a latter-day alternative to plaintiffs whose opponents are distant people, so they do also to plaintiffs who are unwilling to accept the only settlement to which the defendant can be persuaded to agree through indigenous procedures. Sometimes disputants and their respective supporters are unable to find common ground in which a mutual agreement is possible that can be practically executed. Formerly all they could do in this situation was to leave the dispute, the plaintiff seeking to resume it as circumstances seemed to warrant. In effect, by default the defendant was successful; he might not necessarily have obtained a clear settlement exonerating his past action, but at least he suffered no loss. The plaintiff might resort in these circumstances to supernatural means to support his claims, as described in Chapter Eleven. In such an impasse nowadays the plaintiff may go to court; here the court is treated by the Arusha as if it were almost an appeal body taking the case from a lower court. I have heard the Arusha version of the Swahili word for 'appeal' (*olrufaa*) explicitly used for such a court hearing. Although officially the 'court of first instance' (*baraza*) should hear every case *de novo*, merely taking into consideration any earlier, unofficial (i.e. unrecognised indigenous) hearings, nevertheless Arusha magistrates generally show deference to counsellors, spokesmen and notables who have previously been involved. One or two of them are asked to attend the court hearing as witnesses, not only of the facts, but also of previous deliberations. A magistrate may take the opportunity for private consultation with these notable men before he issues his judgement.

The impasse which had been reached must be broken if the plaintiff registers his plaint and persists in pursuing it. A magistrate must hear the case and give judgment without undue delay.[1] If the plaintiff feels confident of his justification for continuing the dispute, he expects to gain at least some satisfaction which the dead-locked moot or parish assembly could not give him. Genuine failure to reach any measure of agreement at all in public assembly and conclave may be the cause of the impasse; but it may also occur because the principal supporters of a disputant hesitate to take the course of persuading him to admit his wrong and to concede the other disputant's claim. Even where many of these supporters are convinced of the necessity of this, they hold back for fear of disloyalty, and for fear of introducing disunity into the group—the inner lineage, the maximal lineage, the age-group—which might result from the disputant's refusal of advice. A counsellor is compelled to consider the unity of the whole lineage in the future, as well as in the present dispute—similarly the spokesman in his age-group. It is a way out to suggest that the adamant disputant take his case to court. The responsibility for decision is thus removed from the notables and supporters, and put on the magistrate who cannot refuse it. He, however, not being a directly interested party, can more easily attempt to deal equitably with the matter. The avoidance of responsibility—a failure of responsibility and performance in a way—is not only the result of a weakness and tergiversation (thought that it may be), but it may be the considered plan of a counsellor or spokesman in his attempt to avoid the possible disunity which might occur by his definitive profession for one side or the other. Where a counsellor, for instance, does not have a loyalty and responsibility to both disputants (i.e. they are of different maximal lineages) he is less likely to recommend recourse to a court. Formerly, I was told, disputes might continue unresolved for many years, being raised again periodically and even into a succeeding generation. Resort to super-natural forces was more prevalent. A resolute counsellor sometimes refused to equivocate, and therefore advocated action against the interests of one disputant and in favour of another of the same lineage: such resolution was sometimes successful, but sometimes it caused the disadvantaged member to withdraw from the group altogether and, with his nearer agnates, to transfer to another clan and lineage. Such changes of allegiance were rare in the nineteen-

[1] Cf. p. 165.

fifties, but genealogical surveys indicated that they were more common in earlier times before the official courts were accepted. There is, then, good reason to conclude that counsellors are justified in recommending disputants to go to court in so far as lineage unity is not irreparably damaged.

In the following illustrative case it might be concluded, so bitter had relations become between patrilateral cousins, that the retention of lineage unity was an empty success; but, as Arusha pointed out, other members of the lineage remained friendly among themselves and with each disputant and his immediate supporters. There was still the possibility of restoring lineage unity, and in fact experience of similar instances indicates that the possibility was a justifiable one in the estimations of the people themselves.

This case is given in rather more detail than previous examples for two reasons. First, it is not possible to appreciate how the impasse was reached, and at what point the unsuccessful but persistent plaintiff resorted to local government procedures—the chief, and later a magistrate—unless some knowledge of the earlier stages of the dispute is available. Secondly, I wish to take the convenient opportunity to give an example of a total judicial process, involving a succession of different and also repeated procedural stages, and to demonstrate how Arusha handle them and with what intentions.

Case 16: This dispute occurred over the ownership of an area of about $3\frac{1}{4}$ acres of land. It occurred between patrilateral cousins, one of whom (the defendant) had sold nearly $2\frac{1}{2}$ acres of it, thus setting off the overt conflict which involved the whole maximal lineage. This lineage comprised the descendants of Miaron (cf. genealogy in Figure 10a). Miaron's oldest son, Siati, had been an early pioneer in one of the higher parishes, probably going there about the middle of last century. He had six sons who survived into adulthood.[1] In his late middle age, as was not unusual for Arusha, Siati used his daughters' suitors and husbands to assist him in pioneering a new farm about one-third of a mile higher up the mountain slopes. The old farm, part of which was scarcely cleared properly, was divided up amongst his three married sons, and it was a part of this land which was disputed now. Everyone agreed that slightly over a third of the farm was allocated to Meyang and his wife, and no dispute had ever arisen there. The plaintiff, Petro, claimed that part of the remainder was allocated to his father and mother by Siati, and part to Lomoni's father and mother. The defendant, Lomoni, denied this, and claimed that his father had been

[1] Historically, one 'son' was a Meru war-captive, and another a Dorobo immigrant.

FIGURE 10.

Case 16: (*a*) *The maximal lineage of Miaron—skeleton genealogy*;

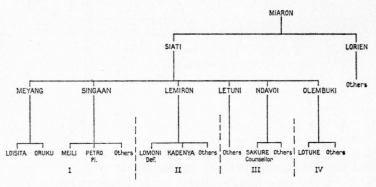

Pl. indicates the plaintiff, and Def. the defendant in Case 16
Broken lines separate the different inner lineages

(*b*) *Diagram of disputed land.*

Area allotted to MEYANG and his wife by SIATI	Area allotted to LEMIRON and · his wife by SIATI	Disputed area Claimed by sons of LEMIRON and by sons of SINGAAN

c. 170 yds.　　　c. 100 yds.　　c. 85 yds.

The shaded area was sold by the defendant, Lomoni, to the sitting tenant. It comprised about $2\frac{1}{2}$ acres.

allocated the whole of the remainder, after Meyang's share was taken out. (See Figure 10b). The difficulty chiefly arose because neither Petro and his brothers, nor Lomoni and his brothers, had ever in adulthood lived and cultivated there. They had all pioneered new farms elsewhere, and tenants had eventually occupied the fallow land. It was to one of these tenants that Lomoni had sold the portion of land which that man occupied. The proceeds of the sale (over 1200 shillings according to the Appeal Court records) were shared by Lomoni and his brothers, with Lomoni, the eldest, taking a larger share because he had negotiated the sale. The sale was witnessed on the sellers' side by Sakure the lineage counsellor (a junior elder), and by Mbaani, a counsellor in the same sub-clan, who lived about three miles away.

The sale was not a secret transaction such as to suggest any fear of its illegitimacy by Lomoni or the counsellors; but Petro did not learn of it until it had been concluded, for he was a bush school teacher and spent a lot of his time away. It is not clear whether his other brothers knew about it—the eldest lived no more than three-quarters of a mile away from the land in question—but there is no suggestion that they raised any objections to the sale at the time when it occurred. Once Petro learned of the sale, he went to see Sakure, the counsellor, to complain. Sakure was (according to his later statement) non-committal, and suggested a conclave between Lomoni and Petro and their brothers. This was held at Sakure's homestead, and by then Petro was supported by Meili, his elder brother. Lomoni lived in a higher parish a mile or so distant, and he brought with him two of his brothers. The conclave was a failure, and was reported to have ended in angry words.

Petro next asked for a moot, and despite the counsellor's reluctance and an initial peremptory refusal by Lomoni, he succeeded in convening one through the support of his patrilateral cousins of inner lineages 1 and 4. The moot was no more successful than the conclave. Lomoni refused to admit any claim of Petro; but that claim was now supported by Loisita and Lotuke, two retired elders, who asserted that they were better acquainted with the facts than any one else alive. The only non-member of the maximal lineage to attend was Mbaani, the counsellor of the linked lineage, who had witnessed the sale. He recalled that many years ago—fifteen or more—he had been invited by the then counsellor of this lineage to assist in the division of the disputed land, on some of which tenants were already in occupation at that time. No division was made, however, for the attempt fell through. Each party claimed this evidence to support him: Petro, because it proved that his father had also claimed the land; and Lomoni, because it proved that no division was made favouring Petro's father. Lomoni claimed that Petro's father had allowed the matter to drop because his claim was unfounded. Mbaani said that he

did not know why the matter was not followed up, but this seems unlikely for he must surely have known what happened, even though it was
not in his own lineage. I assume that he did not wish to commit himself
to either side. The moot ended in a continued deadlock; or perhaps it is
more correct to say that relations between the two parties deteriorated
further, without any sign of a resolution of the dispute.

Petro appeared to be highly indignant about the failure of the moot,
for he made several declarations in public—at a beer club, at a pre-marital
feast and on other occasions—of his alleged rights and the iniquity of
Lomoni. There may well have been some deliberate intent in his actions;
but in any case they stimulated the notables of his age-group (junior
elders) to intervene. Although Lomoni now lived in an adjacent parish,
he had been initiated in the same parish as Petro—where Petro still lived
and where the disputed land lay. Lomoni was also a junior elder and he had
continued to acknowledge the influence of the age-group's notables. At a
beer-drink, when the parish's junior elders were gathered round their
allocation of the beer, one of the spokesmen raised the issue of this dispute between their age-mates. Lomoni was present—but not Petro—and
he explained his case to the group and appealed for their support. There
was a division of opinion: some age-mates were reluctant to discuss the
matter at all, saying that they should not interfere with a quarrel between
near agnates which had already brought ill-feeling to their lineage. They
feared the conflict would invade their age-group, they explained. The
majority of the age-mates desired to attempt reconciliation: feeling generally supported Lomoni and there was talk of persuading Petro to accept
the *fait accompli*, and to reconcile himself with his cousin. A spokesman
suggested a conclave, and Lomoni agreed on the understanding that some
of the notables would approach Petro.

A spokesman and an *engaminin* visited Petro, but he refused the proposal. He was not, he said, prepared to concede to Lomoni, who was his
enemy. Petro's gambit (if that is what it had been) had failed because on
the whole his age-mates were against him, and now he feared the pressures they would bring against him in the interests of reconciliation and
of Lomoni. He told the two notables that he would raise his plaint in the
parish assembly; this they did not want, but they had to accept his intention. Petro said that there were a number of retired elders and some
senior elders who had known well the fathers of himself and Lomoni,
and who would remember the truth of the original allocation of land.
At the parish assembly a few days later, discussion was as fruitless as
before, and no new evidence appeared. One or two older men denied
knowledge of the matter, saying that 'it was all long ago and the affair of
another lineage, not our lineage'—the implication being that they did not
wish to become involved in the matter, as several informants pointed out

to me. Petro and Loisita attempted to press the issue, but had no success at all. Lomoni, however, declared that he was angry at Petro's continued claims and the calumny to which he was subject. He said that he had been ready for the conciliatory intervention of his age group, and then began an acrimonious speech against Petro and his supporters. He was cut short by one of his spokesmen. Both men were censured by notables of their own and of the senior elders' age-group, all of whom expressed the need for peace between agnates and criticised the extension of the conflict into the age-group.

About this time some directly associated disputes began to be raised. Loisita sought to evict a tenant from his land—this tenant being the husband of Lomoni's sister, to whom he had allocated an area at the request of Lomoni's father many years ago. Meanwhile Oruku (Loisita's half brother), who had alleged that Petro had been responsible for his conviction for his possession of illegal spirits, began a field boundary dispute with Lotuke, one of Petro's supporters. Kadenya, the younger brother of Lomoni, then claimed the repayment of a calf he had loaned to Lotuke's son. In suggesting that these disputes were directly connected with the first one, I am giving the views of a number of unrelated informants in the parish, as well as my own and those of Petro himself. The inference was that the maximal lineage was under strain, and that therefore difficulties, hitherto accommodated tolerantly, were being raised as disputes between the two parties to the main conflict.

A second moot was convened to which the lineage counsellor invited two other counsellors of the sub-clan who had not been involved until that time. Not only the dispute between Petro and Lomoni, but the other three also were discussed. Loisita agreed to drop the demand for eviction, and Lotuke's son promised to repay a calf to Kadenya. In the dispute between Petro and Lomoni no further progress was made.

After this moot, the lineage counsellor attempted to arrange another conclave. He let it be known that he was suggesting that Lomoni should allow Petro to share the proceeds of the sale. Lomoni was reported to have decisively rejected the proposition, and to have begun negotiations with the sitting tenant to sell the rest of the disputed land. On hearing of this Petro went to the chief to seek his intervention. The chief summoned both men and a few supporters to his office for a private hearing. He ended the hearing, at which no new feature emerged, by saying that men ought not to sell their land, and that Lomoni had been wrong to do this. He recommended that the two cousins meet with their counsellor and other notables to settle the issue. It appears that the chief was intending to represent public opinion against land sales in general; but Petro returned home claiming that the chief had supported him and called for an annulment of the sale.

The Locus of Dispute Procedure

Informants told me that in the old days there might have been fighting and other physical violence at this point because a complete deadlock had occurred. Petro's only recourse would have been to self-help—a disapproved and illegitimate course, but one not unknown. The lineage counsellor said that he still feared violence might occur. He was on the side of Lomoni, but had never expressed strong support. He was a younger man than almost all of his generation and had had unexpected single responsibility thrust on him when his senior counsellor (a senior elder) died a short time before the dispute broke out. He was not an altogether happy choice as counsellor, and in this affair had been ineffective. Unrelated informants suggested to me that a more forceful counsellor would have assembled such a weight of opinion against Petro, that he would have been compelled to accede and allow his claims to die. Whatever the truth of this, certainly the counsellor was in a dilemma. He wished to preserve the unity of the whole lineage, and Petro had threatened at the second moot that he would secede from the lineage if his claim was not met. The way out chosen by the counsellor was to recommend to Petro that he take his plaint to court. A private meeting of Petro and his open supporters, together with the counsellor, brought agreement on this suggestion; and Petro went next day to register the case.

The magistrate first held a private hearing in his office with the hope (he told me) that he might achieve a reconciliation and a dropping of Petro's claims. He failed, and had to agree to a formal court hearing. I was unable to attend the hearing, but both the official record and the comments of the magistrate and others indicate that nothing new arose. The magistrate found against Petro. Still Petro would not let the matter rest. He appealed to the Arusha Appeal Court, but the judgement of the lower court was upheld, and Petro had to pay the full fees. He threatened to continue and appeal to the District Commissioner, but in the end he did not.

Thus the case finally concluded. The total process had involved a counsellor's conclave, an internal moot, a parish assembly, a second and expanded moot, an abortive attempt at another conclave, a chief's conclave, a magistrate's conclave, a court and appeal court. Associated with these nine stages were a number of separate private meetings of either party to the dispute to discuss arrangements. Although this case covered rather more stages than the average, it was not by any means unusual. A similar kind of land dispute between cousins, in another parish and lineage in 1956-7, covered eleven stages:—two counsellor's conclaves, three successively expanding moots, a headman's conclave (following fighting between the disputants' murran sons), a magistrate's conclave, a court, Arusha Appeal Court, District Appeal Court, and a petition to the Provincial Commissioner for permission to appeal to the High Court. This last was refused. In this case, unlike that of Petro and Lomoni, the conclusion of successive stages did not all favour one disputant.

I have no adequate records of the progress of enough disputes to make a statistical analysis of the number of stages with accuracy and sample significance. Whilst regretting this, I believe it to be more important to demonstrate the kinds of principles involved.

The general principles of procedural action, which have been stated and illustrated above, have been abstracted from both the statements of Arusha and actual practice in specific cases. In order to avoid the impression that they are rigid rules, I have indicated how these principles may for some good reason be ignored in particular instances. The nature of dispute processes among the Arusha can only be understood if it is appreciated that, in some circumstances, virtually any kind of dispute can be dealt with by any one of the public assemblies or conclaves, in an attempt either to obtain a settlement outright, or to further the treatment of the matter towards that end. The members of an assembly or conclave may refuse to attempt to settle a dispute, but seldom do they refuse to suggest a more appropriate procedure; and almost always they make some contribution by the expression of accepted norms and the quoting of relevant precedent.

With the exception of a court, which, at least officially, should make a single hearing and issue a judgement forthwith, no assembly or conclave is necessarily expected to reach a settlement at a first attempt. Even the judgement of a court can be delayed temporarily on the pretext, or perhaps genuine justification, of awaiting further evidence. In that case, the dispute may, on the initiative of the magistrate or notable men of influence, be actively referred to another body in the meantime. Should an out-of-court settlement be reached the magistrate can merely reiterate this in his formal judgement.

As I have noted already, the plaintiff seeks to invoke the particular procedure which seems to him likely to be most advantageous to him in the circumstances. Together with his closest associates—primarily the members of his inner lineage—he attempts to assess where he may expect the most support and the least opposition. The degree of urgency he feels is important, as also his immediate intention in acting as plaintiff: for example, the desire for an immediate, outright settlement together with the appropriate compensation, restoration of rights, etc.; the desire to obtain an affirmation of his legitimate rights but without subsequent action (e.g. the plaintiff's ownership of land occupied by a tenant, but without seeking to evict the tenant); the desire to initiate the dispute preparatory to a definitive hearing of it by another procedure; the desire to test public opinion, to convince wavering supporters of the strength of the plaintiff's claims, and to force the defendant to declare himself. A plaintiff is, of course, subject to the opinions of his associates, and his chosen course of action can be affected by their attitude and by his assessment of their probable support. A disputant, with the solid support of his inner lineage behind him, is in a different position from one who considers that some of his close agnates may give only lukewarm support, or who believes that he may seriously weaken what are in other ways valuable intra-lineage relations. It has been emphasised that both the kind of dispute and the nature of the structural relationship between the disputants are of fundamental importance in the decision; to which may be added the geographical relationship between them both in terms of parish membership and the sheer distance between their homesteads. The determination of choice is dependent on the attitude of the defendant and his willingness to accede to that choice. The defendant's hand can sometimes be forced—he must answer a court order, and can rarely refuse the summons of a spokesman of his age-group on pain of a fine or other punishment; and a refusal to state his argument may jeopardise his case, if it is believed he is merely taking refuge in silence in order to hide his weakness. In a total process relating to a single dispute, the initiative may change hands as the defendant at one stage attempts to make the choice of the succeeding stage. Finally, any disputant is subject to the advice and suggestions made to him by the acknowledged specialists in that field—the lineage counsellor especially, but also age-group spokesmen and notable men in the three sub-systems. Especially when a counsellor does not have allegiance to both disputants (i.e. where they are of different maximal lineages), a disputant is markedly susceptible to his advocacy.

CHAPTER TEN

PROCEDURES AND SETTLEMENTS

I N the last chapter attention was concentrated on the variety of the socially defined places where a plaintiff may raise a dispute and seek to have it discussed; and on the kinds of consideration that determine a choice of locus which, in given circumstances, is thought to be most advantageous. In the course of that account, and elsewhere previously in this book, some mention was made both of the procedural rules which are observed in the process of dispute settlement, and of the factors which lead to a successful conclusion of it. These factors were deliberately under-emphasised in order to concentrate attention elsewhere first; but in the present chapter they become the focus of attention. Here I am concerned in an attempt to show how a satisfactory resolution of a dispute is achieved in this society where, indigenously, there are no judges or other specialist authorities capable of both making and enforcing decisions and settlements.

For the moment I am neglecting the modern local courts and the chief who are empowered with the coercive force of the Central Government, a foreign authority. As should be obvious, from my inclusion of the local government as a third salient sub-system of Arusha society in the context of social control, this temporary neglect does not imply that the courts and the chief can be ignored. They were, by the nineteen-fifties, deeply involved both as a means of dispute settlement and as influences on indigenous ideas and practices.

The Illegitimacy of Self-Help and Recourse to Violence

Unlike the case in a number of so-called, non-centralised societies, there is amongst the Arusha little legitimate opportunity for aggrieved individuals and their supporters to resort to physical violence as self-help. Although, as in any society, individuals may attempt to gain their end by violence or recourse to other unilateral action, this is genuinely disapproved by the Arusha. The person who attempts this by premeditation jeopardises his own case, and lays himself open to counter-claims by his victims. Arusha concede that a man may be so emotionally upset by an injury against him that, in the heat of the moment, he may take direct action against the offender rather than initiate a dispute through the media of discussion. Even this is scarcely approved; it may be understandable and excusable, but a person is inevitably censured by both his own and his victim's notables.

For example, to refer publicly to the non-Arusha origins (paternal or maternal) of a man is considered a gross insult; and younger men commonly attack an offender with fists and stick on such provocation. The proper action is to bring a suit against the offender in the parish assembly, and a calf can be claimed in compensation. Older men do this; but younger men who begin to fight on this account are usually censured by their own age-group spokesman (and probably those of their patrons' group also) later in the parish assembly, and the claim for compensation is most likely to be reduced to a goat, or even only some beer.

Adults often deal peremptorily with children, not of their own family, who offend them. The owner of a field may cuff the herdsboy who allows animals to stray on his land; or he, often she, will beat a child caught stealing ripe maize cobs from a standing crop. This may produce ill-will between the chastiser and the child's parents, but the latter are not likely to gain sympathy from anyone unless the act is viewed as an example of the perfidy of the chastiser, where some deeper dispute already exists. Were the child injured as a result of the beating, then his father might successfully claim compensation in the normal way.

These concern childish misdemeanours of little importance. More important offences are not so tolerantly regarded. The young man who presses his attentions on a girl betrothed to another man, must expect a rough handling from her brothers and her legitimate suitor; but his behaviour is only accepted as partial extenuation if he is injured and claims compensation. The correct procedure is to claim a goat or beer from the young man, and in cases of actual seduction this would be done. In one case that I recorded, a claim for compensation by the father of the seduced girl failed in a parish assembly, and the father was reproved by his age-mates because he had allowed, encouraged in fact, his sons to beat the seducer. The seducer was rebuked also by his patron's age-group. Afterwards, in conversation with men of the father's age-group, I was told that although they warmly sympathised with him, and were themselves much concerned to guard their daughters, nevertheless it would be wrong to countenance self-help of this kind. 'Everyone will fight. There will be no peace in the country. Those murran, they like to fight; but we are elders—are we not big (senior)? We do not want fights; they are bad. We must watch those murran and stop fighting. If there is a dispute we discuss it, but we do not fight.''

Case 17: One evening a junior elder, Johanes, the owner of a store, discovered a man stealing some bottles of beer, cigarettes and other items. This man had them under his cloth, and was leaving the store when the bottles clinked and gave him away. Johanes had been suffering a good deal of pilfering from his store, but had not before caught a culprit. In anger, he attacked the thief with a stick, inflicting bruises and cuts before the man ran off. The thief lived close to the store, and that night Johanes went and stood outside the former's homestead and threatened further violence. He yelled to the thief to come out and fight, and in general raised a furore. A neighbouring senior elder, Olvuko, a distant agnate of the thief, came out from his homestead a short way off and remonstrated with Johanes. I gathered that Olvuko admitted his young agnate's offence (my command of the Arusha language was then poor and was defeated in the noisy argument), but upbraided Johanes for his earlier resort to violence and for his present trouble-making. Johanes, now thoroughly enraged, insulted Olvuko—he ignored the admission of the theft and accused Olvuko of encouraging it. Eventually Johanes went home and quiet fell.

Four days later Olvuko stood up in the parish assembly, and said he wanted to raise the matter of Johanes' behaviour. The night incident had become common knowledge by then and, without waiting for discussion, notables of the age-groups of both Olvuko and Johanes admonished Johanes for his insults to Olvuko. Olvuko stood up again and stated that, although he fully approved of the censure, his real intention was to inform the parish assembly of Johanes' assault on Olvuko's young agnate at the time when the theft was discovered, and his threats of violence later that same night. Johanes then described the theft, gave a detailed account of the items, and claimed a goat as compensation. This was not an unusual claim, and others like it have been accepted by parish assemblies to my knowledge.

Spokesmen of the thief's age-group (senior murran) ignored the claim, however, and concentrated on the assault and threats. They said—without specifying—that Johanes should pay compensation. A senior elder notable supported them, saying: 'Who is Johanes? Is he the chief or the Government? Why does he beat another man? Is he a big man? Did he have permission? No! He is only an *engobiro* (i.e. 'not even a notable', is the inference). He just did it and he asked no one. That is wrong.'

Johanes interrupted here: 'What of my beer? My cigarettes? He is a thief, that man. Thieves must pay. Is that not our custom? Who says he is not a thief? Men are liars if they say.' He turned to the previous speaker —'Why do you not admit the theft and give me the goat? I want a goat.' He continued in like manner for a little longer, until he was eventually pulled down by an age-mate.

The general discussion resumed, concentrating on the assault and neglecting the theft. Finally a senior murran spokesman demanded a payment of beer to his age-group, as compensation for the assault. Senior elders accepted this, and one of their spokesmen directly addressed a spokesman of Johanes' age-group. Johanes' age-mates had kept quiet—a sure sign that they did not support him on this issue. The spokesman thus addressed muttered that he thought Johannes should give the beer to the senior murran. There was a pause but no one of Johanes' age-group attempted to reject the admission. Johanes himself sat still, murmuring inaudibly. The fine of beer was thus the decision of the parish assembly, and it was handed over two days later.

Johanes, by his silence, accepted the decision in the parish assembly; but he then tried to return the assembly's attention to the theft. He was told that that was 'another matter', that he should pay his fine first, and then return to a later meeting of the parish assembly. The senior spokesman of the junior elders began calling to the plaintiff in the next case with some ostentation and fuss; and Johanes must have realised his unpopularity even with his own age-mates. In fact, he never did resume his claim again.

Although this is not an altogether clear-cut case, it shows the general disapproval of self-help. None of these kinds of cases are straightforward: they are complicated by the initial offence which inspired the self-help. In this case, Johanes clearly forfeited sympathy by his insults to the senior elder, Olvuko; and as a storekeeper he was not popular in the parish in any case. These considerations were not unimportant; nevertheless, they were not the crucial ones in the opinions of men in the parish with whom I discussed the whole affair. The parish assembly was not intending to condone theft, or that particular thief; neither was it consciously demonstrating a degree of general antipathy towards Johanes. It was the repugnance for Johanes' resort to a self-help which created the mood of the assembly. Virtually the same collection of men, some months previously, had decided in favour of compensation for a butcher in another part of the parish, from whose shop some youths had stolen meat. In that instance the butcher had not attempted self-help, but had reported the theft to the parish headman and to a spokesman of his own age-group.

Arusha consider the use of violence to be tantamount to an admission of weakness in a man's argument. They also perceive it as an affront to what I may call the integrity and dignity of an individual. It is an Arusha tenet that men are susceptible to persuasion and to peaceful coercion through recognised procedures: but physical coercion against his person, or his property, or his family, is thought to be an inequitable and immoral act. Even when they themselves are not the victims, Arusha appear to be outraged by a man's resort to violence.

Informants often said that violence and self-help were more common in pre-European times: they are doubtless correct in this because the fear of the established government is a modern deterrent against such unlawful action. Nevertheless, Arusha also say that then, as now, self-help was disapproved and was never the norm. One may suggest, in addition, that it was an inefficient technique, it was hampered by the general dispersion of kinsfolk, and it was intolerable among a highly concentrated population such as probably always has existed in this small country since the tribe began. In any case, the idea of the arrogation of force by a self-claimed, injured party is directly contrary to the idea of *discussion* and of negotiation, in which, *inter alia*, the possible rights of the alleged offender can be considered.

It would be false to give an impression of the Arusha as a pacific people of passive and submissive nature. Any outsider who has experience of them would refute that characterisation. The ideal of murranhood contains the notion of young men trained, encouraged and prepared for violence—the spear and sword are a symbol of this —who are quick to take offence, and to act in order to prove and protect honour. This appears to be strongly imitative of the Masai warriorhood norms, but Arusha murran (in the actual rather than the formal role) tend to be divorced from responsibility in family, lineage and parish, and insulated from most dispute processes. Older men often express some fear of the arrogance and violence of murran, who are felt to be scarcely under control. They fear also the psychological pattern which persists into the elderhood. One elder put it to me: 'Those murran, they are bad. They always want to fight and use their sticks. We must stop them, but a father cannot tie (i.e. control) his sons. And we, elders, do not we remember when we were murran—strong and big? Ee, we sometimes want to be murran and fight those who hurt us, who speak bad words. Do you not remember a little while ago, I was angry with Sakure over my field? I wanted to fight then, but I did not because am I not an elder?' (He had been in dispute with Sakure over a field boundary and the use of irrigation water). It is, I suggest, in an attempt to control the inclination to violence of murran, which potentially runs on into elderhood, that murran themselves are largely denied responsibility in society, and that so much counter-emphasis is given to the peaceful solution of disputes through discussion.

As a social anthropologist, I tentatively make this analysis in the face of the apparent contradiction: between, on the one hand, the stress laid on peaceful discussion and on the paramount need for mutually acceptable agreement between disputants, and on the other, the tendency to violence which, in truth, quite often is not suppressed. Whether or not it is an adequate analysis, I wish to make clear that self-help is not only disapproved, but that it is not in Arusha society an effective technique for dealing with disputes. The proper, but also the efficient, method is to raise the dispute in an assembly or conclave, there to depend on one's associates to support one. This raises the further hypothesis that individual self-help is a negation of group cooperation in discussion. Were Arusha lineages and clanship categories more highly integrated, or the parish more unified, this might be a possible explanation; but, as I have shown, Arusha social groups are not notable for their degree of cohesion and cooperation, for these people set so great a premium on the individual autonomy of the family head.

In a rather different way, self-help is the norm. Each man is himself responsible for pursuing any matter in which he feels injured. Counsellors, spokesmen and others will help, but most usually they do not feel an obligation to watch an associate's interests—that is the concern of the individual himself. He must secure the assistance in various ways of those who are linked with him in order to press his claims. As the dispute is dealt with, each disputant continues to look for the support of his own associates; he cannot act without them and there is no established third party to whom he and they can appeal for wider impartial intervention. Third parties are neutral, deliberately and carefully so usually. They do, of course, represent public opinion and socially approved norms, and in this sense may sometimes have a degree of influence. This is not clearly seen by Arusha, who are inclined to resent outside interference, although they are sometimes ready to make use of the moral force of public opinion which appears to support their own case.

Procedures in Assembly and Conclave

With the partial exception of modern, regularly-meeting parish assemblies, an Arusha plaintiff must seek to convene an assembly or conclave through the agency of a recognised man of influence. It would be considered insulting to a counsellor or a spokesman if a man attempted to ignore him, and convened a meeting with the other disputant and his associates. It is most improbable that the defendant would be amenable, and much less the defendant's supporting notables. In any event, the plantiff needs to secure the sympathy, advice and support of his own notables—those men of experience and ability who can do so much for his case. A plaintiff will have made a direct and personal approach to the defendant to attempt to obtain, for example, the return of an unpaid debt or the compensation for an injury; but if the defendant demurs, then the plaintiff is compelled to utilise the accepted channels of deliberation. He therefore must persuade either counsellor or spokesman to make arrangements for a meeting. The plaintiff himself, and his nearest associates, are active in informing others of the time and place of the meeting, and inviting and encouraging others to attend; but a defendant's notables are only susceptible to the approaches of the plaintiff's notables.

Now that parish assemblies all convene regularly (usually on a certain day each week, or twice a month) a plaintiff does not any longer need to seek to convene a meeting especially to consider his plaint. Nevertheless, spokesmen are generally unwilling to have a dispute raised in the parish assembly if they have not been informed beforehand and their general agreement obtained. A parish member, who attempts to raise an unannounced matter, is nearly always told by his spokesman and by the junior elder spokesman to return and present his case at the next meeting when people are prepared for it. Spokesmen themselves say that they should be informed, and regard it as disastrous if they are not. 'How can we discuss a matter (in dispute) if we know nothing of it?' one spokesman said. They are not acting as arbitrators or judges who ideally come to hear a dispute with open minds, uninfluenced by prior knowledge; they act openly as partisans of their own age-mate and should therefore fully understand the case before engaging in dispute with the other party. The defendant's spokesmen and age-mates desire to discuss the matter with the defendant, before they too engage with the other party. Indeed, it is considered to be unfair to a defendant if he does not have the opportunity to prepare his argument with his associates.

A parish assembly meets in some convenient open space roughly central for the population—a piece of waste ground, a grazing paddock, often nowadays the open space near a court or school. A moot assembles in the grazing paddock of the defendant—the paddock adjoins but is not part of the homestead. Conclaves, involving smaller numbers of men and with a notion of privacy, meet inside the homestead of the defendant—often in his own house. Both a moot and a conclave may be held at the homestead of the defendant's counsellor, or that of another notable, if the defendant dislikes the idea of receiving his opponents at his own homestead.

At a moot, the two parties tend to sit on the grass in separate clusters, with an open space in between where the main speakers stand to express their views. The pattern of a parish assembly is less clear because each meeting generally considers more than one dispute, and the alignment of parties is therefore less straightforward. In general men of one age-group sit together: the junior elders tend to cluster towards the centre, senior murran sit beyond them, and senior elders sit near the outer edge. Minors such as junior murran, women and children, who are involved in any of the matters to be discussed, sit slightly apart. The whole meeting may, however, be irregularly seated in large part—especially when it has been in session for a time—because men take the opportunity to greet and gossip with each other irrespective of age-group. Affines may discuss arrangements of mutual concern; agnates from different parts of the parish exchange news; men talk with the parish headman. There is a good deal of movement about the meeting. Not all those present are necessarily interested in every matter discussed, and men often withdraw to one side and go to sleep or engage in a piece of handicraft.

Both moot and parish assembly begin with a short appeal by a senior notable to Engai (the high-god) for his blessing on the people assembled. Then, in a parish assembly, the presiding junior elder spokesman calls on the first plaintiff to state his case; in a moot the plaintiff himself opens the proceedings. Occasionally a notable of the plaintiff speaks first, but this occurs only when the plaintiff himself feels unable to speak adequately—and few Arusha are so inhibited. Where an assembly is renewing its consideration of the dispute, then almost anyone may start the discussion.

Each main speaker in an assembly stands up when he speaks, and usually he comes to the middle, open space purposely left. Most men carry a stick or staff, with which they gesticulate and emphasise points by banging on the ground. Some excited speakers pace to and fro, and become something of a danger to their hearers' feet and faces as they stamp and wave. Whilst he is standing, no one else should attempt to stand and speak, for the first man 'holds the floor', as we should put it, and only yields on his own admission. To stand and speak signifies that a man has a major contribution to make. Brief comments and questions are called out by seated listeners, and generally the speaker replies to them as he goes along; though he may pointedly ignore what he wishes to indicate are irrelevances. Plaintiff and disputant in particular should be permitted to speak for as long as they wish to put forward their argument and counter-argument. An over-loquacious man, or one who seems to wander from the point—or who perhaps succeeds in making no point—is liable to vocal criticism from the assembly, but chiefly from the notables who may begin to recommend the man to finish and sit down. This must be done with caution, for men may complain of having been unable to say what they wanted because of duress; and they tend to become less amenable to ultimate agreement. On the other hand, the speaker's own notables do not want their party's case spoiled by poor or inopportune speaking, whilst the other party's notables may attempt to make capital by deriding a poor performance. Notables, part of whose responsibilities is eloquence, sometimes are impatient of less skilled efforts and attempt to take over from a poor speaker. Few Arusha are, in my experience, inarticulate in meetings; but many ramble and repeat themselves and become involved in contradictions.

The plaintiff is usually followed immediately by the defendant; but the plaintiff or one of his notables may sometimes ask for a witness to speak first to support the argument. Witnesses normally follow the defendant. They are not necessarily formally called, nor in any particular order, and altercation may arise when two of them seek to gain attention at the same time. It is the responsibility of a disputant and his notables to ensure that witnesses do come forward. Facts are frequently in dispute, and an attempt is made to settle those before going on to discussion of the implications and to the effort to reach an agreement.

Case 18: Maru, the plaintiff, began the proceedings in a moot by a short speech in which he claimed repossession of a small plot (about three-quarters of an acre) which, he said, he had pledged to Namoiya for two cattle a year ago. 'Everyone knows my field,' he concluded, 'and everyone knows I have the two cattle here to give back to Namoiya. There is no dispute. Take your cattle and give me the field.'

Namoiya admitted that he had given two cattle, but declared that they were the purchase price of the field, which was not therefore recoverable by Maru. Before he could continue and whilst still standing, Maru's counsellor called out from where he was seated: 'Who knows about these cattle? I was not there (i.e. when the transaction occurred). I know nothing of this. Who says the field was sold absolutely? I do not know. Now then, say, those men who know.'

The counsellor was, of course, well aware of the situation. He wished to indicate, first, that the transaction was not a sale because he had not witnessed it (this is not necessarily correct); and, secondly, that there were witnesses who could affirm the agreement had been only a pledge. Maru's brother and son-in-law were already primed to give evidence, and the counsellor wished to have them speak early.

Namoiya was still standing, but his own counsellor called out that he knew the facts for he had been present at the original transaction, together with Namoiya's patrilateral cousin. Namoiya's counsellor now stood up and Namoiya himself sat down, saying as he walked back to his place, that he had not finished speaking. His counsellor affirmed Namoiya's right to speak again, but said, 'First let us tell the truth. I know this. We cannot discuss this if the truth is hidden.' And he then described the transaction to show that it had been a sale. As he spoke, Maru's brother grew restive, calling out, 'No, that is not so,' and similar remarks. Namoiya's counsellor ignored these and continued to speak, going beyond his alleged factual evidence to review the relations between Maru and Namoiya.

As the counsellor finished, he called on Namoiya's cousin to speak, but before that man could rise Maru's brother strode to the central open space and gave his version of the transaction. He spoke in an angry tone, and accused Namoiya of wanting to steal 'our field, our father's estate (*engithaka e wawa*).' He pulled Maru's son-in-law to his feet, and commanded him to speak. The son-in-law briefly supported the case for the pledge, saying he heard nothing of a sale, and sat down.

Maru and Namoiya stood up simultaneously to speak, and Namoiya's counsellor called out, 'Namoiya speaks. He has not spoken yet. Maru has given his words; let him wait.' Maru bent down to consult with his own counsellor, and then sat down again. Namoiya walked to the centre of the assembly and began speaking again. He ignored the conflicting evidence, and continued his earlier counter-argument. It was only afterwards that his cousin's evidence was given, when the counsellors of both Namoiya and Maru had spoken.

When the two disputants have both spoken, discussion becomes general. Often their respective notables stand out to reinforce the arguments, and they call for others to speak who have evidence or relevant opinion. Anyone present may participate, although the notables and the principal disputants themselves take the chief part. Each party tends to be less tolerant of loquaciousness by secondary speakers, so that their contributions are generally briefer. As the proceedings continue, men of one party whisper together in consulation, and comments are exchanged between the two parties. The phase of suggestion and counter-suggestion may begin immediately after the disputants' opening speeches, or there may first ensue a phase in which it is attempted to reach concensus on the facts. The two phases coalesce; but gradually the exchange of views rather than of facts comes to predominate. When it becomes clear that one side is making a definite proposal, the other side answers or makes its own proposal. A definite proposal must be answered by at least positive dissent—perhaps merely called out by a disputant or his notable without rising to his feet, or perhaps in a full speech. Silence by a party, following the other party's suggestion, indicates approval and agreement; there is no need for explicit verbal assent. 'Men discuss until they agree. They stop and that is the end; there is no more to say.' This was one counsellor's description of the process. Agreement of some kind, at least ideally, is always reached. It may be positive agreement such that both parties concur in a settlement of the dispute; or it may be negative agreement such that they 'agree to disagree', as we might put it.

Thus *Case 18* ended in this fashion: Maru's counsellor, in his third speech to the moot, ended by proposing that Namoiya should cultivate the plot this year (the hoeing season was just beginning) and then should surrender the land and receive back his two cattle. 'No!' called out Namoiya immediately. Maru's cousin stood up where he was and suggested, in a brief speech, that Maru should pay one ox now and the other cow when the land was surrendered in a few months time. A distant agnate of Namoiya called out, 'Let him give the two cattle now.' But, before Maru's party could take this as a proposal, Namoiya himself denied his acceptance of his agnate's suggestion.

There was a pause, and men moved restlessly as an impasse seemed to have been reached. Then Namoiya's counsellor stood up and suggested that Namoiya pay Maru another cow in order to confirm the sale. (Part of Maru's argument had been that two cattle were too low a price for a proper sale) Maru's brother and one or two other of his supporters rejected this proposal with derisive shouts.

Namoiya's counsellor again stood up, and spoke at length of the need for peace and for an end to the dispute. 'End it by giving us our field,' called Maru's brother. The counsellor pointed out the continued disagreement and the ill-effects it had on relations between the disputants. 'Let us go to the chief,' said Maru's brother; 'The court at—,' said another supporter of Maru.

'No, we do not want the Government in this,' said Namoiya's counsellor, 'Let us divide the field, part to Maru and part staying with Namoiya.'

'No, it is all our field,' called Maru, and his brother agreed with him.

'You can keep the cattle, and have part of the field,' suggested Namoiya's counsellor.

There were mixed cries of 'Yes' and 'No' from Maru's party, but Maru himself cut across these to reject the proposal. Namoiya's counsellor got up and walked away to the edge of the paddock; and his action precipitated a wholesale movement of the men in the moot. Namoiya walked off with his cousin and some other men. Maru's counsellor went into the homestead, and quickly the paddock emptied.

There was no attempt to sum up the discussions and to identify the points of agreement and disagreement. There had, in fact, been (as far as I understand it) concurrence that the original transaction had not been specified as either sale or pledge, and also on the kind and quality of the two cattle previously transferred. There was common concensus that the dispute should be settled amicably because, as both counsellors pointed out, the disputants' fathers, though not kin, had been age-mates, friends and neighbours, who had pioneered the land many years ago. Maru, however, persisted in claiming the whole piece of land; whilst Namoiya had shifted to a claim of only part of it, but without any return of cattle. Neither was any mention made of the next step in the dispute. The references to the chief and the local court were not intended seriously, I think; at any event, a counsellors' conclave and then a second moot followed in the next month. At the second moot a settlement was reached by which Namoiya returned rather less than half the plot and gave Maru an additional sheep.

In attempting to indicate the course of an assembly, I have wished to avoid giving an over formal account of procedure. The informality of an assembly is marked. After witnessing a large number of them, I have been impressed by the fact that almost any rule I might try to enunciate can be sometimes ignored for quite good reason. Nevertheless, such pragmatic flexibility does not invalidate an orderly attempt at reaching a settlement. There are general principles of proper behaviour underlying all these assemblies.

Firstly, the spacial segregation of disputants' parties is, in intent, clear. In a moot this is never wholly neglected, although the two parties may mingle irregularly at the edges. In a parish assembly not all the age-mates of a disputant sit with him, but he is invariably surrounded by a cluster of his own closer associates who most actively support him.

Secondly, the right of each disputant to have the full opportunity to argue his case is always respected. He cannot be compelled to give way to another speaker—though he may agree by persuasion—and considerable tolerance is given even to the disputant who clearly tries the patience of both his opponent and his own party.

Thirdly, despite the broad toleration of interjected question and comment from seated members, a second speaker is not allowed to rise and begin talking whilst a previous speaker is still standing. Not infrequently angry disputants, both standing, begin a heated exchange of opinion and accusation; but quickly this is stopped by their notables, with the right of speaking or giving way going to the first man who was standing.

Finally most spokesmen, counsellors, and other notables take their responsibilities seriously and, though avowedly on opposite sides in the dispute, they are generally ready to ally together against unruly behaviour, lengthy irrelevancies, and persistent contumely. It is only by their willingness together to maintain orderly discussion that an assembly can carry on its work adequately. Disputants, with some of their supporters, may quarrel heatedly, but the prominent notables, though not forsaking their allegiance, are generally able to rise above this. I have seen assemblies break up in disorder, but only a few times. On the other hand, I have heard men blaming their counsellors or spokesmen for allowing this kind of debacle to occur, even when they themselves had been among the obstreperous participants.

The emphasis Arusha give to the practical value of discussion —to which reference was made earlier in this chapter—informs the whole proceedings of an assembly and the conduct of men engaged there. An argument by one party is not necessarily expected by Arusha to be wholly truthful and straightforward. They realistically expect attempt at deceit, and are wary of false diversions; and the discovery of these fetches little resentment. Even notables, no less than others, are prepared to lie and deceive on behalf of their own side, and a later admission of the truth is not thought to bring discredit. For example, it eventually was conceded, in the last case cited (No. 18), that no specific agreement had been made concerning the transaction over the plot of land and the two cattle; yet Namoiya's counsellor had declared at length, at the outset of the moot, that he himself had been witness to a sale. This was perhaps not quite the direct falsehood which it might appear, because the transaction, one between friendly neighbours, had foolishly been vague, and a matter of some genuine misunderstanding. Two cattle were more than the usual size of pledge for so small a piece of land, and Namoiya may have expected to retain the plot indefinitely. There had been no time limit established. Nevertheless, a properly conducted sale should be concluded by a ritual transference of the soil from seller to buyer, involving the participation of the wives of each; and there was no evidence that it had been performed in this particular instance. Namoiya and his counsellor could not therefore claim that a completed sale had been made. The counsellor later admitted this, in his negotiations to allow Namoiya to retain a part of the land.

Procedure in a conclave is much more flexible. The men sit close together on stools or on the ground, and do not rise to speak. Discussion is almost conversational, with the give and take and the interruptions which that implies. Occasionally, one or other of the men may speak at length, and in an oratorical tone; but Arusha associate oratory with a standing posture. It is incorrect to stand in a conclave, for intimate argument and reasoning are the aim of the meeting. There is usually the overt cordiality induced by drinking beer or honey-wine together, and the exchange of tobacco, in an atmosphere of privacy. The meeting may be opened by anyone—not necessarily the plaintiff, who at this stage may sometimes not be specifically identified. The general aim is, however, the same as in an assembly: i.e. the exchange of proposals which may produce an agreement. Witnesses as such seldom participate in a conclave; those who are not close associates of either disputant are not invited to the meeting, for they are 'outsiders'. Their evidence can be accepted at second hand from one or more of those actually present. A disputant may, however, decline to accept such evidence, and this can be cause for convening a moot to continue the deliberations.

Case 19: Olepua was claiming bridewealth from his son-in-law, Kidemi, who was procrastinating in his payments. At the conclave, Kidemi eventually agreed to give a cow, claiming that there would then remain but one ox to pay. Olepua disagreed, claiming that another cow was also outstanding. Kidemi then refused to pay anything until his liabilities were determined. Olepua's counsellor recounted the instalments previously paid, together with the approximate dates and the witnesses. Kidemi admitted the counsellor's tally, but again insisted that he had also transferred one other cow in addition. 'Meibuto knows all about that. We talked of this cow yesterday.' Meibuto was Kidemi's neighbour and his agemate.

Olepua continued to deny this payment of a cow. Kidemi's brother intervened to say that Meibuto had told him about it several years ago—the brother lived in a distant parish and did not claim first-hand witness. Olepua then admitted that Kidemi had given his (i.e. Olepua's) married son a cow; he asserted that this was not part of the bridewealth proper, but only an affinal gift. Kidemi and others declared that there were other witnesses than Meibuto, and the implication was that they could be called if necessary to support Kidemi's assertions.

As a listener, I had no means of knowing the truth of all this. The cow could have been either a gift or a bridewealth instalment. Whether the men mentioned were genuine witnesses, and whether they would confirm Kidemi's claim, was impossible for me to say.

Olepua's counsellor suggested to Olepua himself—but not in a private aside, therefore Kidemi and all the others heard—that Olepua should agree to the cow counting as a bridewealth instalment. Olepua was genuinely puzzled, for (as he told me afterwards) he had not treated the cow given to his son as a part of the bridewealth. He still expressed doubt about the matter, but his counsellor and another agnate were prepared to accept the indirect evidence. Eventually Olepua conceded, after obtaining a promise from Kidemi that bridewealth animals would not be given to anyone but himself in the future.

After the conclave, Olepua's counsellor told me that had it been a moot he, at any rate, would have demanded to hear the witnesses. He would also have held up proceedings until Olepua's son could attend and speak. He had not known of the transfer of the cow when the conclave began, but he was prepared to accept that it had been handed over, and that Kidemi had intended it as bridewealth and not as a gift or a loan. The counsellor was pleased with the successful outcome of the conclave, for it ended in considerable amity. He felt that, even had he been wrong about the real nature of the cow (and it was unlikely that he had been), it was preferable to restore good relations between Olepua and his son-in-law. But he added that he would not have dared to have acted as he did, in partly failing to support Olepua, had the meeting been a moot. A readiness to accept Kidemi's assertions, against Olepua's honest understanding of the situation, might have made him liable to public criticism in a moot for failure adequately to support his own party.

I can only give the gist of the counsellor's words, for we were walking home in the rain and I was unable to record them properly. Clearly, however, the counsellor considered that he could act in a conclave more freely than he could in a moot. It may be added, that inside Olepua's house, with beer to drink and a warm fire, in contrast to the wet and cold outside, the atmosphere was one which, to me, seemed conducive to amiability, readiness to make concession, and a desire for a concord. There was a good deal of casual chatter and joking, an air of conviviality, such as could not occur in a public assembly. Not all conclaves are so cordial as this, even between disputants who are not keenly opposed to one another; but most conclaves demonstrate a degree of intimacy which no moot ever gains.

Mutually Acceptable Settlements

Although it might have been preferable to describe the procedures of an assembly and conclave much earlier, it was thought necessary to leave it until this part of the present chapter, because a consideration of procedures must simultaneously involve an examination of the process of reaching a settlement. They are all parts of a single continuum, and inevitably a good deal has been said already on the latter aspect. It is now time to examine precisely what, in Arusha conceptions, a settlement is and how they attempt to maintain it. The question is: in the absence of centralised authority and roles of specialist coercion to which both disputants are subject, and failing self-help, how are disputes brought to a successful resolution? Further, how is the settlement enforced thereafter?

The Arusha answer to questions of this kind is typified by the reply of one counsellor: 'We discuss and discuss the matter (in dispute) and then we agree. When we agree, that is the end. What else is there to do?" In other words, as we have seen in the foregoing cases, the process of establishing a settlement consists of discussion and negotiation, argument and counter-argument, offer and counter-offer, between the disputants' parties in an endeavour to find an area of mutual agreement. Being mutually accepted, the question of enforcement does not arise, or at least only marginally. This is perhaps an ideal statement, but essentially it represents the aim of the Arusha. For them, the emphasis lies in the joint participation of the conflicting parties so that the settlement of their dispute emerges from within—that is, from them together. It is not an imposed decision, a judgement, on the disputants from outside, however rational and equitable that decision might be. As I have insisted previously, outsiders are not concerned, and they remain unconcerned. Except in a moot where the disputants belong to different moieties—and in practice then also—there are always some people who are not even indirectly involved in a dispute. They have no right to participate, let alone act as arbitrators; neither do they wish to do so. Arusha fail to see any positive value in the unbiased judge. He is not, in their opinion, to be trusted for he is not really neutral, but aligned to one party or the other; or if he is neutral, he has no real interest in either party.[1]

To make a perhaps over-sharp antithesis, Arusha dispute settle-

[1] These are common criticisms of a chief.

ment is the result of a positive consent rather than passive acquiescence. This does not mean, of course, that a party to the settlement altogether and necessarily likes the agreement he makes and consents to; but Arusha point out that he does make it and he does recognise —otherwise he would refuse it—that it is, in the total circumstances, the most advantageous he can obtain, even though less than he might desire. Because it is an agreement, and not an imposition, he confidently believes that it will be carried out by the other party. Moreover, what will be carried out is better than the promise of something more but which is not fulfilled at all. For example, in a claim for compensation, a plaintiff eventually accepted two sheep instead of the heifer he had initially demanded. He said afterwards: 'To talk of a heifer is all right, but I have the sheep, and peace also.'[1] That is, he not only gained some compensation but, in addition, peace, *eseliani*—or, one might say, concord, and an end of conflict. Here, this plaintiff was not thinking of the restoration of former good relations between himself and his opponent—they were distantly related patrilineally and of different parishes, and their association was slight. He was thinking of a reasonably satisfactory conclusion of an unpleasant situation.

It is possible, as Arusha are aware, that a disputant may agree to a solution of a dispute and admit to certain liabilities to be met by him (e.g. to pay compensation), but that afterwards he does nothing to put the settlement into effect. To avoid this, wherever possible the settlement is acted upon immediately—generally at the assembly itself, or at a conclave arranged then and held soon after. Almost all disputes are ended in this way in fact, because if immediate action is not possible, there will have to be a further assembly or conclave later to reiterate the agreement—and probably involving a renewal of the earlier pressures and negotiations—and to supervise its practical implementation.[2]

The Arusha are pragmatists, taking the view that tends to see each new dispute as in some ways unique, and therefore to be uniquely dealt with and settled. General patterns are perceivable: Arusha recognise them, and they acknowledge that they influence the process towards another settlement. Pragmatism is certainly limited and

---

[1] Cf. 'a bird in the hand is worth two in the bush.'
[2] This matter and the general problem of enforcement of settlements is discussed in more detail later: see p. 275ff.

directed by accepted norms, most of which are held to be traditionally established by those who are now ancestors. But those norms are guides, and not absolute principles to be rigidly followed. They provide the initial basis for discussion, and they are manipulated during negotiations as seems most advantageous to each disputant. Flexibility is a major virtue; readiness to accept the apparently inevitable is another. This does not mean that Arusha are easily prepared to accept a dilution of their claimed 'rights' against another person, or that they do not argue hotly on their own behalf, railing against the alleged iniquities of that person. In addition, men are aware that too great a willingness, and especially too early a one, to make concession may well be taken as a sign of weakness, and further concessions may then be demanded. Just as the choice of the locus, in which a dispute is raised, is often shrewdly made, so the nature and the timing of proposals, terms and concessions may be carefully calculated. By miscalculation, ignorance and foolishness, and the pressure of emotions, a disputant and his associates may choose unwisely. He may not even appreciate the choices open to him. There is no need to picture Arusha as paragons of calculating wiliness. Proposals and counterproposals are often crudely made, for these people are not sophisticated lawyers.

The Arusha have become fairly well acquainted with the principles and processes of a court, and they will compare their own indigenous processes with those. They are often scornful of the magistrate's judgement—even when they may admit its justice—for they say that a disputant is compelled to accede to the decision; and they criticise the Central Government which enforces such compulsion. They contrast the active role of discussion and agreement by indigenous means, with what they consider to be the passive role of submission to a magistrate. They concede that a disputant is often compelled to accept an indigenously produced agreement, no less than he is compelled to obey the court judgement; they nevertheless distinguish between the two, because the agreement is the result of negotiation, bargaining even, rather freely carried on, which permits him to seek the greatest advantage. Something of this has already been illustrated. It has been shown how a plaintiff may try to go to a fresh locus of discussion, rather than accept the only settlement he can obtain where he is, and in the hope that elsewhere he may be able to obtain better terms.

A useful analogy may be drawn in the contrast between the fixing of the price of a commodity by a government agency according to established and known rules (perhaps by objective reference to an economic index, etc.), and its determination by direct bargaining between a buyer and seller. The buyer would doubtless like a lower price than any he can obtain or expect to obtain, and he may be induced by various means to pay a higher price than he initially offers. Both buyer and seller usually have some general agreement as to the range of prices within which agreement will be struck. This is influenced both by similar sales in the past, and by what they can economically afford. The farmer and a buyer begin their approach and conduct their bargaining in one range for eggs, and in another for beef-cattle. Generally speaking, and with the bargain struck, there is no problem of enforcing it: The commodity is handed over and the price paid. Neither man is compelled by the other to accept a price offer, although the circumstances surrounding each man may give him more or less leeway, from a sale at almost any price, to refusal of anything much different from the initial offer.

An Arusha disputant is subject to a variety of influences in the course of seeking a settlement. It is not intended to suggest that he is really a free agent, and often he is closely limited in his action. Dispute settlement must be a *social* process in which a man is dependent on his associates, whose assistance he requires once a purely personal approach to the other disputant fails. If, for example, a man acknowledges a debt and agrees to repay it, or obtains permission to delay payment, then no dispute arises, for creditor and debtor have established a private agreement with which both are satisfied. If the debtor refuses payment when it is demanded—or even denies the debt—then the creditor's recourse is to established social procedures involving dependence on his defined associates. Such dependence means not only assistance—which is what Arusha themselves always stress—but the liability of constraint. A man's associates, though certainly supporting him, may come to urge, even insist, on a settlement which he would prefer to reject. Not only can he not afford to do without their support in the particular instance, but he is bound up with them in the permanent relationships involved in the groups and categories to which he and they both belong. Thus in a moot, a disputant's closest associates are not only his advisors, advocates and supporters, but they are his near agnates, members of his inner lineage. He is dependent on them, therefore, for much more than assistance in a single dispute, and there are limits on the degree to which he can ignore them. Because of the importance of the lineage, he cannot reject his agnate's opinions to the point of threatening the more general efficacy of group unity, neither can he reject their right to urge a course of action which he dislikes. They can appeal to the value and to the norms of group unity; they may deny him, or at least threaten to deny, the full privileges of membership either directly or by understood implication. Much the same can be said for a disputant's close associates in a parish assembly. It is possible to say that a disputant is judged privately by his associates, who will thus determine their support of him before a wider group. However close they are to him, and however strongly they may support him, they, or some of them, are likely to take a more dispassionate view than he himself does.

Case 20: Thus in a dispute concerning a fight between a junior and a senior murran, in which the junior murran claimed compensation for injuries, the defendant and his age-group at first denied his responsibility, saying that the junior murran had caused the fight and had also injured the defendant. They might have succeeded in their rejection of the plaintiff's claim—certainly they hoped they might. But as the parish assembly discussion proceeded, it began to emerge from the evidence of witnesses and the remarks of both senior and junior elders, that the defendant's adamant stand was unlikely to be acceptable. He himself angrily refused to retract. After a little while, one of the defendant's spokesmen took the defendant and his age-mates aside for a private consultation. On their return to the main body of the parish assembly, the spokesman announced that he thought the defendant to have been in the wrong during the fight. The defendant grumbled disagreement, and the spokesman turned to him and repeated his declaration. 'Let us discuss the goat (the claimed compensation payment),' he announced to the assembly. This they did and the defendant's age-mates were successful in urging that only a payment of beer be made—that is, they continued to support him, and were able to obtain a reduced compensation payment.

A man cannot avoid the pressures of his age-group unless he moves to live in another parish, where he will be a stranger and forfeit the advantages of support he can legitimately ask of his age-mates in his own parish. In practice it is nowadays extremely difficult to move, for land is not easily available elsewhere and a man cannot well afford to quit his own land where he is. He might attempt to reject his age-mates' advice and opinion, but life would then be intolerable in his parish for they could refuse support in other ways, or at least give it weakly and tardily. A man would be almost an 'outlaw' in his own parish, not only in respect of support in future disputes but also in other kinds of assistance, in leisure activities, in participation in the parish affairs, etc. He would tend to become socially isolated.

A man may attempt to break away from part of his inner lineage, if he can retain the support of his own brothers. Lineage fission is the possible result. If his brothers refuse to support him against other agnates in the lineage, or if they are insufficient in number to establish a viable group, the dissident is relatively powerless. He may threaten refusal of his support in the future, but the rest of his agnates can continue to support each other and can afford to ignore him. Again he is in danger of social isolation.

There is another factor involved in these situations. In the case briefly described above (No. 20) the defendant's age-mates were prepared to support their fellow in one respect—i.e. a reduction of compensation payment—if he would submit to their advice in the other respect—an admission of guilt. Negotiation is not limited only to the opposing party, but is involved also within one's own party. There is also both a moral and psychological aspect. That defendant's age-mates urged him to act as he should as an individual, and also as he should as a member of his age-group. Secondly, he was, by implication, promised approval and esteem for proper behaviour towards his age-mates, i.e. he could earn group approval. It must be noted that he did not earn group disapproval because of his fight with and injury of the plaintiff, a member of a different age-group— indeed, that was rather approved of; but he was in danger of disapproval because of his continued rejection of his age-mates' opinion. By assenting to their opinion, he shifted directly from a possible disapproval to a positive approval; that is, not merely from disapproval to a neutral midway position offering no reward but only escape from penalty.

Arusha pressures appear most usually to be framed both as appeals to right behaviour, and as promises of positive approval by a man's associates. In the case cited, the claim to compensation by the plaintiff could no longer practicably be rejected, as the defendant's age-mates perceived; but they were ready to praise him for his submission and his acknowledgement of guilt which allowed the dispute settlement to continue, and to be concluded successfully. In the following discussions over the size of compensation, several of his age-mates spoke of his right behaviour in his admission. Others afterwards assisted him in carrying the compensation beer to the plaintiff's homestead, and in other general ways they demonstrated group loyalty to him.

More distantly linked supporters of a disputant—his patrons' age-group in the parish, or distant agnates and members of patrilineal categories in moot and counsellors' conclave—are more easily able to take a dispassionate attitude. By 'dispassionate' I do not mean a neutral or unbiased attitude, for they continue to be his supporters and continue therefore to seek his best interests. They are, however, often able to perceive those more clearly than he, or even his close associates, can. They are likely to be more influenced by accepted behavioural norms, and by the inchoate but not unimportant public opinion. Recognised notables—spokesmen, counsellors and others—have an accepted responsibility towards members of their groups to make objective assessments of possible action, and to urge their opinion on disputants. They are the skilled and experienced negotiators, and disputants are inclined to acknowledge this and therefore to accept their advice. Herein lies the diplomatic skill with which notables must work; they negotiate not only with the other disputant and his party, but also within their own party. They must not appear to give way too readily to the other party, as if deserting their own side; yet they need to investigate the reactions of the other party to possible proposals. Thus proposals made early in dispute discussions are usually tentative, often indirectly phrased, allowing room for withdrawal or manoeuvre. Many counsellors in particular are adoit in this procedure.

More distantly related supporters join with a disputant's closer associates in their expression of approval in his accedence to their advice and constraint. Euphoria is often evident among all the participants in a dispute settlement if it is genuinely successful and in effect mutually acceptable. But among a disputant's own supporters there is commonly a most marked sense of euphoria centred on the disputant himself. I was repeatedly impressed by this, as are the Arusha themselves.

On one occasion, following the successful conclusion of a moot, I went to the defendant's homestead an hour or so later. There he was sitting with his inner lineage, his counsellor and a number of other supporters. They were drinking beer together, and showed every sign of amity and even cheerfulness.

'Come and drink beer,' someone called to my assistant and me. 'We are truly one inner lineage (*engang*) here,' said the defendant's cousin, and there were murmurs of agreement. 'Ee-ee, and one maximal lineage (*engaji*) also,' added the counsellor. As we sat drinking, there was a good deal of talk about the lineages, including reminiscences of pleasant times in the past. Later, conversation turned to arrangements for the men to attend a post-natal meat feast at the homestead of one of their number.

In the preceding moot, concerning a dispute in respect of a divorce, the defendant had lost the custody of a small child which he had been claiming, and he had eventually accepted a smaller bridewealth repayment than he had at first demanded. The dispute had been lengthy: the defendant had been adamant through the course of an earlier conclave. His counsellor, with a distant senior agnate and a neighbouring notable of the same sub-clan, had together been the prime movers in urging the defendant to drop his claim to the child. They obtained the agreement of the father-in-law to repay immediately the instalments of bridewealth previously transferred; but then differences arose concerning the number of animals and other wealth involved. After listening to the conflicting evidence about largely unwitnessed transactions over a period of some two years, other Arusha and I were unable to assess the truth of the matter. Eventually the defendant agreed to accept a repayment of one cow and three sheep, instead of the two cows, three sheep and some money which he had lengthily claimed. Objectively, therefore, the defendant had lost a good deal—especially the legal custody of the child.

Nevertheless, in his loss I discovered him not in bad humour, and showing no sign of resentment against his associates who had come to urge him to accept the final settlement. They made it abundantly clear to him that they were not deserting him, and that they much approved of his willingness to accept less than his demands and to end the dispute. His nearer agnates, members of his inner lineage, had not played much part in the final negotiations—apparently content to allow more distant associates to take the responsibility of urging the compromise. But they did not dissent, and they took pains to show the defendant their loyalty to him, and their approval of his final action. The defendant did genuinely accept the settlement; he appeared to hold no animus against his supporters, and became the centre of reiterated lineage unity. This conclusion was borne out in the following months, as the defendant continued amicably to cooperate with his agnates in the normal way, and to seek the advice of his counsellor.

Dispute Settlement Between 'Related' Persons

The nature of negotiations between the two disputants, each with his supporters, is appreciably affected by the nature of relations existing between them, both in general terms and in respect of the particular matter in dispute. Where the disputants have been in some mutually valuable relationship, then they both have an interest in maintaining or restoring it. Each is inclined to accept compromise for the sake of the relationship; but at the same time each has a measure of bargaining power to use against the other. This is immediately obvious in the case of directly contractual situations, such as a dispute between father-in-law and son-in-law over bride-wealth (Case 21 below), or between a stock-owner and herdsman (Case 22). But a similar situation arises when a dispute lies between members of the same nuclear group—an inner lineage or age-group. Here again, each disputant has something to offer to induce the other to modify his claims or to acquiesce to a settlement. Thus in the first instance the considerations are the maintenance of the marriage and the affinal tie, or of the herding arrangements; and in the second instance, the maintenance of group unity, reciprocal assistance and mutual activity. In both kinds of situation, reconciliation between the disputants is most important, so that a successful resolution of the affair should go beyond the dispute itself.

On the other hand, disputants may have had little or even no significant relationship between them prior to the affair which precipitates their dispute, and they seek no particular relationship thereafter. In that event the bargaining power of each against the other is both weaker and of a different order. The process of reaching a settlement is different in those kinds of situations, and this is demonstrated in the following case-histories.

Before beginning this examination, it is necessary to revert to the problem of the connection between pragmatic negotiation and the socially accepted norms of the Arusha. There has been, from time to time, a good deal of debate among anthropologists on the meaning of law in non-centralised, non-literate societies—including the proposition that such societies have no law, but only custom. It is not intended to engage in that argument here, for it is one which is too concerned with semantics and not sufficiently with social realities. Therefore I shall content myself by asserting that among the Arusha there are, as in any society, commonly enunciated and accepted norms of behaviour. Arusha speak of *embukunoto*, pl. *imbukunot*. These norms are well known, and each is similarly enunciated everywhere in the country. Not all transgressions of norms precipitate disputes, of course; only those which seem to a person to injure his interests or welfare are, or at his volition can be, made subject to regulatory procedures. This is not a handbook of Arusha customary norms, or 'customary law', and therefore I can afford to ignore a precise definition of 'injure' or 'interests'; for in examining the process I shall confine myself to those transgressions which precipitated active disputes.

Whilst it would be incorrect to say that an agreed settlement of a dispute never wholly conforms with the relevant, socially accepted norms, it is true to say that such precise conformity is the exception. Before I began to understand the general principles of the Arusha dispute process—but often having already recorded some of the norms from informants—I was frequently puzzled by the gap between the details of an agreed settlement and the declared norms. The norms themselves were invariably quoted during dispute discussions, and this confused me further. I noted that the Arusha themselves were not worried by this gap; indeed they seldom commented on it, although it was sometimes large. After beginning to appreciate Arusha concentration on compromise, which would provide a mutually acceptable resolution of a dispute, I was almost inclined to describe them as cynical opportunists. If by that is meant 'unprincipled', it is a wrong description of the Arusha in these matters. Clearly they recognise norms, and they hold them in great respect: they are what make Arusha different from other peoples with whom they come into contact. In their modern opposition to outside influences, and their desire and attempt to preserve their distinct way of life, they have in fact come to emphasise these norms, rather than passively take them for granted. They are, then, guided by their principles of right behaviour, and they use them as the bases of claims to rights; but they accept an imperfect world in which an individual does not and should not expect to gain all the ideal rights prescribed by the approved norms. But equally, men hope to be able to avoid some of the obligations implicit in those norms. It is perhaps significant that the Arusha have no word that can be translated as 'justice', nor does any such concept appear in their ideology. It is an irrelevant consideration. They are prepared to agree to something which is as near to their claims as possible in the particular context of the strengths and weaknesses of the two parties to the negotiations. Further, they believe that undue insistence on one's 'rights' under these norms may well conflict with obtaining an effective settlement, and with establishing or maintaining otherwise satisfactory relations. Every dispute begins as the plaintiff contrasts, directly or by implication, the divergence between the defendant's behaviour and the relevant norm. The defendant's reply is usually to attempt to show that no real divergence exists; or, if it does, that some overriding and more general norm necessitiates it. The process of negotiation continues from there.

The next case to be considered has been selected because it illustrates quite clearly the place of the socially accepted norms in a 'contractual' context. It relates to the transfer of bridewealth on which the norm, or set of norms, is well established. Inquiry among informants, as well as the statement of men in assembly and conclave, showed no significant variations in this.

A proper and completed marriage—involving the establishment of certain marital rights and statuses, and including the filiation of children—is made by the transfer of a fixed bridewealth, *engaputi*, composed of specified, named animals as follows (though not necessarily in this order):—

Nondoye, female calf; *embalelu e ngashe*, ewe; *wakiteng*, ox; *gidedani*, ox; *olker*, male sheep; *olcani le menye*, he-goat; *olcani le ngoto:* he goat; *sotwa*, female calf; *waker*, ewe; *olker le kwokwo*, male sheep; *enger e kutukaji*, fat old ewe. Occasionally, for ritual purposes, a wife's father of Meru or Chagga patrilineal origin may demand another ewe, *enger o lmasali*.

The total contains four cattle and seven small stock, with possibly an eighth sheep. The animals are distributed in the bride's family by established rules. Transfers of other animals and material goods are obligatory during the betrothal period, and some of these are recoverable on divorce; but they are not part of the bridewealth proper. The latter is transferred by instalments, as requested by the wife's father after the wedding, and often several years after. The norm of an Arusha bridewealth has been detailed in this way in order to show its explicit nature. The only proper modification said to be allowable is that nowadays an equivalent cash payment may be substituted for an animal, although such payment is described by the name of the animal it represents.

Case 21: Roikine had married the daughter of Temi about seven years previously, and she had borne him four children. There had been no major troubles in the marriage. Roikine had transferred to Temi in bridewealth one female calf (*nondoye*), an ox (*gidedani*) and six small stock. Temi's son, the brother of Roikine's wife, now had to meet demands for a cow as a bridewealth instalment to his father-in-law. At the same time, both Temi and his son were fined for non-payment of tax for two years, which, together with the unpaid taxes, cost them the price of an ox. Temi therefore sent his son to inform Roikine that he must now give the animals outstanding in bridewealth. Roikine refused, saying he had no animals for the purpose, and those he had were thin and in poor condition. A few days later, when Temi was accompanying me on a tour of a recently pioneered area on the edge of his parish, he took the opportunity to visit Roikine's homestead there. Roikine again said he could not at the moment afford to transfer the animals, though he admitted to us his unfulfilled liability for them. Temi insisted that he must have them, especially the two cattle, and he explained the reason for his request at this time. The visit ended by Temi declaring that he would not accept Roikine's refusal. He told me, as we walked away, that he would go and see a lineage counsellor of his sub-clan who lived in the same parish—the counsellor of his own maximal lineage lived about five miles away—and discuss what to do. This he did that same day. He also consulted with a patrilateral cousin, a member of his inner lineage, who lived nearby. The counsellor, Kisita, agreed to convene a conclave. For six days nothing further occurred; and then at the regular meeting of the parish assembly, Kisita took the opportunity to speak with the younger brother of Roikine's father and with Roikine himself, both of whom were attending the assembly. A conclave was agreed to, and it was arranged to hold it in Roikine's homestead three days later. The next day Temi sent a young son to inform his two brothers who lived elsewhere, inviting them to attend. One brother arrived the evening before the conclave and slept the night at Temi's homestead. The other brother came the next morning and, together with their cousin, they all went to Kisita's homestead. Temi told me, during the conclave, that they had discussed the dispute with Kisita before walking to Roikine's homestead.

The conclave began about two p.m. It was held under a tree near Roi-kine's house. Roikine was supported by Olaimer, his counsellor, by his father's brother, his own brother, and a neighbouring agnate of his maximal lineage. After some desultory conversation, Kisita began the discussion proper by speaking of Roikine's marriage, saying it was a good marriage without quarrels and trouble. Two of the children were playing nearby, and Kisita pointed to them and asked rhetorically whose children they were. 'Are they your children, Roikine?' he inquired. Roikine assented with a murmur.

'Truly, it is good you have children,' said Kisita, 'but you have not finished the bridewealth. They are not yours. No, you cannot have animals and children.' He referred to the animals that should be given to Temi as bridewealth.

'He has given bridewealth,' said Olaimer. 'Has he not given? Has there been trouble about bridewealth? No, Roikine is a good affine. Who can say he is not? Does he not live well with his wife? They are his children —is she not his wife?'

'Ee, but he has not finished the bridewealth,' Temi interrupted. 'What about *wakiteng* and *sotwa*?' These were the two outstanding cattle.

'Well, let us discuss the bridewealth,' replied Kisita.

There followed a lengthy listing of the items already transferred, including the pre-marital items not specifically part of the bridewealth. Temi grew restive as this continued, and he whispered to his brother a number of times. Finally he interrupted the discussion and said, 'Yes, those cattle are all right. We agree, we agree. What about *wakiteng* and *sotwa*? Those are the big (i.e. important) ones now.'

Olaimer protested, saying that it was important to be certain about the whole bridewealth transaction; and he resumed discussion of the transferred items. My assistant, who sat with me, whispered that he thought that Roikine and Olaimer were trying to establish that Roikine had hitherto been a good son-in-law. He was doubtless correct in his inference, because, when the listing of items was completed, Roikine began an account of the occasions when he had helped Temi in the ways a dutiful son-in-law should. He referred also to the time when his wife had been ill, describing how he had been to a diviner and had obtained Temi's permission to perform supplications to his (Roikine's) father and ancestors. His wife recovered as a result, he claimed.

Temi listened and murmured assent now and again. Once or twice Roikine's brother interjected that he could bear witness to some event recounted by Roikine.

All this took over an hour to complete. When Roikine stopped, Temi again asked about the two outstanding cattle. 'They have not been given. Give them now! I want them.' And he explained why he needed them, emphasising that he had a genuine need and that it was not merely an arbitrary demand which he was making. Temi's brother briefly endorsed this explanation.

'Now, where are these cattle?' asked Kisita. 'Have you cattle?'

Roikine admitted he had, but said he had only two cows, an ox and a calf. 'We want milk to give the children. Are they not to drink milk? What will the grandfather (i.e. Temi) say if the children are hungry? No milk?' He turned directly to Temi; 'Do you want the milk of the grand-children? Are you not a grandfather?'

Temi's cousin suggested that Roikine had other cattle. This remark was not followed up because Roikine reverted to an explanation of his need of the cattle. Temi's elder brother interrupted to declare that Roikine could give the ox and one cow, and still have milk for his children. 'One cow stays, and it has a calf,' he said, 'A cow is like a herd for it will bear calves and soon there will be many. It is wrong to hold on to other cattle when there is bridewealth (to pay).'

Roikine replied quickly, 'No, it is impossible. I want those cattle.'

A pause followed this, then Kisita began to say that he had heard that Roikine was wanting to buy a piece of land adjacent to his own. This was apparently new information to everyone, for there were ejaculations of surprise.

'Who told you that?' Roikine exclaimed. 'What do you know? I have bought no field.' Olaimer, his lineage counsellor, echoed his words.

Kisita replied, 'Olorombot there (i.e. Roikine's neighbour) is my kinsman, is he not? He has come to talk with me about selling a field. Am I not the counsellor? Why should he not talk with me? He says you want to buy that field there.'—he pointed to an area of land just beyond where we were sitting—'He speaks of cattle and money.'

There was silence. A man who could consider buying a field must have wealth—cattle were indicated—and he ought to pay his bridewealth debts if he has wealth. I learned afterwards that Olaimer had not known of Roikine's intentions in this matter, and his ignorance appeared to explain his silence during the rest of the conclave, and was a factor in the dead-lock which now quickly arose.

Roikine attempted to deny any intention of buying land, but an ex-plosive snort and a noisy spit from Kisita expressed the doubts everyone felt. Roikine reverted to the need for milk for his children, and he spoke of using the ox for ploughing work.

Temi's elder brother, to whom Roikine was a virtual stranger, slapped his stick noisily on the ground, saying, 'Give us the cattle, give us the cattle. Ee, to buy land! With our cattle! Are they not bridewealth, those cattle? Give us the cattle.'

Roikine murmured dissent.

Temi's elder brother spoke again, addressing Temi himself. He recommended that Temi take his daughter back to his homestead and away from Roikine, until such time as Roikine would pay the outstanding instalments of bridewealth. Roikine should also, he said, pay an extra cow to recover his wife, and should apologise to Temi. (Such a payment is common practice when a wife deserts her husband because of maltreatment.)

'No,' replied Temi, 'No, that is wrong. Roikine is a good affine. You have heard; and my daughter, she has done nothing wrong. She is content here at Roikine's homestead. This is her homestead now; this is a good marriage. Have I not grandchildren, small murran?' Although technically perhaps able to break the marriage, or threaten to do so, he had no wish to do so, even in the light of Roikine's obduracy. Temi was a rather gentle, elderly man and anything but a trouble-maker. His brother, I knew, thought Temi rather weak; the brother himself was an impulsive and rather irritable person.

The brother shouted, 'Take our daughter to the homestead! Take her, I say! We want the cattle.' He jumped up and walked away out of sight beyond the house.

Temi reiterated that he did not want the marriage broken, and did not intend to take his daughter away. There was a silence after this. Kisita got up and walked away. Olaimer and Roikine's father's brother began a low conversation between themselves. My assistant whispered to me that the conclave was finished in disagreement. Temi then got up and, with his other brothers and his cousin, walked off. They were joined by the first brother and by Kisita, and all left the homestead together. It was about three thirty p.m.

To sum up the results of the conclave: there had been ready agreement on the amounts of bridewealth already paid and still outstanding; and agreement on the good relations in the marriage and between father-in-law and son-in-law. There was disagreement as to whether Roikine could afford to hand over the two cattle—no mention was made of the sheep outstanding. The disclosure of Roikine's negotiations to buy land threw doubt on his declared inability to fulfil his bridewealth obligations. Thus both the norm in general and its particular applicability in this instance were clear. It was clear also that, although Temi had the right to take his daughter away because of Roikine's refusal to give the two cattle, he was not prepared to do so. Roikine appeared to depend on Temi's compliance and might have succeeded had it not been for Temi's irascible brother. Neither spokesman had altogether committed himself to a specific stand— Roikine's counsellor, because of his ignorance of the proposed land purchase.

No mention had been made of what, if any, steps Temi would take next. He probably had not then decided; but it may have been partly decided for him, because his elder brother on his way home that afternoon, called at the homestead of Ndaanya, the counsellor of their own maximal lineage, and recounted the course of the conclave. Apparently he urged that a moot be convened, for next day a son of Ndaanya came to Temi's homestead to obtain further news. Three days later Temi and his cousin went to visit Ndaanya, and spent the night at the latter's homestead. On his return, I learned that Ndaanya would attempt to convene a moot. Some time later Roikine visited Temi, bringing a little beer as a present; but he did not offer to hand over any animals. I assumed that he was hoping to influence Temi to drop the whole matter; but if this was so, he failed. The moot convened eight days later. In the meantime, Temi had sold an ox to a neighbour, in order to pay the court fines and overdue taxes by the date decreed in the magistrate's judgment.

The moot was held at Roikine's homestead on a grassy flat some distance from the houses. Roikine and Temi were members of the same clandivision of Molelian clan, and thus the operative, dichotomous segments were the sub-clans. The main participants, seated in their separate groups, were as follows:—Temi and his two brothers, the neighbouring cousin with his brother and an autonomous nephew (i.e. the inner lineage complete); Ndaanya, the lineage counsellor; Kisita, the counsellor of the linked maximal lineage; and a senior elder of the sub-clan who was also a parish spokesman. There were about ten other men with them all of whom, near neighbours, were members of the maximal lineage or the sub-clan. With Roikine were his father's brother, his own brother who lived nearby, another brother and a cousin (the inner lineage, but not entire); Olaimer, the lineage counsellor; a notable of the lineage and a notable of a linked lineage, both of whom lived in the same parish; and two other distant agnates. There were also eight other supporters, members of the sub-clan. In addition there were a number of onlookers who sat to one side, and whom I joined. Altogether over forty men were assembled there, all but a few of whom were positive participants. The moot began at about eleven a.m.

Casual gossiping died down, and some whispering ensued between Temi and his supporters. Temi then rose and went to stand in the space between the groups. He said that he came to collect his two cattle owing in bridewealth. He pointed out that Roikine had not attempted to deny the debt, and that it was a proper claim that he was making. He explained his need for the animals. It was a brief speech, quietly made.

Roikine went to the centre and began his counter-argument. He more or less repeated what he had said earlier in the conclave. He spoke of the good relations between himself and his wife, and his father-in-law. He enumerated the children; and he began recounting the bridewealth instalments already paid. In the middle of this, Temi's elder brother called out, 'Yes, we know all this. You have given some cattle, but not all. Tell us you will give us two more cattle. That is it, two cattle.'

Roikine answered that it was not merely a question of two cattle, but also one of a marriage and affinal relations. 'He wants to break off affineship,' he said, pointing at Temi's brother, 'But Temi does not. He knows I am a good affine.' And he continued his account of the marriage and of his behaviour towards Temi. Temi's brother muttered, but was quieted by Ndaanya. Roikine's speech was a long one. He did not attempt to discuss the outstanding instalments of bridewealth, but built up a picture of idyllic affinal relations.

Olaimer, Roikine's counsellor, followed him but merely affirmed Roikine's own account.

Temi's brother, who had attempted to interrupt Olaimer, then stood up, but he was pulled down by Temi, and Ndaanya rose and went to the centre.

Ndaanya began with some polite remarks about the parish (in which he was a stranger, of course) and gave formal greetings to Roikine's supporters. He stood with his back to his own supporters, leaned on his staff, and spoke quietly to the opposing party. He agreed that Roikine had been a good son-in-law, but said that Temi had been an even better father-in-law, for he had been tolerant in his bridewealth demands. He reiterated the norms of bridewealth, counting the animals on his fingers and bending over each finger to indicate an animal paid. He paused with two outstretched fingers and said slowly, '*Osotwa*; *wakiteng*. Those are what we want. They are not yet given. Why? Are they not part of the bridewealth? Yes, we all know they are. Roikine admits it, and we all know the custom. We do not want to quarrel; we want our cattle.' A supporter of Temi called out his approval, and there were general murmurs of assent on that side of the moot.

'I hear,' continued Ndaanya, 'that Roikine has cattle. He can give cattle to us then. I also hear that he wants to buy a field. Kisita says this is so.' Kisita called out that it was so. 'But who can buy fields when there is bridewealth?' Ndaanya went on. 'To buy a field is good if another is foolish enough to sell. But Temi wants his cattle first; that is right. You must agree, it is right. Who can say no? We Arusha have always given bridewealth; it is our custom from long ago and it has always been so. Did not the big men long ago do this? You, Roikine, you say you have been a good affine; but good affines give bridewealth. We want no other words, only cattle. You have cattle—I have heard that you have cattle although I have not seen them—so give us the cattle.'

248

Roikine's father's brother spoke next. He argued that a good father-in-law should be generous to a good son-in-law, and not make heavy demands for bridewealth when the son-in-law cannot afford to pay. Several of Temi's supporters called out, 'He can pay,' 'He has the cattle,' and similar remarks. The notable of Roikine's lineage spoke next, virtually repeating the previous speaker's remarks.

Roikine came forward again and spoke. He now admitted to having some cattle, and he admitted to his hopes of buying the adjacent land. He explained that he had only a small piece of land at the moment, not enough for his family to live on. In fact he had approximately seven acres in this region, off the mountain slopes where rainfall is low and soils are poor. With the requirements of rotational cultivation of maize and beans, and the need for grazing for both his own and his brother's cattle, his submission of an inadequate amount of land was, I think, reasonably correct. The area he hoped to buy was some three acres in size; it adjoined Roikine's present land, and had never been cultivated by its present owner, who had a large holding.

Roikine's counsellor, Olaimer, stood up again. He spoke of Roikine's small holding of land, explaining how Roikine had been a late pioneer in the area and so had less land than most of his neighbours. He described Roikine as a hard worker, who nevertheless was scarcely able to feed his family and at the same time to produce enough crops to sell for cash. Temi's elder brother called out, 'We all have only a little land these days. I have only a little, but I give bridewealth to my affine.' Olaimer replied that Temi's brother was fortunate enough to live on the mountain slopes where rain and soil are good and bananas are plentiful. He spoke at length of the difficulties of cultivation in this semi-arid region, and then explained Roikine's good fortune in having the opportunity to obtain more land by purchase. He appealed to Temi not to prevent his son-in-law buying the extra land—for the sake of Temi's daughter and his grandchildren. He obtained a murmured assent from Temi that he did not want to prevent this. Olaimer then said that he knew that Temi had already met his court fines and paid his taxes, and that therefore the need for bridewealth was less than it had been. He concluded by appealing to Temi to delay his demands.

Temi then spoke, explaining that his own son must take an animal to his father-in-law (that son had so far given no instalments at all after three years of marriage). Roikine's father's brother then called out, 'Take a calf, then. There is a calf; take it.' This was applauded by some of Roikine's supporters.

Temi whispered with Ndaanya and his elder brother, and eventually called out that he agreed to the calf. 'That is *wakiteng*,' announced Olaimer. There was no reply from Temi's side, and thus acceptance was indicated.

After a pause, Ndaanya stood up and went to the centre of the moot. '*Wakiteng* is good, but now *sotwa*—the female calf, we want that,' he declared. He argued that there was no disagreement that this item of bridewealth was owing, and since Roikine had agreed to give the one animal, he must agree to give the other also.

Roikine stood up and said that he could not give a further instalment if he was to buy the piece of land. 'One male calf is enough,' he said, 'that is all now. I have no more cattle.' There were immediate calls of 'No,' 'That is not good enough,' and the like from Temi's party. Roikine, still standing, again said he could give no more, and then went and sat down.

Temi's brother stood up in the middle of his party and shouted that Roikine must give the second animal. 'This case has gone on for a long time,' he continued, 'and we want it finished. We do not want all the trouble of another meeting to discuss this. I say, let us finish it. Are we not all here? Do we not agree about *sotwa*? That it must be given by Roikine? Give it, I say; we have discussed too long. We want the calf, not words.'

Ndaanya did not rise, but called out, 'That is right, that is right. Ee, our *sotwa*! Give it!'

There was a pause after this, and then the counsellor, Olaimer, went to the centre again. He said that he had already pointed out that Temi no longer had the pressing need for the second animal from Roikine, because he had paid his taxes and court fines. 'A good affine does not claim bridewealth for nothing. You, Temi, you have no need now. Your son can use the *wakiteng* to give to his affine as bridewealth; that is good. Why do you keep on saying that you want another ox? Why? Leave your son-in-law; let him buy the field and care for your grandchildren. Later, when you need an ox, Roikine will give it. He is a good son-in-law, and he will give then. We all know that he has no cattle now.'

Temi's party consulted together in whispers, whilst the other side waited. After a few minutes Ndaanya rose and said that Temi wanted the *sotwa* animal now. Although the taxes were paid, they had cost an ox from Temi's herd, and this he wished to make good from Roikine. This was a legitimate claim, not a capricious one, Ndaanya asserted.

Roikine's brother came forward to say that it was obvious that Roikine could not give the *sotwa* animal immediately; but he too, like Temi's brother, wished to see the case settled. Temi's brother interrupted him by calling out, 'Give us *sotwa* and finish. You can finish the case.' Roikine's brother replied, 'All right, perhaps my brother can give after a little while—after a few months. Take *sotwa* when the short rains come.' Silence followed this suggestion, thus indicating the agreement of Temi's party. Olaimer then stood up and spoke of the satisfaction that the agreement brought; and he concluded by turning to Roikine, saying he must give Temi a sheep later on, at the time of the short rains. This caused whispered discussion among Temi's party, but no audible dissent, whilst some of Roikine's supporters called out their approval. Roikine himself remained silent.

The moot ended in this way after about three hours of discussion. The participants remained seated where they were, talking quietly, until Roikine's wife brought out beer from her house. Temi sent a murran to a neighbouring homestead where his own contribution of beer was waiting, and this too was brought to the moot. The men dispersed about half an hour later, having drunk all the beer.

The agreement was that Roikine should give Temi a male calf immediately, and this was to be the *wakiteng* animal. Arusha always describe *wakiteng* as a large, fat ox, and it is an important bridewealth animal because it establishes the full affinal status of the two parties. Thereafter they address each other as *wakiteng*, and the son-in-law is regarded as escaping the ascribed inferiority to his wife's kin to which he has hitherto been subject. Nevertheless, despite its well-understood importance, Temi had agreed to accept a calf in lieu of a fine ox.

Secondly, it was agreed that a sheep should be given to Temi by Roikine within a fairly short, specified period—the short rains could be expected after about five months. This sheep was to be regarded as the equivalent of the outstanding *sotwa* heifer. This had not been clear to me, and I had assumed that the promise of a sheep was only to fulfil the other outstanding obligation of a small animal, *olcani:* but it was explained to me afterwards by Roikine's supporters that in addition to the *wakiteng* ox, only the *sotwa* heifer had been discussed in the moot, and therefore the promised sheep could only refer to the latter item. This, it turned out, was in fact the case. About six months later, at a conclave on Temi's incentive, Roikine handed over an ewe which was dubbed *sotwa*, despite the great differences in value between a heifer and an ewe. Neither in the moot, nor at the time of the later transfer of the ewe, was mention made of the still-outstanding small animal. This should be a castrated male, preferably but not essentially a goat. Temi told me later that he had not forgotten it, saying that he would claim it when he had need for it.

In this fashion a mutually acceptable resolution of the dispute was made. To the participants in the moot, the acceptability of it was obvious—a number of them chided me because, at the time, I tactfully hinted that it might not work. They were entirely justified in their expectations for the agreement was honoured fully, and the two animals handed over and publicly named before witnesses of both sides. If Temi afterwards attempted to claim that the calf had not really been the *wakiteng* ox, or the ewe not really the *sotwa* heifer, he would have had no valid justification. In addition, the friendliness of the affinal relationship had been retained and no threat to Roikine's marriage was made. Roikine was, moreover, able to retain sufficient animals to go ahead with his land purchase negotiation; he completed this a few weeks after the moot.

This was the first major bridewealth dispute whose treatment I had been able to observe. The substitution of less valuable animals for the specified items impelled me to make particular inquiries on this matter. This led to the discovery that often, although not invariably, there was such substitution. More than that, the substitute was sometimes almost only a nominal item, where the difference in value was greater than it had been in that first case—e.g. perhaps only a few shillings, whereas a good cow had a market price to the Arusha of over two hundred shillings at that period; or perhaps some beer and a length of cloth. In some cases—a minority, I think—an item was agreed to be waived altogether by the father-in-law. Of course there were also instances where the father-in-law had taken his married daughter back to his homestead, until her husband would agree to transfer the claimed animals. Arusha admit that such a father-in-law acts within his rights over bridewealth, for the daughter is not a proper wife until all bridewealth is transferred. Nevertheless, most informants concurred with Temi's position in the above case, where he was clearly unwilling to risk breaking up an otherwise satisfactory marriage and affinal link. Sons-in-law are aware of this, and are ready to take advantage of it.

On the other hand, a wife sometimes takes advantage of the dispute to desert her husband whom she no longer likes, and divorce follows. If the husband then wishes to retain the children of the marriage, he must pay the outstanding bridewealth quickly and his bargaining power is slight. A plaintiff-claimant does not then agree to an inferior substitute for the specified items.

Thus the negotiating-strength of the disputants varies according to the circumstances of each particular case. Sometimes the 'letter of the law' is rigidly applied; sometimes a greater or lesser deviation from it is agreed to. Such variations from the norm of bridewealth are not new in the ethnographic literature, and in themselves would scarcely have been worth comment, had not Arusha often emphasised the specific constitution of a 'proper bridewealth' containing explicitly described items. What is more important for present purposes is, that the possibility of departure from expressed and socially approved norms exists in reference to most, perhaps all norms, the transgression of which may precipitate a formal dispute. It can be said that in the process of discussions and negotiations towards a mutually acceptable resolution of a dispute, there is most usually a departure from the applicable norms in the end result. For the Arusha, one might say that it is what a plaintiff *can* obtain (after, if necessary, long negotiations) which is important, rather than what he *ought* to obtain.

This can be illustrated for a quite different kind of dispute, but one in which still there is an element of bargaining power on either side.

Case 22: Ngatieu had a small farm on the mountain slopes. His mother's brother's son, Moruo, had a large farm in the peripheral lowlands. It was arranged that Moruo would pasture and look after some of Ngatieu's animals (four cattle and three goats) for which Ngatieu himself had difficulty in finding adequate feeding on his own farm. This is a fairly common agreement; sometimes the accommodating herder agrees because of kinship obligations only, but often there is a negotiated contractual arrangement between the two men that the herder shall receive some kind of payment—a young animal, money, foodstuffs such as bananas which the herder cannot grow, etc.

Shortly after placing these animals with Moruo, Ngatieu went on a journey to Kitumbeini, a mountain area in Masailand where an agnate had settled. When he returned after about two months and visited Moruo, he discovered that one of his oxen was missing. At first Moruo declared that it had strayed and he had been unable to find it. Ngatieu was unwilling to accept this story and, on making inquiries in the neighbourhood, he learned that Moruo had slaughtered the ox and sold some of its meat. Confronted with this, Moruo admitted his offence, and offered Ngatieu an ox plus a sheep in compensation. Ngatieu refused this, and went to request his lineage counsellor to arrange a conclave. Meanwhile Moruo continued to look after the remaining animals belonging to Ngatieu.

The conclave was held at Moruo's homestead, and Ngatieu was accompanied there by his lineage counsellor, a brother and a notable agnate of his maximal lineage. Moruo was supported by a counsellor of his clan-division, a neighbouring parish spokesman of his maximal lineage, and a patrilateral cousin who lived a mile or so away. I was not present at the conclave, but I knew both Ngatieu and his counsellor quite well, and the result of the meeting was clear enough. It was a matter of local gossip at the time.

Moruo immediately admitted his guilt and again offered an ox plus a sheep. The approved norm in such a case of theft, where the stolen animal has been killed and eaten, is an equivalent animal plus three others as compensation (*enyamu*). The compensation, say Arusha, may be reduced by one animal where the thief is a kinsman. Ngatieu demanded two cattle in compensation in conformity with this norm. In this case the eventual agreement was that Moruo gave Ngatieu an ox in return for the stolen beast, and paid a male calf in compensation plus a gift of three *debe* (12 gallons) of beer delivered to Ngatieu's homestead.

Moruo, although admitting his offence, naturally wished to pay as small a compensation as possible. His negotiating strength lay in the fact that, despite his misdeed, Ngatieu still wished if possible for his animals to be maintained by Moruo on the latter's lowland farm. Ngatieu had no-one else to whom he could turn for this service. None of his nearer agnates had a lowland farm where grazing was available, and he had previously quarrelled with his sister's husband in whose cattle camp he had formerly kept his beasts. Since making the arrangement with Moruo, Ngatieu and his adult son had hoed up over half of his own grazing paddock in order to plant coffee and bananas, thus he could not contemplate taking his animals back to his own farm. Finally Ngatieu's only other son (about ten years old) could no longer be depended on by his father as a regular herdsboy, because he was attending school full-time. Usually a man sends a son with any animals he puts out to another homestead, and one of the advantages of Ngatieu's arrangement with Moruo was that there was no need for this. Moruo had a number of sons capable of all the herding work which was necessary.

On the other hand, the herding arrangement was advantageous also to Moruo. He obtained extra milk, the promise of a female calf in due course, and the expectation of occasional gifts of bananas from Ngatieu. He did not wish to defy Ngatieu's claims to the point of causing him to remove his cattle altogether. In any case, Moruo had committed the theft; and at one point Ngatieu had angrily spoken of taking the matter to court where, since the evidence was ample, Moruo was likely to be made to pay the full compensation and to incur the possibility of imprisonment in addition.

In the agreed settlement, Ngatieu obtained a larger compensation then that initially offered. Before his own supporters and those of Moruo, the total animals of Ngatieu were paraded and inspected. It would be difficult in the future—at least so Ngatieu hoped—for Moruo to attempt chicanery again. Moruo escaped with a smaller compensation payment than Ngatieu initially claimed, and he avoided the threat of court proceedings. For both men the useful herding arrangement was retained. The conclave was ended by a performance of ritual reconciliation (*olmomai*) between the two men before their supporters, so that further offences or further accusations of offences by either would bring supernatural punishment.[1]

A final example follows of a dispute in which the conflicting parties had negotiating-strength against one another, but of different kind than that involved in the previous two cases. In this instance the disputants were members of the same inner lineage: each attempted to use the cause of continued lineage unity and the value of the restoration of agnatic cooperation as a lever against the other.

Case 23: (Cf. the accompanying skeletal genealogy). About ten years before the dispute itself arose, Kadume's mother had separated from his father, Makara; and taking Kadume and the other children with her, she went to live on her own brother's farm in the adjacent parish. There in due course Kadume was initiated. Makara remained on his farm alone for he had no other wife, and he came to depend a good deal on his immediate neighbour and half-brother, Soine, and his wife. On Makara's death his land was occupied by Soine.

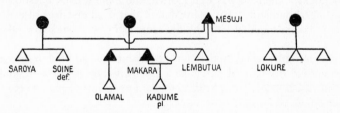

Later Kadume married and shortly afterwards, as a mature adult and autonomous family head, he obtained the two cattle and three goats left

[1] See pp. 288-90 below.

by his father. Although these cattle were stalled in the house of his wife on the land of Lembutua, his mother's brother, an arrangement was made for them to graze in the daytime in the paddock of Soine. Kadume was accepted as a full member of the inner lineage founded by Mesuji.

About a year after the establishment of the grazing arrangement, Kadume claimed possession of all of his father's land which Soine was then cultivating for the fourth or fifth season. Soine refused to give up the land and, after a quarrel, refused to allow Kadume to continue to graze his animals in the paddock.

Kadume went to the lineage counsellor who convened a conclave of the inner lineage. This ended in failure and further quarrelling. Soine held to the arguments that Kadume's mother had deserted Makara and left him wifeless and uncared for, except by Soine himself and his wife; that Kadume had never cultivated his father's land; that Soine himself had only a small farm, but that he had rightful claims in the estate of Mesuji (i.e. the land Makara had inherited from Mesuji); and finally, that Kadume already had a piece of land on his mother's brother's farm where he was living. Soine found some support among his brothers, but Kadume was supported by Olamal, the son of his father's full-brother. The suggestion by the counsellor (a member of a different inner lineage), that Kadume should resume grazing his animals in Soine's paddock but drop his claim to arable land, was angrily rejected by Kadume.

Later, at Kadume's insistence, the counsellor convened an internal moot which was held at Soine's homestead. In addition to all the members of the inner lineage and the counsellor, there were present nine members of the maximal lineage who lived nearby. Kadume, who was only a senior murran and not yet occupying the actual role of elder, had persuaded a lineage notable, Kirevi, to speak for him. Kirevi began the moot, and he argued that Kadume, the only adult son of Makara, had the right to inherit his father's land now he was a big man (*olkitok*—implying maturity in this context). The land was well known, and there was no question as to its proper boundaries. He pointed out that Kadume had already inherited Makara's animals, and by the same right he should now take the land.

Soine, in reply, relied on the same arguments he had used in the earlier conclave. He emphasised particularly his own shortage of land, and his claimed rights in Makara's land which had previously been a part of the single estate of Mesuji, their father.

Kadume called out, 'Brothers do not inherit, it is sons who inherit. That is the custom of long ago.' This fetched murmurs of assent from some of the men present, but a retort of, 'Not always,' from Soine himself.

Kirevi stood up again, and reiterated what Kadume had just asserted. He then introduced overtly the subject of the inner lineage. 'You say,' he addressed Soine directly, 'that you inherit from your brother because of your father's estate of long ago; but what of your father's *engang*, *engang* of Mesuji? (*engang* referred not only to the former family of Mesuji, containing both Soine and Makara, but to the lineage founded on Mesuji). Is there not one *engang*? Do you want to break it and spoil it?' He described the ideal behaviour of close agnates, and then went on; 'And what of your father? Will he not be angry and send trouble to his sons who quarrel and fight? Do you not beg Mesuji? He truly is the big one (principal ancestor), and our big ones do not like quarrels among their children.' He stressed the notion of ancestral wrath, and a dead father's desire for a strongly unified lineage among his sons. Kirevi continued, 'And Kadume, is he not big (mature) now? Does he not take part in *olmakoko* (ancestral rituals) with the others? He is one of the lineage.'

Kirevi's three principal points brought calls of approval from, among others, the lineage counsellor.

Olamal, the autonomous patrilateral cousin of Kadume, spoke briefly. He pointed out that he and Kadume were only small (junior) in the lineage, whilst all the other members were their fathers. He said they did not want to seek control of lineage affairs while their fathers remained alive. Nevertheless he and Kadume were no longer children; they were both married men, heads of their own families, and they had rights in the lineage. He accused Soine of trying to drive Kadume out, and said that Mesuji, the lineage founder, would certainly send illness and trouble to them all because of Soine's actions. But in addition, he and Kadume were beginning to gain seniority and soon they would be the important members of the lineage as their fathers became old men, dependent on their juniors. 'Shall we help you then?' he asked Soine and the other fathers. 'If you do not help us now, why should we help you then? We are your sons, you are our fathers. Help us! Give us our land!'

The counsellor commended Olamal for his speech, but said that he must look after his fathers in their old age whatever they did now. Then, turning to Soine, the counsellor said that perhaps it would be a good thing to talk of giving Kadume his father's land. (I can only suggest here something of the oblique way in which the counsellor phrased his proposal. It seemed to me that whilst sympathising with Kadume, the counsellor feared rousing the hostility of his peers, i.e. Soine and the others). Lokure, the eldest of the third set of brothers, agreed aloud that they should consider giving Kadume the land. Silence followed this statement, signifying agreement on the point. In effect Soine had tacitly expressed his willingness to allow Kadume some of the land, for when he spoke he entered immediately into a consideration of what part of the land Kadume might occupy.

Kadume broke into Soine's speech to demand that he be given the whole of his father's land; but Soine replied that Kadume had land already at his mother's brother's farm, as much almost as Soine's own farm. 'Does Lembutua (the mother's brother) want to drive you away? Are you and he not friends?' Kadume was silent, but, stirred by the insistence of Soine and the counsellor, he admitted that Lembutua did not want to evict him from that land. 'And have you not planted coffee there? Ee, and bananas and trees also?' Kadume agreed that he had. 'Then you have a farm,' announced Soine; 'And you do not need all of Makara's land. Take that portion beyond the bananas—that is yours.' He indicated the area referred to.

There was some discussion, and then the members of the moot all walked over onto the land in question nearby. The establishment of the new boundary took some time—about half an hour—and a good deal of bargaining, but it was successfully concluded in the end. The result was that, despite the enunciated norms of inheritance, Kadume obtained only about half of his father's land, and Soine retained the rest.

The moot resumed discussions back at Soine's homestead, as the counsellor reminded the members of the inner lineage that this was a settlement of the final inheritance of Makara's estate—a settlement which had not been made after his death, because his sons were then but children.

'Who is the inheritor of the calf?'[1] He asked. Since Makara's full brother was also dead, this role fell to Saroya, the eldest half-brother of Makara's *olwashe*. 'Saroya wants a calf from your father's herd,' the counsellor formally told Kadume. After further negotiation, Saroya agreed to accept a female goat in lieu, and a son of Soine was sent to fetch it from Kadume's homestead. It was later formally handed over to Saroya before the witnessing members of the moot.

The whole moot concluded by retiring to Soine's house to drink beer in commensal cordiality. Agnates took the opportunity to congratulate both Soine and Kadume on the success of the agreement, and on the conclusion of the inheritance settlement.

Dispute Settlement Between 'Unrelated' Persons

Although in Arusha, all people are structurally related to all other people through the patrilineal descent system, nevertheless those who live more than a few miles apart, and whose patrilineal link is relatively remote, may be said for practical purposes to be 'unrelated'. In that case, when such people come into dispute their bargaining

---

[1] *Olaijungoni le ngashe*: the nearest agnate of the dead man, who, on behalf of the inner lineage, takes a calf from the deceased's herd as an affirmation of the inheritance and as a renunciation of any further claims by the lineage against that herd.

power against each other is unaffected by considerations of mutual advantage and reconciliation. There tends to be instead a greater emphasis on ideal norms of behaviour as justification of claims, and more effort is made to appeal both to public opinion and to the less deeply committed supporters of the other disputant. As will be demonstrated, the norms are still guides rather than dogmatic rules, and a good deal of toleration occurs. The settlement itself must still be one to which both disputants agree and therefore one which they will make practically effective.

Earlier in this chapter, in Case 20 at page 236, it was shown how a man's supporters may come to be convinced that he must in some respects give way to the claims of his opponent. There, in a parish assembly, a senior murran was persuaded to admit his guilt in a fight with a junior murran; he was induced to do this by his age-mates. The plaintiff—or more precisely one of his patrons' age-group acting for him—had directed his advocacy towards the defendant's age-group and also that of the senior elders. In this case, however, the process took place within a single parish and therefore the defendant and his supporters were acting in a situation of pre-existing relations between age-groups within the unity of the parish. Therefore the disputants were not altogether 'unrelated'. In the following case a dispute is examined where the social distance between the two parties was much greater.

Case 24: Raraya, a senior murran, was betrothed to the daughter of Lavilal, a man of a different parish. Raraya had already begun to make the usual series of pre-marital gifts, and Lavilal had his daughter's clitoridechtomy and initiation completed. Kidenye, a junior murran from a parish above five miles distant from Lavilal's homestead, became friendly with the girl, unbeknown to either Raraya or Lavilal; and eventually, with her agreement, he abducted her to his married brother's homestead, where he seduced her. The brother, Baraa, came to the homestead of Lavilal next day, bringing a sheep and beer, and a request that Lavilal consent to the marriage of his daughter to Kidenye. Lavilal refused to discuss the matter, and he refused also to accept the gifts in order not to commit himself. The girl returned home on her own later that day.

Lavilal thereafter consulted with Raraya, who refused to surrender his betrothal rights and demanded that Lavilal should claim compensation from Kidenye and Baraa. Lavilal then went to discuss the matter with his lineage counsellor who lived in another parish. Raraya accompanied him to urge the case, for he believed (and correctly, as it turned out) that

259

Lavilal was likely to be slow to take action. The counsellor suggested a conclave between Lavilal and Baraa, and this was held some days later at Lavilal's homestead. Baraa came accompanied by two paternal cousins, a counsellor of a lineage of his sub-clan, and a notable of his lineage. Lavilal was supported by his counsellor, a brother, a cousin and a lineage notable. Raraya attended with his father's brother. Baraa continued to press the idea of marriage between his brother and Lavilal's daughter; but Raraya, followed by Lavilal, would not consider the proposal, and the conclave broke up after only a brief meeting.

Some days after the conclave the girl again spent a night with Kidenye at Baraa's homestead, and Baraa sent a message again the following day asking Lavilal to agree to the proposed marriage. Lavilal refused; and, urged on by Raraya, now asked his counsellor to convene a moot. But this was extremely difficult to arrange. Baraa, and Kidenye also, refused to agree and claimed that no wrong had been done which Lavilal's agreement to marriage could not put right. Baraa's lineage counsellor lived over ten miles away and made no effort to join with Lavilal's counsellor in arranging a moot: he did not positively refuse, but merely took no apparent action. The dispute remained in abeyance for about two weeks, when the girl again went to Baraa's homestead—this time for two consecutive nights. Then she disappeared, and both Kidenye and Baraa refused to say where she was. (She hid at the homestead of Baraa's mother's brother for two days, before returning home).

Incensed by this fresh offence (as it seemed to him), Raraya raised the matter in the parish assembly of his own parish a day or two later. At first the junior elder spokesmen refused to listen to him: they said that Lavilal and Baraa and both their counsellors lived elsewhere, and it was no concern of theirs therefore. Raraya replied that he wished to confront members of the parish who were agnates of Kidenye and Baraa—two patrilateral cousins—and also the counsellor of a maximal lineage of the same sub-clan as those men. The counsellor and one cousin were present, and they denied knowledge of the matter at first. Raraya insisted that they should see that a moot was arranged and he gained the general assent of several spokesmen of the parish who, though not connected with either party directly, were prepared to express public opinion in favour of a moot. Shortly after that, Lavilal's counsellor raised the matter publicly at a bloodwealth assembly where large numbers of Arusha were collected. He too gained general approval in favour of a moot. A number of Baraa's agnates were there and, though not speaking, signified by their silence that they accepted the proposal. There were further delays, but eventually a moot was arranged, and largely as a result of these tactics. Thus Raraya and Lavilal had accomplished their first task—a task which would have been fairly simple had the disputants been more nearly related by descent or parish.

The moot was a complicated one. Raraya and Lavilal refused to meet at the homestead of Baraa, the defendant and it was agreed to meet on the site of his parish assembly. Lavilal, the formal plaintiff, and Baraa, the defendant (representing his junior murran brother) were supported by their counsellors, agnates and other notables. Raraya, the real plaintiff and effective force behind the plaint, also attended with some of his agnates and the counsellor of a lineage linked to his own in the same sub-clan. Lavilal and Baraa were of different moieties; Raraya was of the same moiety as Baraa, but of course clearly he was not supporting Baraa, as ideally he should by structural definition. It was a large moot, partly because of the three parties who were involved, and partly because the dispute had become a matter of much gossip and therefore numbers of men attended to hear it argued. The supporters of Raraya and of Lavilal sat together, with the conventional open space separating them from Baraa's party.

Lavilal opened the moot by stating his claim against Baraa—compensation of an ewe and beer, and permission to use ritual means to prevent Baraa acting as the accomplice of his younger brother in the future.[1] Raraya followed immediately. First he described the whole history of the affair (Lavilal had not attempted this), and then he stated his claim against Kidenye—a female calf and two sheep in compensation,[2] and permission to use ritual means to prevent Kidenye consorting with the girl again. Raraya also asked Lavilal to affirm that his daughter would still marry him. Raraya's speech was long, histrionic and clearly aimed at Baraa's supporters rather than Baraa himself. Raraya appealed to several of them individually by name, but never addressed Baraa himself personally.

Baraa then replied and denied any offence. He ignored Raraya, and urged Lavilal to agree that the girl should marry Kidenye: he offered to pay the virginity fee to Lavilal and to bring pre-marital gifts. Thereafter in succession three of Raraya's supporters, in similar speeches, censured Baraa and Kidenye, and appealed to the latter's counsellor and others to admit Raraya's claims. Baraa's counsellor began to defend Baraa and his brother, but quickly became involved in a running debate with Raraya and his supporters—the counsellor standing and being subjected to a succession of questions and comments from the men of the party of Raraya and Lavilal sitting opposite. 'Has not Kidenye done wrong?' Has

[1] He asked permission to use the *emuty*, 'cooking-pot' oath; cf. p. 290ff.

[2] If Raraya was to marry the girl he would be responsible for paying the fee for the breach of the girl's virginity (*ingishu e ngilata e ngeju*), whether or not he himself had deflowered her. His claim for compensation from Kidenye was equal to this fee. This is a conventional claim in such circumstances.

not Baraa done wrong?' 'Why did the counsellor not help to convene a moot earlier?' 'Are not Raraya's words right?' and so on. The counsellor parried as best he could, and eventually sat down again, leaving his speech unfinished. A patrilateral cousin of Raraya, a senior elder spokesman of his own parish, stood up next. He repeated the claims of Raraya and Lavilal; he spoke of the opinion expressed in Raraya's parish assembly and at the bloodwealth assembly. He ended by challenging Baraa's supporters to deny that Kidenye and Baraa had done wrong, that a girl could be 'stolen' from her father, and that the claim for permission to use ritual coercion was a good one.

When this speaker sat down, amid commendatory remarks from his own side, the members of Baraa's party began a low discussion among themselves. Baraa's counsellor then stood up and suggested that the ritual oath be performed a few days later. Tacitly he had thus admitted the claims of Raraya and Lavilal. Raraya called out to inquire about the compensation claims, and the counsellor suggested that these be discussed at the subsequent meeting. Silence followed this proposal, indicating assent. The time of the next meeting was arranged and then the moot broke up.

The disputants met again six days later. This time it was a conclave attended by Raraya, two of his agnates and his lineage counsellor; by Lavilal and one of his brothers; and by Kidenye and Baraa with their counsellor, a related counsellor and another agnate. A day or two before the conclave met, Baraa had visited Lavilal, taking a gift of beer. He had pleaded with Lavilal to drop his claim for compensation and Lavilal had agreed. Therefore at the conclave only Raraya's claim was outstanding. First the ritual oath was performed by Raraya against Kidenye and Baraa together, before the assembled witnesses. It bound them not to have any further contact with Lavilal's daughter, 'Not to speak to her or even to see her.' I was told that Kidenye or Baraa and the girl must thereafter strictly avoid each other, turning off a path if they happen to be walking towards each other. When the ritual was completed, Baraa went to bring a large ewe and a half-grown male goat which were already tethered to one side. These he offered to Raraya as compensation for his and Kidenye's offence. He said also that Kidenye would take beer the next day to the homesteads of both Raraya and Lavilal.

Here I must report my own failure adequately to record the proceedings. I had not witnessed this form of ritual oath before, and had become involved in talk with my assistant and one of the participants concerning it, so that I missed much of the rest of the brief conclave. Therefore I am not certain how far Raraya objected to the payment of the two animals instead of the legitimate compensation he had originally claimed—i.e. a female calf and two sheep. It appeared, however, that arrangements had been made before the conclave between Baraa and Lavilal. Lavilal would accept a virginity fee of two animals from Raraya; so that Raraya was content to receive only those in compensation from Baraa, because he would merely pass them on to Lavilal. My assistant was of the opinion that Lavilal had accepted this compromise in order to end the whole dispute quickly and without additional trouble. Raraya was satisfied by his performance of the ritual oath, his freedom from further commitment in the matter of the virginity fee, and his hope that now his marriage would go forward.

This last case illustrates the difficulty which arises, when the disputants are 'unrelated', in bringing a dispute to discussion. My conclusion, supported by the opinions of uninvolved Arusha, is that Baraa had hoped first to force the hand of the girl's father to accept a *fait accompli*. Failing in this, he had hoped to avoid the consequences of his actions—in which he was supported by his counsellor—by refusing to convene a moot. The plaintiffs met these tactics by a refusal to be thwarted: by appeals to public opinion to support the demand for a moot, and by challenging the defendant's supporters (especially his lineage counsellor) to deny in public that an offence had been committed. This strategy was successful, at the expense of the girl's father who agreed to take smaller payments than he had a right to by the accepted norms. Had the father refused to take a smaller virginity fee, and had he insisted on a compensation payment from Baraa, the dispute might not have been settled so readily. There was, of course, never any real question that Kidenye and Baraa had committed injuries against both the girl's father and her betrothed suitor, and ultimately this was where the plaintiff's strength lay in the dispute.

Most serious disputes occur between people who are directly and fairly closely related to one another in one or more ways— members of a single lineage, or of a single parish, affines, contracting parties to a mutual agreement, etc. These are the people who, because of their relationships and co-activities, are most likely to come into dispute. Arusha indigenous procedures are on the whole able to deal with these relationships because the procedures themselves emerge out of the social sub-systems in which these relationships operate. 'Unrelated' people are less likely to come into serious dispute; but when they do, indigenous procedures are cumbersome and not altogether efficient. Injuries may have to be tolerated under the circumstances because of the difficulty, perhaps impossibility of taking useful action. The following case is an example of this.

Case 25: On his return home one evening, Lamal discovered that a sheep was missing from his paddock. His son, the herdsboy, was shelter-ing in the house because of the cold and damp (it was the rainy season) and knew nothing of it. Immediately Lamal went off to try and trace the animal, and he claimed afterwards that he found its tracks in the mud leading to the nearby stream and a small watering-place. There some women told him that Maliten had earlier been watering a flock of goats and sheep. They said also that no other person had been at the stream for some time; but they denied any knowledge of theft or even suspicious action by Maliten. Next morning Lamal sent his murran son to make enquiries in the neighbouring parish beyond the stream, where Maliten lived. The son returned later to report that he thought Maliten was the thief, because he had learned that Maliten had killed a sheep at his home-stead the previous evening. Maliten, however, had denied the theft, saying that he had slaughtered one of his own animals. Lamal's son could ascertain no reason why Maliten should have killed an animal, and this was a matter arousing suspicion because Arusha do not usually kill merely to eat meat.

Lamal and Maliten were related only by their common clan, and Lamal had no near agnates or other close kin in Maliten's parish. After consulta-tion with a nearby cousin and with a lineage counsellor of his sub-clan who lived in his own parish (his own lineage counsellor lived about eight miles away), Lamal went to see the headman of Maliten's parish. The headman denied knowledge of the matter, but promised to investigate. Whether or not he did so, nothing further came of this attempt to press the case. A few days later, therefore, and after consultation with members of his inner lineage, Lamal went again to his local counsellor to ask him to arrange a conclave with Maliten. The counsellor was apparently sceptical of the evidence which Lamal had obtained, and the subsequent failure to obtain a conclave may, therefore, have been partly the result of a lack of zeal by the counsellor. Maliten and his associates refused to agree to a conclave; and he was supported in this by a lineage notable who lived nearby and whom the counsellor also visited.

Lamal refused to accept the stalemate; and a few days later he attended a meeting of the parish assembly in Maliten's parish. He went accompanied by his paternal cousin, and he gained the introductory assistance of a spokesman in Maliten's parish with whom he was friendly—they were sons-in-law of the same man, and members of the same age-set (though not, of course, of the same age-group). At the parish assembly Lamal was told that he could not present his case because Maliten and his agnates were not present. The junior elder 'chairman' said that they (i.e. members of the assembly) knew nothing of the dispute and could do nothing; but after some argument Lamal obtained permission to attend the next meeting, and the parish headman agreed to notify Maliten of this. The following week (now about three weeks since the alleged theft) Lamal again attended the parish assembly, and this time he was able to present his case. Maliten and his father's brother both denied the accusation outright; and they expressed indignation at false charges against him in their own parish by a stranger. The junior elder 'chairman' declared that he thought that Lamal had no evidence to substantiate his case; and he went on to say that people in his parish were not thieves and liars. He made reference to the recent case of a proved thief in Lamal's parish, and told Lamal to look elsewhere. The rest of the assembly remained silent. Lamal made a brief justification of his accusation, and challenged Maliten to say why he had slaughtered a sheep that evening of the theft. No-one attempted to reply to this after Lamal sat down, and instead the assembly began discussion of another matter. Soon after this, Lamal and his cousin left quietly.

In conversation afterwards with men present at the assembly meeting, I found that some of them suspected that Maliten might have been the thief. I asked one of these why he had not supported Lamal's request for discussion of the case—Maliten had flatly denied the accusation, made no attempt at explanation, nor called any witness. My informant replied: 'Why should I? Lamal is a stranger here; no kinsman of mine, not a neighbour (i.e. not a member of his parish), not an age-mate.' I pressed my question again, suggesting that an elder of some importance, such as he, should have intervened to ensure that Lamal received proper consideration. 'Why?' asked my informant, 'it is no affair of mine. And Maliten, he is of my parish. Why should I speak against him? Yes, he is not my kinsman; but we are neighbours and we have peace here. Why should I spoil peace here to support Lamal?'

In the event Lamal was defeated. He attempted to persuade his local counsellor to obtain permission for him to use a ritual oath against Maliten; but the counsellor advised against it, and suggested that Lamal should go to the counsellor of his own lineage if he wished to take that course. The counsellor also advised against taking the matter to the local court. Lamal discussed the affair with members of his inner lineage, and they too tended to support the counsellor's opinions on the uselessness of further action.

Whether Maliten was in fact the thief was never determined, nor even publicly discussed. The dispute was settled in effect because Lamal was forced to accept his failure to bring the matter to proper negotiation. Presumably he had thought his evidence good enough to warrant pressing the dispute, or he would not have persisted so long, for he had no previous animosity towards Maliten to provoke him. It is possible that he would raise the matter again later as occasion permitted; as it was he was thwarted. Firstly, because of indifferent support by his local counsellor and near agnates, who prejudged the issue and appeared to have found Lamal's case too weak; and secondly, by the cold reception he received in Maliten's parish. I do not think that he expected a favourable solution in that parish assembly; probably he intended only to force Maliten's hand so that a patrilineal conclave or moot might be arranged.[1] These tactics failed, as I have described. Had Lamal's evidence been stronger, it is possible that he would have succeeded in bringing the matter to discussion in some way. Again, had he been related to Maliten by some fairly close link, he would have been in a better position to exert pressure even though his evidence was poor. Finally, had the injury been of a graver kind, he might have persisted longer and have insisted more strongly on the active support of his kinsmen. As it was, Lamal had lost a sheep and continued to believe he knew the thief; but he eventually accepted (at least for the time being) the fact of his inability to take action.

A possibility open to Lamal was to have taken the case to the local court, for this has become a recognised way of dealing with 'unrelated' disputants.[2] Similarly a dissatisfied disputant—plaintiff or defendant—may appeal to a court where the indigenous processes seem to him unsatisfactory. An alternative possibility is to attempt to obtain the support of the chief or a magistrate by an appeal to them to consider the ignored plaint. The chief, or magistrate, can call a conclave in his office which the defendant and his close associates cannot easily ignore. This, like the appeals to public opinion made by the plaintiffs in Case 24, forces the hand of the defendant. He is virtually compelled to attempt to make some answer to the charges. As a result of a chief's or magistrate's conclave, the plaintiff is usually able to obtain a moot or counsellor's conclave, and, supported by public opinion, he is in a strong position to gain at least some settlement. Usually neither chief or magistrate himself seeks to impose a settlement—although that can happen.

[1] Cf. Case 1, p. 182.
[2] See p. 204ff.

Rather he is content to have brought the two parties together. He declares the appropriate norms, indicates his opinion on the kind of settlement that is warranted, and enjoins the two parties to arrange a subsequent meeting.

The Local Courts

The procedure in connection with a court is briefly as follows. A formal dispute between Arusha is begun by the plaintiff applying to register a case with the court clerk. The acceptance of registration and of payment of the appropriate fee presupposes the opinion of the clerk, and also of the magistrate perhaps, that a *prima facie* case exists. The magistrate may make enquiries if he has doubts, and, as I have shown previously, he may recommend alternative out-of-court procedure. Often a plaintiff is accompanied by his parish headman, or a reputable related notable, who can affirm the validity of the plaint. Once a case is registered, it must be heard in the court within a few days, unless the plaintiff himself agrees to its abandonment. It becomes the magistrate's responsibility to fix a time for the hearing and, if necessary, to issue summons to the defendant and witnesses to appear.

In the court, the magistrate and his clerk sit at a table on a dais at one end of the open-walled courtroom. The 'court elders' also usually sit on the dais, or at least nearby, together with one or more court messengers. Litigants, witnesses and the general public sit in the main body of the courtroom, but in no particular order. A person giving evidence comes to stand before the dais.

The plaintiff should first state the nature of his charge and claims. If the magistrate does not already know—and usually he does—he then asks the defendant whether he admits the claim or not. If the defendant denies it, the plaintiff states his case, and this is usually followed immediately by the defendant in reply. Thereafter the supporting witnesses of each party are heard, and any neutral witnesses such as a parish headman, medical orderly, policeman, etc. Magistrate, clerk or court elder may interrupt any witness to elucidate testimony or to obtain further information; they may also cross-question a witness or confront him with conflicting evidence.

Most or all of the evidence is given in the Arusha language, but the court clerk makes a written summary in Swahili, the official language of the court. After each witness completes his testimony, the summary record is read out to him (orally translated by the magistrate, if necessary). The witness can require alterations of the record—though usually he does not—and finally he attests it by his thumb-print or signature. The plaintiff or defendant, who are primarily self-responsible for their respective cases, may speak more than once if they wish to rebut evidence or develop their argument further. Finally, and after consultation with his clerk and the court elders, the magistrate sums up the evidence and argument, and then issues his decision, giving the reasons for it. This also is recorded in summary form by the clerk, and signed by the magistrate.

The contrast between this procedure and those followed in indigenous assembly and conclave is well marked. The magistrate sits apart from the disputants and others; the whole proceedings are more formal, this being especially underlined by the process of recording and attestation of evidence. A court hearing is usually much briefer than one in assembly or conclave. Witnesses' statements are noticeably shorter, and there is little or no discussion directly between the two parties to the dispute. Evidence and argument are directed mainly at the magistrate, for it is he who must be persuaded by virtue of his dominant role in the court. Proposals and counter-proposals are seldom made. The decision-making phase is entirely monopolised by the magistrate, who issues his finding together with any *obiter dictum* he sees fit.

The two features of judicial procedure in a court to which chief attention is directed are, firstly, the obvious one of the dominating authority and coercive power of the magistrate; and secondly, the nature of a magistrate's decision and its relation to the relevant, established norms of behaviour.

A court is established by powers and forms external to Arusha society. Its existence and competence are created by a legal warrant issued by the Central Government of Tanganyika—actually by the Provincial Commissioner with the approval of the Governor. The powers and procedures of a court are laid down in the Local Courts Ordinance, 1951, and all courts are subject to the supervision and revisionary control of Government officials. These officials—and especially the immediately supervisory District Officers—are advised not to require too great a formality in court procedure, nor to force

English law-court practices upon African magistrates.[1] In the Arusha Chiefdom, however, and unlike some areas of Tanganyika, there is no tradition of more or less formal courts upon which the modern local courts can be based. Their existence as well as their authority depend essentially on the power of the Central Government and the alien-established local government system. The procedure followed by a court must be largely of an imported kind; and it has inevitably tended, therefore, to be patterned on English-style court procedure, as successive District Officers have required in the light of their varying experience with other African local courts in the territory. Arusha magistrates are roughly aware of the nature of judicial procedure in courts (e.g. in the township) presided over by English magistrates and judges, and these provide a more relevant model than the indigenous procedures of their own society. Additional formality of an alien kind is required because of the necessity of written records of testimony, and also in order to preserve the dignity and authoritarian role of the magistrate himself.

The magistrate has a defined and sanctioned authority which no indigenous notable holds, and which is foreign to Arusha culture. He acquires this directly from his appointment and continued support by the Central Government. Within the limits of his ascribed competence, his authority is unavoidable. Furthermore, he exercises this authority not only to uphold court procedure, but to issue decisions *ex cathedra*, as a neutral party to disputes before him. His decision is binding upon both parties in a case, in that his order must be obeyed and his award to one disputant must be accepted by the other. But although a magistrate has this authority, he also has an explicit obligation to exercise it—that is, an obligation to reach a decision, and one which he cannot avoid. Ideally, he should do this entirely on the evidence presented to him without personal consideration for either party.

In parenthesis, it may be noted that, whilst acknowledging the indisputable authority of a magistrate, Arusha often suspect his impartiality. They find it difficult—sometimes impossible—to accept the idea of unprejudiced decision, for they can scarcely conceive of a man who is not susceptible to pressures. In the past, some magistrates have certainly been guilty of accepting bribes or other induce-

[1] Cf. *Local Government Memoranda, No. 2 (Local Courts)*, 2nd edition, Government of Tanganyika, Dar es Salaam, 1957, passim.

ment to bias their decisions. Unsuccessful disputants are ready to blame their failure on the magistrate's partiality, rather than on the evidence and the law. But in any case a magistrate himself is a member of an age-group and parish, or an inner and maximal lineage, and of a clan. He cannot entirely divorce himself from his obligations in these groups; but most Arusha do not expect him to do so.

Nevertheless, despite his position of authority—and also his somewhat atypical nature as an educated person—a magistrate is, of course, culturally conditioned by his own society. In principle therefore, he is mindful of the value which Arusha place upon discussion, negotiation and a mutually acceptable settlement in disputes. He is aware of the nature of compromise which permeates indigenous judicial procedures, and on the whole accepts its rationale. As far as I could ascertain, magistrates approve of indigenous principles; they do not perceive their courts as competitors attempting to replace assemblies and conclaves. This is the reason why a magistrate often attempts to refuse registration of a civil case (i.e. a dispute between private individuals), either commending the potential plaintiff to his lineage or parish notables, or arranging a conclave in his own office. This is not an essential part of a magistrate's formal duty; but the fact that it is so commonly done is most important to the total contemporary pattern of dispute settlement in this society. The magistrate, if not his court, is thus a part of the system of negotiation procedure typical of his culture.

If a dispute nevertheless comes to his court, despite his conciliatory efforts, a magistrate seldom refuses to take cognisance of any previous indigenous proceedings, and the opinions of the notables concerned. Usually one or more notables are especially requested to attend the court hearing in order that they may inform the magistrate of previous events. They do not necessarily give formal evidence, but may discuss the matter with the magistrate before the court opens. Magistrates have said that they prefer to have the guidance of such notables in any dispute which is at all serious in itself, or may have important repercussions in a related situation. Undoubtedly a magistrate's weighing of the evidence may be biased by his understanding of the need for a compromise settlement, and the need for the reconciliation of disputants where they are related in some way. It is difficult to assess the significance of this because it does not appear in the court record, and not always is it evident even

in the course of a hearing. It is certain, however, that lineage counsellors in particular do take care to advise the magistrate—not just
to gain his favour on their own side, but to assist him in a mutually
satisfactory solution insofar as a magistrate is able to go in that
direction.

To some extent, therefore, a magistrate is able (and is expected,
by Arusha) to depart from rigid adherence to the 'law'—stated norms
and established precedents—and to imitate indigenous aims and
methods. If, however, one of the disputants is adamant in his
legalistic claims, the magistrate is severely limited in a way the
notables are not, by the threat of appeal and fear of revision.[1] Unlike
the notables and other supporting associates of a disputant, a magistrate has no means by which he can bring strong pressure to bear in
an attempt to gain a reduction of a plaintiff's claims, or an admission
of guilt from a defendant. He cannot use his magisterial authority,
for it has no substance here. There are no sanctions at his disposal
to back his efforts at persuasion towards compromise—much as he
may perhaps prefer compromise. A disputant is unlikely to be
considerate of the approval or disapproval of a magistrate, since
those affections are of no importance to him. The magistrate has no
authority to threaten other loss of privilege or to promise reward
for compliance. He is an unrelated person and therefore in that sense
powerless. His formal, neutral role of judge can make him easily open
to criticism, reprimand and over-ruling if his court decision is not
in comformity with the objective facts and the law.

Thus, for example, a magistrate hearing a dispute such as that in
Case 21 (p. 243ff.), concerning failure to pay outstanding bridewealth,
must state the norms and rule accordingly. He could not order that a
male calf be substituted for a large fat ox, or a goat for a heifer, as
was agreed in the moot in that instance. Or at least, he could not
unless the plaintiff voluntarily agreed to accept the inferior sub-
stitutes. This might occur, but a survey of court records indicates
that it is not usual, once a plaintiff has determined to go to court;
and where it does occur, it appears that it is largely the persuasion
of the defendant and of the notables of both disputants which is
important, rather than that of the magistrate himself.

The magistrate, whilst making his judgement conform to the

---

[1] Court records are inspected monthly by the District Officer, who can order a
revision of any judgement which seems necessary to him.

'law,' may add a recommendation that the successful litigant show generosity to his opponent. An actual case illustrates this fairly common feature.

Case 26: Sendu was allocated a piece of land in a peripheral pioneering area by the chief in 1941, and in the following year he allowed two of his younger brothers to have the use of part of it. In 1954 one of those brothers died, and the other, Leshiloi, claimed the field which the deceased had cultivated. Sendu refused, asserting that all the land was his by right of its legitimate allocation to him by the chief. In the subsequent quarrelling, Sendu sought to evict Leshiloi altogether, and eventually he appeared as plaintiff for that claim in the local court.

I have no information concerning pre-court procedures; but in the court itself, in 1955, the magistrate awarded the whole area of land to Sendu. In his judgement, the magistrate noted that there was no evidence at all to indicate that Sendu had shared the original allocation, and there was ample witness (the ex-chief and the parish headman) to the legality of the allocation itself. So overwhelming was the evidence in support of Sendu, that both the Arusha Appeal Court and the District Commissioner's Appeal Court upheld the first court's finding without amendment.

In each of the three successive courts, the magistrate pointed out that the chief ought to have made provision for Sendu's brothers when he made land available to Sendu himself. More emphatically, each magistrate declared that it was Sendu's duty to assist his younger brother (Leshiloi was his half-brother) and to give him the use of some land. The magistrate of the Arusha Appeal Court actually advised Sendu to allow Leshiloi to remain on the land cultivated for twelve years by the two younger brothers; the magistrate of the local court and the District Commissioner in his Court merely counselled the general obligation to be generous and to observe fraternal responsibility. These were all merely *obiter dicta*, and the actual judgements awarded the whole area to Sendu.

The fact that Sendu had taken the dispute to court indicates fairly clearly that he was dissatisfied with any settlement he could obtain otherwise. In my opinion, the lineage counsellor and notables would never agree to a man evicting his brother from land which the latter had occupied and cultivated for so many years. Their constraint must have failed to move Sendu—or alternatively there was not time to make if efficacious before Sendu resorted to the court, an action they could not easily prevent. Had there been no possibility of a court hearing, the final solution would almost certainly have followed the lines of the magistrates' moral admonitions. I base this opinion on a number of similar cases decided in moot and conclave, and on discussions with Arusha informants.

In discussing Case 23 (pp. 255-8) with a magistrate, he was certain that, had the case come before him in court, he would have awarded all the disputed land to the son, Kadume. This decision would be based directly on the rule that a son has the right to inherit his deceased father's land in precedence to his father's brother. I pointed out that, in the moot in question, the father's brother, Soine, had been allowed to retain part of the land. The magistrate commented that it had been a good settlement in the circumstances. It had, he said, taken account both of Soine's special relationship with his brother before the latter's death, and of Soine's shortage of land in contrast with Kadume who had a farm on the land of his mother's brother. Additionally, the magistrate noted, the settlement had been such as to permit full lineage unity to continue without great strain. 'Those men (i.e. counsellor and notables) were right,' he declared. 'They know the custom of inheritance, but they also know the people of the lineage and their affairs. But I cannot judge like that for I am a magistrate of the court. I must follow the custom. The law[1] is that a son inherits his father's property. If I fail to follow the law, people will say that I am wrong—and the chief and District Commissioner too.' He continued: 'But how could I persuade Kadume to give way and let his father's brother keep some of the land? He would say that I am not his kinsman, nor his counsellor. Oh yes, he listened to his counsellor and his elder father, for they are near (i.e. closely related) and they are seniors in that lineage.'

A magistrate's exhortation is sometimes heeded by a successful litigant, especially if the other disputant seeks a moot or, more likely, a conclave in an attempt to use the weight of the court's admonitions. This often does not occur, however, because of the bitterness engendered by the conditions leading up to and during a court hearing. A magistrate is in much the same position as many early doctors in Africa, who complained that they had difficulty in building up a medical reputation among the people because they tended to receive so large a proportion of hopeless or badly delayed cases.

The still persisting notion that courts are alien-imposed institutions; the failure to understand the principle of the impartial judge,

[1] He used the Swahili word, *sheria*.

and disbelief that such a judge usefully exists; the antipathy to imposed settlement of dispute; the dislike of court formality; these are the bases of Arusha lack of faith in the courts, and their lack of enthusiasm for them. But, as indicated above, they also see what, to them, are unsatisfactory solutions of disputes. In addition, for most Arusha, the indigenous procedures and the settlements they provide continue to meet people's needs. On the other hand, as already discussed in the previous Chapter, the courts are attractive to some disputants:—those who wish to attempt to avoid the necessity of compliance with the pressures and sanctions of their associates, and those who can scarcely pursue their claims at all by available indigenous means. Sometimes, also, notables are ready to pass on the onus of difficult and unpopular decision to the magistrate, who cannot refuse. Thus disapproved in general as they may be, the courts are fairly well established in Arusha society and, even by Arusha standards, serve some useful purposes.

CHAPTER ELEVEN

ADDITIONAL MEANS OF COERCION

COERCION of a non-violent kind is integral to the indigenous
process of dispute settlement among the Arusha. It is a
moral and sociological kind:—appeals to past precedents,
and to custom established by the ancestors; appeals to right behaviour, and especially right behaviour to close associates (near
agnates, age-mates); threats of disapproval and ostracism, and
promises of approval, fellowship and cordiality; threats to curtail
rights and privileges, and offers to maintain or even increase them;
appeals, both emotional and practical, to the cause of group unity.
Examples of these have been given in the preceding chapters. Such
coercion is aimed not only at the disputant himself, but also against
his supporters who can influence him. It may be directed, too, by a
man towards his own associates with the intention of stimulating
their support and loyalty. The whole pattern of discussion and
negotiation, both in public assembly and in conclave, is permeated
by pressures and counter-pressures, with the object of persuasion
and constraint, in which reference to the commonly accepted norms
of right behaviour is but one factor. Ideally, but very often in
practice, the dispute is resolved by an eventual, mutually accepted
settlement, to which either side concurs because it is felt to be the
most advantageous one that can be obtained with an expectation of
its proper fulfilment in the circumstances.

But although the agreed solution is mutually accepted, Arusha
are well aware of the remaining practical considerations of putting
it into effect. They recognise that a disputant, who finally admits to a
liability and agrees to meet his obligation to pay compensation, etc.,
may do nothing about it afterwards in the hope of avoiding his
material responsibility. To prevent this, there are two common
techniques. One is to insist that the agreement be put into effect
immediately, before the assembly or conclave disperses. For example,
the new field boundary is physically marked out there and then,[1]

---

[1] Cf. Cases 13 (p. 200), and 23 (p. 255); and the conclusion of Case 6 (p. 278).

or the animal required in payment is handed over on the spot.[1] This is generally the most satisfactory method, for then no problem remains; but such immediate action is not always possible, and it may not even be desirable. Instead the alternative method is to arrange for another meeting, usually in the form of a conclave, at which the final details are worked out and the agreement implemented. This meeting occurs within a day or two following the occasion of reaching the agreed solution.[2] In these instances a man has time, for example, to obtain the animal required and bring it to his creditor— he may have to send to a cattle camp, or to beg it from an agnate; or it may be more convenient to meet later at the site of a disputed boundary, perhaps some distance from the current meeting.

One or other of these procedures is usually possible; but when they are not feasible—because, for instance, the agreement is that an offender pay an animal when he can obtain one, or at a specified future time—then there is likely to be difficulty. It may be the case that a disputant merely wishes to obtain public recognition and affirmation of his claimed rights—the ownership of land occupied by his tenant, or a tenant's right to plant coffee trees, or the right of a father-in-law to unpaid bridewealth. Such affirmation is sometimes thought valuable as an insurance against a possible denial of rights in the future; it is not, however, always a certain insurance if many years pass before positive action is taken to claim the rights materially. Witnesses become dispersed or die, or their memory fades; and above all the pressures and negotiating strengths of the two parties may change in the meantime. If the agreement is to be put into effect after an interval, it may happen that purely personal persuasion is sufficient. This was so in connection with Case 21 where it was agreed that the son-in-law should hand over a bridewealth item 'at the time of the short rains', about five months after the moot was held (page 250). More usually the creditor or right-holder must convene another meeting to press his delayed claim. The original agreement may then be reiterated and honoured by immediate action, or the whole negotiation may have to be restarted. In the latter case the eventual agreement is not necessarily the same as that originally made, for this depends on the negotiating strengths of the two parties at the time. In other words, for the Arusha an

[1] Cf. Cases 8 (p. 194), 21 (p. 243), 22 (p. 253).
[2] Cf. Cases 12 (p. 200) and 24 (p. 259).

agreed solution of a dispute is not a complete settlement until it is put into practical effect. A disputant who attempts to obtain a postponement of his liabilities is possibly indicating his actual dissatisfaction with the solution. He may be able to avoid his liability, and thus by default gain an effective settlement in his own favour—just as he may by avoiding discussion of the dispute altogether, as in Case 25 (page 264).

The mutual acquiescence of the parties to the agreement is specifically affirmed at the conclusion of the dispute—i.e. at the end of the meeting in which positive agreement is reached—as each disputant provides beer for the assembled participants for a communal drink. Occasionally the offender—if one is clearly evident, and his offence is a major one—may be required to kill a goat or sheep for a meat feast at the same time; or only the offender supplies beer in recognition of his fault and the lack of provocation by the injured person. In any case, the idea is that by sitting and drinking together the two parties (each a disputant and his supporters) acknowledge their accord. Arusha are not naive enough to think that the mere act of drinking together creates friendly relations; they do say, however, that men who drink together tacitly declare their lack of particular enmity and conflict. Further, the fact of the beer-drink can be quoted in the future as proof that the settlement was indeed agreed to by both sides: this can add to the negotiating strength of a disputant if the agreement is not honoured, or if the matter is re-opened for some reason at a later time.

Where a dispute lies between two hitherto 'unrelated' or weakly related persons, it may well be the case that, although accepting and honouring the final agreement, one or both of the disputants feels somewhat resentful. Arusha prefer ideally that this should not be so, and to some extent they are prepared to make efforts by continued negotiation to alter the solution to meet persisting objections. Nevertheless a man feels little or no obligation to establish specifically friendly relations where none existed before, if by doing so some surrender of his claim is required. Where the disputants had pre-existing relations of some importance, however, every effort is made to adjust the final agreement so that friendly relations are restored or recreated.[1] That is to say, reconciliation of the disputants is only important—and then it is very important—in these kinds of

[1] The conclusion of Case 23 is a pertinent example; see pp. 257-8.

instances. As Gluckman has rightly pointed out in a different social context, 'if a dispute arises between two people who are comparative strangers to each other, there is no need for the court to reconcile them, since they are associated by a single contractual or delictual relationship which can be adjusted by a clear decision.'[1] But even between closely related disputants it may prove impossible to obtain genuine reconciliation, despite conscious efforts. Just as with 'unrelated' persons, the dispute ends in mutual agreement for practical purposes, but animosity remains.

This was the situation at the conclusion of *Case 6* (cf. pages 190-1). This was a dispute between patrilateral cousins of different inner lineages, where the precise boundary between their adjacent fields had never been marked. The action of one of them (the defendant) in hoeing up a narrow strip in the indeterminate boundary area, caused the other cousin to begin a formal dispute. At the moot, despite censure for his precipitate action, the defendant gained the land. The plaintiff was constrained to agree to this solution, and he participated in the marking out of the new boundary; but he was not reconciled to his cousin. There had been a long history of minor quarrelling between them, and to me it appeared that the defendant too obviously showed his pleasure at the outcome of the case. The plaintiff walked off as soon as the boundary marking was completed, and shouted that he would not stay and drink beer. The defendant had his contribution of beer brought out to a shade-tree near the new boundary, and the remainder of the men sat down to drink.

Members of the inner lineage of the absent plaintiff were clearly restless, and soon one of them went to the plaintiff's nearby homestead. As a result of this, beer was carried out to the assembled men by the plaintiff's wife. After a show of drinking with the others—to indicate their lack of animosity—members of the plaintiff's inner lineage gradually moved off and retired to the plaintiff's house, where they sat and drank beer with him. They attempted to persuade him to join the main drinking party, but he refused. In brief, he sulked at home. Members of his lineage, wishing to show loyalty and friendliness both to him and to their other agnates of the internal moot, were in a dilemna. Some returned to the group under the tree, some remained in the plaintiff's house, and some went to and fro. The plaintiff remained in his house until the moot had dispersed, and he told his near agnates that although he agreed to the settlement, he did not feel any friendship for his cousin.

[1] Gluckman 1955, p. 55. Note also his criticism of some writers for their overemphasis on the place of reconciliation in African judicial processes, at p. 78.

To the people concerned, this was a serious failure. The particular point at issue had been settled, and both parties had shown public agreement. The wider issue was not settled; and in fact not long after there was further trouble when the former defendant accused the other of allowing his cattle to stray unattended. As far as I could assess the position—the plaintiff at other times was a good informant and most helpful to me—the animosity between the two cousins arose out of incompatible personalities and somewhat irascible temperaments. At least no critical conflict remained such as might create persisting hostility between the two men's inner lineages and threaten the integrity of their maximal lineage. Whether or not the particular dispute is solved, in some cases the dissatisfaction is so great, and it is expressed at inter-group level, that the dissident inner lineage secedes altogether and attaches itself to another maximal lineage and clan. Although unusual, there are a number of authentic instances in Arusha; but I was unable to document one sufficiently well to discuss it here.

In Case 6 the particular dispute was settled, but sometimes even that much success is impossible. A disputant—probably abetted by his supporters—persistently refuses to submit to a settlement despite the pressures of his opponent, because in the circumstances the pressures available are inadequate in comparison with the factors involved in the dispute, or because high emotions cloud a man's practical assessment of the situation. A defendant may even refuse to participate in negotiations, or he may delay arrangements intolerably. An example was given in Case 24 (page 260) where appeals to public opinion were eventually successful; but such appeals may well fail. A disputant may refuse to compromise in his claims or denial of claims; he may attempt to avoid keeping his agreement, or it is suspected that he may do this; it may be thought that he will repeat the same offence again. Sometimes the evidence is so poor or contradictory, and misunderstanding so complete, that neither disputant is willing to shift his ground, and their supporters—especially their notables—cannot perceive where a balance lies. Sometimes an offender is unknown (e.g. a thief, when property has disappeared) and there is need to try to compel his disclosure. In all these kinds of circumstances there is a failure of normal processes. This may mean complete frustration for a disputant, and the matter is left unresolved; although that also means a virtual success on the part of a recalcitrant disputant. There is, however, the possibility of recourse to certain institutionalised means of positive coercion, which are available both to individual disputants and to notables acting on behalf of the groups which they represent.

The Arusha have an ambivalent attitude towards these additional means of coercion; the means are approved and are defined by well-known, regular procedures, yet their use indicates some failure in ordinary processes which people are not always willing to recognise. They are, on the whole, not lightly resorted to, and Arusha prefer to do without them if they can. In the majority of cases they are not used, partly because they are not needed, and partly because of this antipathy. A number of them depend on supernatural power, which is a direct negation of the possibility of human abilities. Supernatural coercion is especially marked by its application to the enforcement of a settlement where doubt remains as to the adequacy of the settlement itself, or of it actually being carried out.

In the following brief account there are described first, the non-supernatural means of coercion—the deliberate delaying of consideration of later disputes, physical coercion, and fines. Secondly, there are described the curse, available to notables, and the various forms of ritual oaths.

The Ability to Delay Consideration of Later Disputes

Arusha say that participants in a dispute should not concern themselves in any subsequent dispute until the first one is settled. This applies not only to the disputants themselves, but to all their supporters, including the notables who, because of their responsibilities, are involved with more disputes than an ordinary person.

The rule is most easily applied in homicide cases. Thus if such a case concerns members of different moieties, no other homicide case can be dealt with until it is settled. If killer and victim are of the same moiety, then cases confined to the other moiety can be treated, but not those of the same moiety. Arusha explain this by saying that simultaneous consideration of two cases by the same group of people would result in confusion and conflict of interests. They also say, that in order to maintain equity among members of a moiety, in respect of the obligations to give cattle for bloodwealth and the privilege to receive cattle, it is necessary to complete one transaction before beginning another. And finally, it is said that the dead victim may resent the postponement of bloodwealth payment in his case, whilst later victims are satisfied, and therefore he may in his anger send misfortune on the living.

The victim's agnates, the principal plaintiffs, who cannot obtain satisfaction, attempt to take advantage of this rule by drawing attention to subsequent cases which are being delayed. They seek to gain the support of the plaintiffs in those cases in bringing pressure to bear on the recalcitrant or procrastinating defendants.

This same rule is held to apply to other kinds of dispute, but it is less commonly invoked and is less satisfactory. Homicide involves at least a whole moiety, and possibly both of them; it is treated by special procedures and raises important issues, both moral and material.[1] The failure to settle, say, a bridewealth dispute affects only a relatively small number of people: even if the disputants belong to different moieties, their effective supporters are confined to their own agnates and to local members of the moieties. Nevertheless it sometimes happens that a disputant can raise objections to any of his supporters participating in another case (a case of any kind, not merely another bridewealth dispute) whilst his own is delayed by alleged intransigence on the part of the other disputant. It is at least good propriety that a counsellor should inform an agnate, whose dispute is unsettled, that he wishes to proceed with another dispute. The agnate may object; he hopes then to stimulate his counsellor's efforts and those of his other agnates on his own behalf. He may hope to gain the support of the disputant in the second case. At least he raises a protest against the unsatisfactory condition of his own case, and may influence public opinion in his favour.

The following two cases illustrate both the usefulness and the weaknesses of such attempts at coercion:—

Case 27: A land dispute between Ndasiken and his neighbour had reached an impasse. The disputants were members of different maximal lineages of the same sub-clan. At this time Yozef, a man of a third lineage of the sub-clan, became a plaintiff in another dispute. Yozef's own lineage counsellor lived at a distance; and therefore, as he had become accustomed to do, Yozef approached the counsellor of Ndasiken's lineage, who lived fairly near to his own homestead. This counsellor agreed to assist Yozef and negotiations were begun to convene a conclave. On hearing of this, Ndasiken immediately protested to his counsellor, saying that the latter

[1] Cf. my account in Chapter Seven.

should not take up a case for an outsider whilst his own dispute was unsettled. It is difficult to assess the effective results of this. Certainly the
counsellor, in deference to his agnate, did not continue actively to support
Yozef; nevertheless Yozef was able to manage without this assistance by
going instead to his own counsellor, and by obtaining other supporters
at a conclave without calling upon members of the lineages of Ndasiken
and his disputing neighbour. But an awkward situation had been created
for the counsellor and others. Ndasiken had drawn marked attention to
the unsatisfactory state of his own dispute (in which he was the plaintiff),
and the deadlock became a matter of public comment. Members of Yozef's
lineage and others of the sub-clan declared their opinion that Ndasiken's
dispute should be quickly settled; and they complained of their inability
to claim the support of members of the two lineages concerned in Yozef's
cause. It appeared that efforts were renewed in Ndasiken's dispute. A new
conclave was held—earlier there had seemed to be little value in this—at
which both Ndasiken's counsellor and a notable of Yozef's lineage admonished the defendant to agree to a settlement. At a subsequent moot,
a week or two later, a settlement was agreed to. This might have occurred
in any event, but at least it is likely that negotiations were speeded up.

Case 28: In different circumstances, similar tactics were used in a parish
assembly. A long drawn-out dispute between two men of the same age-
group remained unresolved as dusk approached, and men wished to go
home. It was agreed to renew the discussion at the next meeting of the
assembly, one week later. The difficulty in this case arose because the
defendant, who had admitted his offence, refused to agree to the compensation demanded, despite persuasion from his age-mates (junior elders).
During the week before the next meeting, the plaintiff let it be known that
he would insist on a settlement of the dispute before the parish assembly
began to consider any other matter. At the renewed discussion little or
no progress was made. After about an hour had passed in profitless argument and some acrimony, other members of the assembly began to grow
restive. One called out to protest, saying that he had a matter to raise
which he had been unable to introduce the previous week. A little while
later, the parish headman called out that he had news from the chief to
announce. The defendant suggested that consideration of his dispute be
adjourned until later. The plaintiff immediately rejected this, and instead
began to appeal to the men in the assembly, not only because of the rightness of his claim for compensation, but now because of the increasingly
intolerable delay, he had general opinion on his side. A close friend of
the defendant attempted to object to these pressure tactics, but he was told
by a number of other men to sit down and be quiet. Men of the other
stream (senior elders, senior murran) who had taken little direct part in

the dispute hitherto, now began to act as the plaintiff's supporters. Quickly the defendant gave way and agreed to the compensation demanded. A tentative effort to fix a smaller compensation was similarly rejected—not only by the plaintiff, but by virtually the whole assembly.

In this case, had a possible settlement not been fairly clear, the plaintiff might have been compelled to give way in his intention of monopolising the parish assembly. Because, at a parish assembly meeting, usually several different matters are dealt with—and not all concern disputes, of course—members are often not ready to tolerate delays, and disputants are advised to return another time. The defendant probably hoped for that in this last case, but the plaintiff had the stronger grounds and so achieved his intention.

The Use of Physical Coercion
Both spokesmen and counsellors may, under certain circumstances, order murran to seize a man's animals required for compensation, or order men to compel an age-mate to attend an assembly. The notables of one disputant cannot order such action against the other disputant: this would be presumptuous, and might lead to fighting, and it would be unlikely to facilitate the dispute process. The use of physical coercion is therefore limited to the action of the notables against their own party. It means that a man is so obdurate, or so guilty, in the eyes of his fellows that they feel justified in taking direct action. There is, in other words, a virtual breakdown in normal processes.

An example of this has already been given in Case 15 (p. 204) where a junior murran, having failed to take part in communal road-clearing work in the parish, refused to pay the fine and threatened to refuse to take part in the work on the next occasion. Spokesmen of his patrons' age-group ordered his age-mates to go and seize a cow of his and slaughter it immediately (the original fine had been a sheep). Junior murran spokesmen led the group of age-mates who carried out this task. There was general approval of the action.

A similar example occurred in a moot. The murran brother of a defendant failed to attend, although he knew that his evidence was required. The lineage counsellor, in some anger, ordered the defendant and his other near agnates (i.e. the inner lineage) to go and fetch the absentee. This they did, and the cowed man quickly appeared. The moot resumed, and the counsellor continued in his support of the defendant.

In both these instances, the person against whom action was taken was a murran. This is commonly the case. The action itself may be taken by his age-mates or his agnates, but the authorisation is most likely to come from an elder notable. When the recalcitrant is himself an elder, the use of force is rare. Notables are unwilling to order force against an elder; they cannot well order murran to execute the action and other elders tend to eschew the responsibility. I have seen junior elders compulsorily summoned by some of their age-mates at the spokesman's orders, but without physical force. Arusha say that an elder's propery might be seized, but I have no clear example of this occurring. I heard a counsellor obliquely threaten an agnate of elder status with force, when the latter refused to agree to a generally accepted division of land inheritance; but the threat was not followed up, and probably no one expected it to be.

What was said earlier about Arusha dislike of violent self-help,[1] applies in this case also. Here, the resort to violence is regarded as legitimate, in that notables act on behalf of and with the agreement of their group. Nevertheless, there is a notion that there is no need for this recourse, because discussion and negotiation are possible and preferable. Physical coercion, occurring as it does when negotiation breaks down, comes to represent such a breakdown; and men do not wish to acknowledge failure of normal procedures. Further, as explained previously, notables are unwilling to gain a reputation for authoritarianism, or to advertise the fact that their influence is weak enough to require bolstering by force.

Fines

The imposition of a fine, *sogo*—some beer, or an animal to be slaughtered and eaten—is confined almost entirely to what may be broadly paraphrased as 'contempt of court'. That is, fines are punishments for intemperate behaviour in assembly or conclave, especially behaviour insulting to the notables:—for example, publicly accusing notables of failure to give proper support, imputations against their characters, wilful disregard of reasonable direc-

[1] See pp. 216-21.

tives aiming at an orderly procedure, brawling or rowdy behaviour
(e.g. by a drunken person) and the like. Notables are usually most
tolerant of men's behaviour, and only take action where the whole
meeting is disturbed and when, therefore, there is general resentment against the offender and agreement on his punishment. Many
interruptions of a standing speaker are allowed, until they begin to
prevent the speaker from making his points; a spokesman will often
tolerate derogatory remarks from an age-mate, unless the latter
begins to be aggressively libellous, and especially if he includes
several notables in his attack.[1]

Fines are more common in connection with the parish assembly
or intra-parish conclaves, and in that context they have been dealt
with already in Chapter Three.[2] They are infrequently imposed in
moots or in counsellors' conclaves. As with orders for physical
coercion, fines can only be imposed by a notable of the group of the
offender—an age-mate by his spokesman, or an agnate by his
counsellor. Other notables who are affronted must persuade the
offender's own notables to take the action.

An important feature of a fine is that it is usually provided by the
offender at his own homestead, where it is consumed by the members
of his group, or at least the more notable members, together with
him in commensality. In age-group contexts, heavier fines involving
an animal are sometimes brought to the parish assembly site, or some
other public place, there to be consumed by all age-mates of the
offender. The idea is that the culprit begs pardon of those he has
offended: they accept his apology by the act of accepting and consuming his fine; and there is a reconciliation of all concerned. The
intention is not mere punishment—not even mainly that—but the
opportunity for the re-establishment of proper and cordial relations.
There is the same notion which applies to the provision of beer
by disputants at the conclusion of a dispute settlement.[3] Every
effort is made to give the offender the chance to show that he remains
a full and accepted member of the group, and for all to show that no
resentment remains. As my field assistant put it: 'A court makes a
man pay a fine, but who knows where the money goes? Perhaps the

[1] Cf. Case 6, p. 190, for an example of the imposition of a fine for insulting behaviour
to spokesmen.
[2] See pp. 62-4.
[3] See p. 277

magistrate eats it; perhaps the Government. But an Arusha fine is not money; it is beer, and we all drink it together. We are friends then. Is that not so? Is that not right?'

The Curse

A curse (*oldeket*) is made by an appeal to the high-god, Engai, to punish an alleged offender. The belief is that if a person is indeed an offender, Engai will perceive this and send misfortunes on him as punishment. There is no idea of coercing Engai to take action, for he will only punish if he sees that a wrong has been committed. The action of cursing is to describe the alleged offence, and then make the appeal to Engai by raising both arms above the head and raising the eyes towards the sky. The name of Engai may be uttered, or merely a repeated ejaculation of wordless awe—'E-e-e-e!'—but sometimes no sound is made at all.

Almost anyone can curse anyone else, especially a kinsman, in an attempt to visit punishment upon him. But in dispute proceedings only a notable—usually only a spokesman or counsellor—does so, never a disputant. Only infrequently is this done, and I was unable to record a good example of it. Threats of the curse are rather more common, but still not frequent. It is believed that Engai, who is omniscient and omnipotent, will send great misfortune (probably death) unless the curse is quickly revoked. A notable does not wish to take so drastic a step against one of his own close associates, and it would be a grave offence to curse a member of another group (lineage or age-group). Arusha say that the curse is only used in the event of such extreme contumacy by a person that his group's interests are directly and seriously threatened.

In one instance of which I was told, a man was preventing the completion of an inheritance settlement by his long, persistent refusal to accede to his half-brothers' demands over the division of the dead father's land. The counsellor and all other members of the lineage wholly supported the half-brothers. The man himself, at the second internal moot, began to accuse his agnates of injustice and threatened to seize the portion of land he claimed. He directly insulted both the counsellor and his father's brother. These two men, exasperated and incensed, cursed the man and the moot broke up. The next day the man went to beg the counsellor's pardon: he brought a conciliatory gift of beer and some meat. The curse was lifted, and the man agreed to accept the required inheritance settlement.

Ritual Oaths

There are four kinds of ritual means which the Arusha use in connection with dispute settlement. They differ in their applicability and degree of efficacy, but there are certain features which they have in common and which throw light on Arusha conceptions and aims in their dispute procedures.

Firstly, the suggestion to use one of these ritual means is almost always made by a disputant, and he himself becomes the protagonist in the performance. Secondly, none of these means may be used without the permission of the notables supporting each disputant. Nowadays a court will also give permission for their use; or the chief or a magistrate may make a strong recommendation for them to counsellors or spokesmen. Arusha emphasise this because, they say, it is possible for some of these rituals to be carried out secretly and nefariously, 'like sorcery', in an attempt to circumvent the agreed settlement of a dispute, or in disapproved self-help. Furthermore it is considered wrong to use them unless the other disputant agrees. They are only properly performed before the public witness of the notables of both disputants; the notables ensure the correct procedure, but take no active part in the performance.

Thirdly, they are resorted to when the settlement of a dispute is felt by one of the parties to be in doubt, or when he suspects it may not be adequately carried out, or in an attempt to prevent a repetition of the offence. They may sometimes also be used where settlement cannot be reached, either through failure to achieve any agreement, or because the offender is unknown by the evidence available. That is to say, they are used when normal processes are thought to be inadequate, or even altogether useless. Arusha say that if a dispute is genuinely settled by a mutually acceptable agreement, then there is no need for ritual action, i.e. the invocation of supernatural powers. As an outside observer, I agree with their contention.

Fourthly, these ritual means all operate by producing illness or death in an offender. Proof of their operation can be determined by a recognised diviner. The effects of the ritual, or further effects, can only be avoided by the confession of the offender and by his making due restitution. In some cases, confession must be accompanied by ritual removement of further danger.

The Arusha have no explanation of the forces which they believe to be set in operation by these rituals; they merely assert that the rituals are efficacious. None of the rituals involves the recognised powers of the ancestors or of the high-god. The ancestors are sometimes said to be angry at discord between their living descendants, and it is thought that they may send misfortune as a sign of disfavour. Whilst these beliefs symbolise the needs of agnatic unity, I know of no cases where by themselves they had jural significance. No instance came to my notice where the course of a dispute was affected primarily by the assumed intervention of the ancestors.

There are no ritual means of constraining disputants or witnesses to speak truthfully in assembly or conclave. It is expected that disputants and their supporters will attempt to evade the truth where it might harm their interests; supporters' prime concern is to their own party, and this comes before objective veracity. Arusha are aware of judicial affirmations, for they have to submit to these sometimes in a court; but they say cynically that such affirmations are useless, for people still lie to a magistrate.

General supernatural forces, activated ritually, are not used as means of punishment. Men are concerned to obtain their rights, and to be materially compensated for their injuries or deprivation of rights. They are not concerned with punishment as such, for that seems to them to serve no particular purpose. If an offender belongs to one's own group, the need is for reconciliation and recreation of working relations; if he does not so belong, then one has no interest in his behaviour once compensation is obtained. Wrongful behaviour is, of course, recognised at a general moral level; but a man has no responsibility for those who are not related to him and who do him no injury.

Brief accounts of these ritual oaths are given in sufficient detail to illustrate their use and significance in judicial processes. I am not concerned here with their intrinsically supernatural and symbolic nature.

Olmomai: Arusha say that this ritual oath brings 'peace' (*eseliani*) to two related disputants.[1] Its use indicates a failure to establish

[1] Cf. p. 233 above.

genuine reconciliation between them, whilst there remains resentment, and perhaps mistrust, which may nullify the agreement or bring a renewal of the act which precipitated the particular dispute. As far as I know, it is used only between related men in dispute procedures; similar threats to an agreement where 'unrelated' men are concerned, may be countered by the use of one of the other oaths described later. *Olmomai* may also be used where personal relations between related men have become so strained that mutual recrimination produces virtually irresolvable conflict in which particular issues are so inter-mingled that material settlement scarcely meets the case. In effect the oath then binds the men to good behaviour, and for that reason notables often advocate its use when they fear the persistent quarrelling and bitterness between two members of their nuclear group.

The oath has a general usage outside specifically dispute procedures, when it is desired to reinforce and also symbolise the ideally friendly relations between certain people. Occasionally all the members of an age-group undergo it together; and the women of a parish may perform it, during an anti-witchcraft drive, as an affirmation of their lack of intent to harm each other.

In the context of dispute procedures, it is normally the plaintiff who suggest its use after an agreement has been established. Then it is incorporated into the implementation of the settlement. The plaintiff becomes the protagonist, and the defendant is the subject of the oath. The protagonist provides a goat to be slaughtered, and pieces of its tongue, heart, gallbladder and breast-meat are taken and cooked separately. The protagonist stands erect, before the witnessing notables, and the subject crouches or sits at his feet. The subject's clothing must be removed, or at least carefully loosened—all knots, button and pins being unfastened—in order that there be no hindrance to the supernatural forces invoked. The subject is then fed pieces of the meat on a stick proffered by the protagonist, who at the same time briefly recounts the dispute and the agreement. He finally eats some of the meat himself.

Thereafter, should either man break the agreement, or should the subject repeat the offence, it is believed that he will sicken. The symptoms are marked dryness of the mouth and a painful tongue. Most Arusha say that only non-fatal illness comes from disregard of this oath; but some informants declared that a man could die unless he confesses to his new offence and asks the other man for pardon, thus acknowledging his obligation to make amends. All are agreed, however, that only the two men taking the oath are liable to be affected, in the case of failure to observe its terms. For this reason, *olmomai* can be used between near kin, because it will not endanger any of their mutual kinsfolk. Other ritual oaths have a wider range of effectiveness, and therefore they cannot be used between kin.

Olemwua: This is used only in connection with disputes concerning land, and where, despite his acquiescence to the settlement, one of the disputants remains dissatisfied. This man takes a handful of soil from the disputed land and throws it over the other disputant, saying at the time words to the effect that, 'if this land is not really his, he will die'.

In this case the supernatural forces are believed to cause the death of the man if he wrongly holds the land in question. They may also kill his wives and children, or anyone else who cultivates that piece of land. A diviner is said to be unable to diagnose the operation of this oath from a single death among those subject to it, but only if two or three deaths occur close together.

This oath is particularly liable to nefarious use. It may be performed clandestinely, the soil being thrown on the subject's house or inside his homestead without his knowledge. A man may perhaps attempt to mix some soil from another field, obviously not claimed by the subject, so that the latter will be attacked illegitimately. Some cases have occurred where a man has had soil thrown at him by an angry disputant passing by. Spokesmen of the parish in which the land lies impose a fine of an ox, and declare the oath void in such circumstances. Where the illicit operator lives in another parish, the spokesmen sometimes make a plaint to court, and fines of between fifty and one hundred shillings have been successfully imposed by magistrates during the nineteen-fifties.

Emuty nadanyi, 'breaking the cooking-pot': This is the most commonly used ritual oath among the Arusha. The descriptive phrase is a euphemism, for the object used is a special piece of stone, a little larger than the hand. In most parishes one or two men own these 'pots', which they hire out for a fee of, nowadays, fifty to eighty shillings. The stones are said to have come from Pare, Kahe or Taveta countries, and are not obtainable locally.[1]

They are kept covered with the leaves of certain trees, whose botanical names are unknown to me,[2] and are buried when not in use lest they accidentally kill anyone who sees them. To 'break the pot', the protagonist partly uncovers the stone, and with it in his hands he walks round the subject; who sits by an *engoiyapia* tree. As he does this, he informs the stone of the facts of the case as previously directed by the witnessing notables. In making the oath, the 'pot' is addressed directly, for it is believed that the stone itself is the agent of power.

Thus on the occasion of its use in connection with Case 24 (page 262), the murran, whose betrothed girl had been seduced, gave a brief summary of the affair and the settlement agreed to. The girl herself, the seducer, and his elder brother, were all pointed out to the 'pot'. Finally it was bidden to kill any of them if they contravened the agreed settlement. After this, the 'pot' was immediately covered up and taken off to be returned straightaway to its owner.

This ritual practice is most commonly used in disputes over land and over marital rights, although it is not confined only to these. There is some danger in its use for the protagonist: if he is making a wrongful claim, the 'cooking-pot' is said to discover this and to turn its attack on him.

Case 29: Thus one land dispute ended with the field being retained by its occupant, largely because the origins of its initial ownership were no longer clear, some seventy years after it had been cut out of the forest. The plaintiff was persuaded to acquiesce by his counsellor and agnates, who saw no chance of shifting the defendant. The plaintiff agreed finally on condition that he might 'break the cooking-pot' against the defendant; permission was given when the defendant himself did not object, and the ritual was performed. Some months later the plaintiff's child died, and soon after his cousin's wife also died. Many Arusha asserted that this was the work of the 'pot', and said that the plaintiff's claim to the field was therefore false. Nevertheless, the plaintiff made no attempt to seek the removal of the oath, and he insisted to me later that his claim was a true

[1] Similar objects were used by the Chagga. Dundas recorded that they are called *nungu*, literally 'cooking-pot'. According to him they came from Taveta and Kahe. He described one as a piece of lava. Cf. Dundas, 1924, p. 174ff., and plate at p. 192. Also, Gutman 1926, p. 619ff. The Meru neighbours of the Arusha also use this device.

[2] These are *embibiye* and *oloiyaniyaa* trees.

291

one. The results of divination in this case were indeterminate as to the cause of the two deaths.

Unknown offenders are sometimes dealt with by this means.

Case 30: My field assistant's house was entered and some money stolen, whilst he and his wife were temporarily absent. Despite enquiries, there was no clue to the thief, and so he attended the next meeting of the parish assembly to ask the spokesmen for permission to 'break the pot'. He was told that if the thief was not discovered within a week (the time elapsing before the next meeting) he would be given permission. The parish headman was ordered to help in the search. No more information was obtained, and my assistant received permission a week later. In carrying out the ritual, he showed the 'pot' his house, the open door, and the place where the money had been, and he explained to it exactly what was missing. He assured me that the thief would be sought out by the 'pot' and would die, even if we did not learn of the death, unless that person came immediately to confess. No-one did come to confess, and my assistant felt that his main object in performing the oath had failed. He found no satisfaction in his steady belief that the thief would soon die.

An activated 'cooking-pot' attacks not only the individual against whom it is directly used, but also any members of his maximal lineage, including the wives of members, and their livestock. Its action is arbitrary within that range; although my limited information on its operation indicates that distant agnates are seldom alleged to have died as a result. Because of this potential range of its operation, the 'pot' may not be used by a man against an agnate. In cases where circumstances warrant resort to ritual means between disputing agnates, the lineage counsellor gives permission only for the *olmomai* oath, the action of which is limited to the protagonist and his subject. The wider range of the 'cooking-pot' is an indication of its strong power. The inference is that, being liable to its attack, the agnates of a disputant will take care to assure themselves that he is not in the wrong, and that he does not in the future transgress the agreement reached in the settlement. But Arusha do not overtly emphasise this point.

Many Arusha have told me that the 'cooking-pot' is a certain killer in cases of transgression—more certain than any other ritual procedure. They speak of it with some awe; and during its actual invocation it is handled and used with great care, lest it accidentally directs its attentions to a by-stander. Occasionally, men use the 'pot' clandestinely to attack an opponent. If this is discovered, the miscreant is liable to a fine of an ox, and must also bear the expense of stopping the 'pot's' action. In one case in 1955, a man who 'broke the pot' without permission was prosecuted in a local court, at the instigation of the subject's counsellor and spokesman. He was fined 150 shillings with the alternative of three months hard labour, and his two accomplices were fined 100 shillings each or three months hard labour.[1]

If a death occurs—or a severe illness likely to lead to death—which is divined as the result of the action of the 'pot', the only remedy is for the disputant to take a female calf to the original protagonist (or vice-versa, as the case may be) and acknowledge his wrong. The person thus shown to be in the right, obtains the 'pot' which was originally activated, kills a goat and smears some of its fat and undigested stomach contents over the stone, informing the 'pot' that it should no longer kill. Any adjustment in the dispute settlement can then be made in view of the offender's public confession.

Edanggai: This is a particular flower which is buried, in front of witnesses, in a piece of disputed land, or inside the homestead, of a disputant. If the subject is in the wrong, he and members of his maximal lineage become liable to death as the flower rots in the earth. This oath is seldom used, and I have no record of it. Informants stated that it is an especially fast working device, and that it is an alternative to the 'cooking pot' in its nature and scope.

The question remains: how efficacious are these supernatural practices in dispute settlement? First, I reiterate that the use of these coercive measures at all indicates a partial failure of normal dispute processes. If a mutual agreement is properly reached, and if it is accepted by both the disputants and their closer supporters. then there should not need to be any recourse to such coercion. Therefore, if one or the other disputant asks for permission to use a ritual oath, he is straightaway indicating his reservations concerning the settlement and the good faith of his opponent. This in itself can be salutary, in that notice is given that a man is going to be especially

---

[1] This is an example where it was difficult for the injured party and his notables to bring indigenous action against the offender (who illicitly used a 'pot'). The latter lived in a parish some seven miles away. Therefore they chose the more certain, because authority-backed, local court.

watchful of his opponent—notice is given both to his opponent and the notables of either party.

Despite long endeavour by the Lutheran Mission, still the great majority of Arusha (especially of older people) retain their indigenous beliefs in the supernatural. They continue, therefore, to have faith in the genuine efficacy of these ritual procedures. This is demonstrated, in one way, by general demands that modern local courts not only recognise these procedures as valid, but actually authorise them in particular cases. Since all magistrates and court clerks (being educated men) are at least nominal Christians, their willingness to acknowledge and make use of these rituals is all the more striking.

The continued belief in these rituals is also shown by the high indignation invariably demonstrated when they are used without the proper permission of the notables or a court. In part, of course, this indignation comes from resentment by a person who, being subjected to the rituals, is thereby accused of offence, actual or potential. But it goes beyond that to include resentment, and even fear, that a man should be made subject to a ritual oath when its imposition is not properly made and witnessed. I have mentioned how these oaths may be used so as to gain a desired result by chicanery: the *olemwua* oath can be subverted by illicitly using soil from a field obviously not belonging to the people involved; a 'cooking-pot' may be told to attack a victim without just cause. People believe that they may be made ill or killed by such improper practice, because they believe in the efficacy of the ritual devices themselves. The 'cooking-pot' in particular is regarded with much apprehension: care is taken by keeping these objects buried when not in use, by retaining the special leaf-covering except during the actual invocation, and by hurriedly returning them to their owners (avoiding people on the way) after use.

A few Arusha are convinced sceptics. Most of these are found among the Christian converts; but by no means all converts are entirely disbelieving of the efficacy of the traditional oaths, and most are inclined to agree to their use rather than court unpopularity by public disagreement and disapproval. There are some non-Christian sceptics, whose experience or disposition has brought them to disbelief. It was impossible to estimate their number, because they did not willingly confess to their position and sought to remain unnoticed. In one case, the sceptic was an old man (retired elder) of unusual vigour and intelligence, who admitted to me privately his unbelief. He used his conviction for his own personal ends, for in land disputes with his neighbours, he successfully curtailed complete discussion of the conflicting claims by declaring his readiness to submit to ritual oath. Twice this strategy succeeded: he held the disputed land (of which he carefully took physical possession), allowed the 'cooking-pot' to be 'broken' against him, and asserted that he would not quit the land until the supernatural forces showed him to be in the wrong. He effectively disarmed his opponents in each dispute and made it almost impossible for them to refuse to accede to his plans. Men grumbled, saying this was no way to conduct negotiations; but they agreed nevertheless. Some of them, but by no means all, suggested that the old man was deceiving them, that he had special protection against the 'cooking-pot', and was wrongfully obtaining land which belonged to others. On the other hand, if few Arusha are sceptical, many hope to avoid the consequences of the supernatural forces released by these oaths. In discussion with me, some Arusha admitted that it seemed that the oaths were not always efficacious; or, it was said, their action is so long delayed (i.e. for many years) that they do not any longer affect the particular dispute. Men subjected to ritual oath, appeared to hope that they would avoid the consequences. At least I know of no case where a disputant refused an oath because, being in the wrong, he feared the results. Some notables did sometimes express these fears. Instances occurred where permission to apply an oath was refused, because notables were not sure of the innocence of the potential subject. But expression of such doubt by a disputant's supporters gives his opponent the advantage he requires to improve the settlement to his own advantage. Sometimes it is clear that one of the disputants must be in the wrong—e.g. when both claim ownership of a whole field—and yet this seems not to deter them from using a ritual oath.

Inadequate as my records must be in these kinds of cases, it is clear that there are more cases of oaths being administered than there are of illness, death and confessions of offence as a result. Divination is not unequivocal. One diviner said that he hesitated to make a diagnosis in such cases, because he disliked to become involved in other people's disputes. I would suggest, too, that some protagonists of ritual oaths are well aware that they themselves are in the wrong (e.g. illegitimately claiming a piece of land), and that therefore they resort to the ritual as a means of emotional release, and as an expression of antagonism towards the opponent.

My conclusions are that these ritual oaths are but weakly efficacious in determining the offender in a dispute. This suggests itself because of the empirical fact that so few disputes are resolved when recourse is had to oaths; but also because people optimistically hope to avoid detection, although believing in the oaths in a general way. The rituals are, however, more useful in deterring future wrongdoing. Again this seems to be empirically true. The reason is not only because people believe in the supernatural powers so that they fear to offend. Public warning is given by the protagonist to his subject that the latter's good faith is not altogether credited, and therefore his actions will be scrutinised. If the dispute is later renewed because of alleged bad faith or another act of offence, the weight of opinion is likely to be on the side of the protagonist. Finally, it must be remembered that the large majority of cases do not involve any recourse to ritual means at all, and they cannot be described as normal agents in the Arusha dispute process.

*   *   *

At the beginning of their work on the Cheyenne Indians, Llewellyn and Hoebel assert dogmatically that 'law has the peculiar job of cleaning up social messes when they have been made'.[1] In this book I have described the same job of social control as that of settling disputes; and I have in part followed Llewellyn and Hoebel in concentrating on particular disputes in order to see how they were settled, and how social control works among the Arusha. In their analysis of the Cheyenne material and the issues it raises, those authors write: 'in many groups and cultures it has happened that authority has become attached less to persons than to patterns of action ("procedures") or to norms for action. . . . There can be recognised procedures for settling grievance, say, by treaty and composition, or by oath, or by ritual combat, with no official even to mediate or preside. . . . As soon as the course of behaviour shows, recognisably, authority in procedures or persons for cleaning up trouble-cases, or authority in standards whose infraction is met not only by action, but by action carrying the flavour of the *pro tanto*

[1] Llewellyn & Hoebel 1941, p. 20.

official, at that point the peculiar institutions called "legal" have become perceptible.'[1] It is likely, then, that Llewellyn and Hoebel would designate Arusha processes of dispute settlement as 'legal'. Whether it is useful to identify all these processes in different societies by the word 'legal', or as 'law-ways', is at least arguable; nevertheless those authors do demonstrate an important aspect of similarity in such processes in terms of authority and regularity. Whilst retaining this understanding of the common thread of similarity, it still remains to distinguish different kinds of process, different kinds of authority and regularity. There are several ways of doing this, according to the results desired, and I suggest one here which arises from my analysis of the Arusha data.

During my field investigations among the Arusha, and afterwards during the preparation of this book, I was constantly aware of an essential difference between the dispute processes of the Arusha and those of peoples who have a recognisable system of courts and judges—for example, the Lozi as described by Gluckman.[2] Clearly there is a crucial difference in the general methods of decision-making and decision-enforcing in these two cases. One way of dealing with this is to conceptualise two polar types of process—judicial and political—between which there is a graduated scale where, ideally, particular systems could be placed according as to whether they are more judicial or more political in their nature.

By a judicial process I mean one that involves a judge who is vested with both authority and responsibility to make a judgement, in accordance with established norms, which is enforceable as the settlement of a dispute.[3] For example, in a generalised account of the judicial process in Central Africa, Epstein writes: 'Arguments are presented, witnesses are called or supporters heard, until *finally the matter is concluded when the acknowledged spokesmen of the group give their opinions on the case.*'[4] The obvious implication is that some person (or group of persons) is recognised as holding the obligation

---

[1] Llewellyn & Hoebel, p. 268.

[2] Gluckman 1955. It so happened that I first read this book whilst I was in the field among the Arusha.

[3] *The Oxford English Dictionary* defines 'judicial' as follows: 'Of or belonging to judgement in a court of law, or to a judge in relation to this function; pertaining to the administration of justice; proper to a court of law or a legal tribunal; resulting from or fixed by a judgement in a court.'

[4] Epstein 1954, p. 2—my italics.

and the power to make a binding decision: he may be the accepted head of the group to which both disputants belong, or he may stand outside it and exercise a power given to him by the higher political authority to which all are subject. Epstein also notes that 'a court of law . . . has to find a way through the tangle of conflicting evidence, and in the end arrive at some conclusion on the case before it.' He emphasises what he calls 'the necessity for decision' on the part of the court, and that decision is reached 'by reference to the acknowledged norms of the group'.[1]

The purely political process, on the other hand, involves no intervention by a third party, a judge. Here a decision is reached and a settlement made as a result of the relative strengths of the two parties to the dispute as they are shown and tested in social action. The stronger gains the power to impose its own decision, but it is limited by the degree to which its opponent, though weaker, can influence it. In this case the accepted norms of behaviour relevant to the matter in dispute are but one element involved, and possibly an unimportant one.

Of course these are theoretical models only. Probably no judges are entirely neutral, partial neither to one side or the other, nor to one kind of settlement rather than another. Judges may be susceptible to personal pressures and inducements from disputants; they may be subject to interference by the political authorities of their society, or they themselves may be the political authority and concerned to further its aims and interests. That is to say, the judicial decision is likely to be affected in some degree, crudely or subtlely, by pressures applied by or on behalf of the conflicting parties in the dispute. Similarly, disputing parties in a political context are to some extent, and perhaps considerably, influenced by the accepted norms of behaviour in situations similar to that which has raised the dispute. Commonly each party appeals to its own interpretation of the practical application to the norms, as a means of justifying its stand. It may be important to gain the support of public opinion, or of men of prestige and influence, and this may be possible by demonstrating coincidence between the party's claims and established practices; but there may be other ways also, such as the offer of a *quid pro quo*. The contesting parties may, if their strength seems about equal, accept

---

[1] Epstein 1954, p. 2. Epstein's description applies, of course, to the local courts and appeal courts established in the Arusha country by the modern local government.

the intervention of a conciliator in order to resolve the deadlock. Each party only accepts the conciliator's suggestion or finding if it appears to be tolerable in the circumstances; yet to some extent he represents the norms of the society and he makes a judgement on behalf of the society.

In brief, the processes of dispute settlement in any society combine in some degree both judicial and political elements. On this kind of conceptual scale the Lozi and Arusha would occupy positions near the opposite poles, judicial and political respectively. As I have shown, in their indigenous social system the Arusha recognise neither judges nor any other roles of authority or of neutral arbitration. Their leaders—spokesmen, counsellors, notables— are accepted as men of influence by virtue of their approved characters and abilities: they are advocates of the group to which they belong, and they work for the benefit of their own side in a dispute. They are in no way able or expected to take a neutral or judicial stand. The solution of a dispute between Arusha does not come from authoritative decision, but through agreement resulting from discussion and negotiation between the parties which are in conflict. Each party is a disputant and his relevant supporters.

Thus Arusha dispute processes have a nature which can be characterised as mainly political, rather than judicial: they concern conflict and struggle between opposed parties in the attempt to reach a decision on particular issues. Without cynicism on their part, Arusha would doubtless subscribe to the sometime definition of politics as 'the art of the possible'. It is not just a case of what an injured person *ought* to obtain in compensation, but what he *can* obtain, that matters—not what an offender ought to give, but what he cannot avoid giving. The precise resolution of the conflict depends on the relative strengths of the parties: this involves not only an assessment of the alleged offence against the commonly accepted norms, but also the extent to which each party can affect or threaten the interests of the other, the need for accommodation demanded by common interests, and the ability to make use of more general processes and forces in the society (e.g. the opposition and rivalry between adjacent age-groups). Arusha are inclined to view each new dispute as a unique phenomenon, to the solution of which the ideal norm and past precedent provide only the initial basis for negotiation. Because there is no adjudicatory body, each party uses whatever means it can (short of armed force) to press its own advantage; and almost always, each is susceptible to social pressures of some kind from the other.

Because of this nature of dispute processes in Arusha society, I have not found it either empirically or analytically valid to adopt Gluckman's hypothesis of the 'reasonable man'. Insofar as this concept 'corresponds closely with the concept of "the *role* of a particular *status*" '[1] Arusha, like other peoples, have some idea of it which they more or less explicitly put into words, and which can be readily inferred from their behaviour, at relevant times. Among the Arusha there is, too, a commonly accepted range of toleration allowable in the behaviour of a person in a specific role—an integral attribute of the 'reasonable man' which can be described as 'reasonable expectations'. In effect, though not altogether as a conscious technique, Arusha do allege an offence, and deny accusation, by reference to reasonable expectations; but, as described earlier, discussion of a dispute is by no means limited to an attempt to establish the validity of such a reference. It would seem that the use of the technique of the reasonable man and reasonable expectations must be directly associated with judicial processes of social control, where the judge requires a stable standard of reference. And such a standard is most distinctively associated with judicial processes which involve emphasis on impartiality in judgement. It is surely not coincidental that Gluckman should also state of the Lozi, among whom he perceives the operation of the reasonable man, that 'a marked feature in all judgements is the emphasis that the court decides by evidence and reasoning, and without favour';[2] and 'even where judges are striving to reconcile disputants who are kinsmen, they will not do so at the cost of glossing over wrongdoing'.[3] The contrast with Arusha policy and practice is clear.

In Arusha, the degree of convergence between normative standards (taking into account reasonable expectations) and the details of actual settlements can vary considerably, according to the relative distribution of bargaining power between the two parties. A plaintiff may hold no power at all in effect, and therefore is not able even to

[1] Gluckman 1955, p. 129.
[2] Gluckman 1955, p. 61.
[3] Gluckman 1955, p, 358.

start active negotiations.[1] On the other hand, he may have such a monopoly of power that the defendant must merely accede to demands.[2] These are the two extremes. Although it is most improbable (and perhaps impossible) that a plaintiff could have a monopoly of power without his case conforming closely to accepted norms, it certainly cannot be suggested that where he has no power he is entirely unsupported by them.

Most disputes find bargaining power shared between the conflicting parties, and the resolution of the matter is not a case of reaching a decision as to which disputant is supported by the norms, and to what extent. Neither party is willing to agree to a resolution of the dispute to which it is not compelled—and a party is not compelled only by appeals to norms. A defendant may perhaps even concede that his behaviour was a breach of the relevant norm, but he still attempts to avoid the normative consequences of it—and he may succeed. In Case 22, to take a single example, the herdsman admitted that he had slaughtered and consumed one of the animals for which he was responsible, and which was the property of the plaintiff. There was, then, no dispute as to the breach of the norm. But the herdsman endeavoured to avoid paying the full amount of compensation for this breach; and he succeeded to some extent, because of his bargaining strength in the particular situation between himself and his kinsman, the owner of the animal.[3]

These processes and inter-party struggles can only be understood in terms of the social system in which the participants are involved in ordinary social life. The composition and strengths of the two conflicting parties in a dispute, the identification of leaders and the scope of their influence, the particular social situation in which negotiations occur (assembly or conclave), and the general social context within which the processes operate, are all direct functions of the sub-systems of Arusha society. It has therefore been quite essential to describe these sub-systems in some detail (albeit necessarily in rather abstract form). I have attempted to show how the process is affected according to the nature of the relationship between the disputants, and by the nature of the matter in dispute. It is also affected by the largely conscious choice of procedure, and therefore

[1] e.g. Case 25, pp. 264-5.
[2] e.g. Case 8, p. 194.
[3] See pp, 253-4.

of supporters, by the disputants themselves as they seek to gain personal advantage from their joint social context. This choice, however, is made within the limitations arising out of the social system itself. In effect, then, I have not only been describing the processes of dispute settlement, part of the mechanism of social control among the Arusha, but I have shown the major sub-systems of this society in action in one particular connection. Furthermore, I have been concerned to show the nature of the interaction between these sub-systems, each of which is founded on markedly different sociological premises; although this present account has not attempted to cover the total range of that interaction.

BIBLIOGRAPHY

BEIDELMAN, T. (1960). The Baraguyu; *Tanganyika Notes & Records*, 55.

BERNARDI, B. (1955). The age system of the Masai; *Annali Lateranensi*, 18.

BOHANNAN, P. (1957). *Justice and Judgement among the Tiv;* London, Oxford University Press.

COLSON, E. (1953) *a. The Makah Indians;* Manchester University Press.

(1953) *b.* Social control and vengeance in Plateau Tonga society; *Africa;* 23, 3.

DALLAS, D. (1931). The sacred tree of Ol Donyesha; *Man*, 31, 43.

DUNDAS, C. (1924). *Kilimanjaro and its Peoples;* London, Witherby.

EPSTEIN, A. L. (1954) *Juridical Techniques and the Judicial Process* (Rhodes-Livingstone Paper No. 23); Manchester University Press for the Rhodes-Livingstone Institute.

FORTES, M. (1945). *The Dynamics of Clanship among the Tallensi;* London, Oxford University Press.

FOSBROOKE, H. A. (1948). An administrative survey of the Masai social system; *Tanganyika Notes & Records*, 26.

(1956). The Masai age-group system as a guide to tribal chronology; *African Studies*, 15, 4.

FRANKENBERG, R. (1957). *Village on the Border;* London, Cohen & West.

GLUCKMAN, M. (1955). *The Judicial Process among the Barotse of Northern Rhodesia;* Manchester University Press.

GULLIVER, P. H. (1953). The age-set organisation of the Jie tribe; *Journal of the Royal Anthropological Institute;* 83, 2.

(1955). *The Family Herds;* London, Routledge & Kegan Paul.

(1957) *a.* A history of relations between the Arusha and the Masai; *Conference Papers of the E. African Institute of Social Research*, Kampala, Uganda.

(1957) *b. Report on land and population in the Arusha Chiefdom;* Tanganyika, Provincial Administration.

(1958). The Turkana age organisation; *American Anthropologist*, 60.

(1960). The population of the Arusha chiefdom; *Rhodes-Livingstone Journal*, 28.

(1961) *a.* Structural dichotomy and jural processes among the Arusha of Northern Tanganyika; *Africa*, 31, 1.

(1961) *b.* Land shortage, social change and social conflict in East Africa; *Journal of Conflict Resolution*, 5, 1.

Bibliography

(1962). The Evolution of Arusha Trade; in Bohannan, P. (ed.): *Markets in Africa*, Evanston, Northwestern University Press.

GUTMAN, B. (1926). *Das Recht der Dschagga;* Munich, Beck.

HERTZ, R. (1960). *Death and the Right Hand* (trans. R. & C. Needham); London, Cohen & West.

HUNTINGFORD, G. W. B. (1953). *The Southern Nilo-Hamites* (Ethnographic Survey of Africa, E.C. Africa Part 8); London, International African Institute.

KRONENBERG, A. (1961). The Logarim favourite beast; *Kush*, 9.

LAMBERT, H. E. (1947). *The use of indigenous authorities in tribal administration: studies of the Meru in Kenya Colony;* Cape Town, Communications from the School of African Studies, N.S. No. 16.

(1956). *Kikuyu Social and Political Institutions;* London, Oxford University Press.

LEACH, E. (1957). Aspects of bridewealth and marriage stability among the Kachin and Lakher; *Man*, 57, 59.

LLEWELLYN, K. N. & HOEBEL, E. A. (1941). *The Cheyenne Way;* Norman, Oklahoma University Press.

MAYER, P. (1949). *The lineage principle in Gusii society;* London, International African Institute, Memorandum No. 24.

MIDDLETON, J. (1961). *Lugbara Religion;* London, Oxford University Press.

NEEDHAM, R. (1958). A structural analysis of Purun society; *American Anthropologist*, 60.

(1960). The left hand of the Mugwe; *Africa*, 30. 1.

PRINS, A. H. J. (1952). *The Coastal Tribes of the North-eastern Bantu* (Ethnographic Survey of Africa, E.C. Africa Part 3); London, International African Institute.

RUEL, M. (1962). Kuria generation classes; *Africa*, 32, 1.

SOUTHALL, A. (1952). *Lineage Formation among the Luo;* London, International Africa Institute, Memorandum No. 26.

TUCKER, A. N. & MPAAYEI, J. T. O. (1955). *A Masai Grammar;* London, Longmans Green.

Acknowledgement is gratefully made to Professor Max Gluckman for permission to quote from Gluckman 1955; and to the Oklahoma University Press for permission to quote from Llewellyn and Hoebel 1941.

INDEX

305

Index